Nation Making

Emergent Identities
in Postcolonial Melanesia

Edited by
ROBERT J. FOSTER

Ann Arbor

THE UNIVERSITY OF MICHIGAN PRESS

1998   1997   1996   1995   4   3   2   1

A CIP catalogue record for this book is available from the British Library.

Library of Congress Cataloging-in-Publication Data

Nation making : emergent identities in postcolonial Melanesia / Robert
J. Foster, editor.
    p.   cm.
    Includes bibliographical references and index.
    ISBN 0-472-10558-2 (alk. paper)
    1. Melanesia—Politics and government. 2. Ethnicity—Melanesia.
3. Nationalism—Melanesia.   I. Foster, Robert John, 1957–   .
JQ5995.A91N38   1995
329.5′4′0995—dc20   95-8775
                             CIP

Contents

Acknowledgments

All but one of the chapters in this volume originated as papers presented in the session, "Nationalism and the Making of National Cultures in Melanesia," that I organized for the 1991 meetings of the Association for Social Anthropology in Oceania (ASAO) in Victoria, British Columbia. (Ellen Facey joined the project after the ASAO session.) I would like to thank the members of the audience at that session for their comments and suggestions. I would also like to acknowledge the contributions of several participants in the session who were unable to prepare chapters for this volume: Wari Iamu, Michael O'Hanlon, Pamela Rosi, Donna Winslow, and Laura Zimmer-Tamakoshi. John Kelly did an exemplary job as the discussant for the session and graciously accepted the charge of writing an epilogue for the volume. I have consulted him frequently in preparing this collection and thank him in particular for his generous assistance. Martha Kaplan and Ed LiPuma have also given me helpful advice and support. The careful reader reports of James Carrier and Nicholas Thomas have improved the volume substantially.

The first of several rounds of revisions to the papers was begun while I was a Visiting Fellow in the Department of Anthropology of the Research School of Pacific Studies, Australian National University. I would like to thank both the department and the school for generously allowing me to use their various and many resources. My visit to Australia was made possible by funds from the Australian-American Educational Foundation and the American Council of Learned Societies.

Robert J. Foster

Introduction:
The Work of Nation Making

The chapters in this volume examine the process of nation making in the former colonial states of the southwestern Pacific: Fiji, Papua New Guinea, the Solomon Islands, and Vanuatu. These states attained formal political independence in the years between 1970 and 1980. Relative newcomers to nation-statehood, they arrived quietly and quickly—not through noisy, protracted struggles for liberation, but mainly through the instigation of their colonizers.[1] Anticolonial resistance, which surely did occur, did not provoke broad-based national consciousness, not even temporarily. In Papua New Guinea, the Solomons, and Vanuatu, local-ized secessionist and/or anti-independence movements developed in an-ticipation of decolonization; in Fiji, the most vocal anticolonial move-ment mirrored and celebrated Indian nationalism.

Since independence, then, political elites and local intelligentsia in these states have undertaken in earnest the work of producing images and ideals of nationhood. They have generated a steady discourse of custom and tradition that seeks to ground national distinctiveness in definitions of indigenous ancestral ways (Facey this volume; see also Jolly and Thomas 1992, Keesing 1989, Keesing and Tonkinson 1982, Lindstrom 1990, and Philibert 1986). Much of this discourse is official discourse. It is inscribed memorably, for example, in the preamble to the constitution of Papua New Guinea.[2] Accordingly, nationalism in post-colonial Melanesia largely takes shape as state functionaries try to na-tionalize state structures rather than as collections of "peoples" try to create or seize state structures as their own.[3]

It might well be the case that this state project proves futile, des-tined to attain only the most juridical sense of "membership" in the international system of states, for the new Melanesian states must effect their transformation into *nation-states* under conditions of intensifying economic dependency and accelerating transnationalization of capital and communications. These states, moreover, must construct images and ideals of unitary identity in the face of more than the usual heterogeneity—linguistic, sectarian, regional—much of it the legacy of divisive colonial rule (see Howard 1989). The job of naturalizing connections between culture (nationality), people (nationals), and place (territory) thus seems more unnatural than usual (see Ferguson and Gupta 1992).

It might also be the case that there is something antiquated about the attempt to nationalize the state, especially with regard to securing a protected internal market. We should ask with Balibar (1990) whether the nationalization of states is only possible today along the peripheries and semiperipheries of the late colonial world system, for the Western European center of that system might be edging toward a "postnational" phase more in line with the flexible structures of a post-Fordist global economy (Jacobsen this volume; Kelly this volume).

Undeniably, however, postcolonial Melanesia remains an active site of nation making. State officials and public intellectuals have been joined by and resisted by a variety of other agents in producing images and ideals of nationhood. These agents—corporate advertisers, village "big men," visionary mystics—demonstrate that state agencies neither monopolize the discourse of tradition nor control the various appropriations of official discourse by unofficial agents. At stake are both the terms in which all these agents identify themselves to themselves and to each other, as well as the future lives premised upon these identities. It is this active and contested construction of collective and personal identities, all in the name of "the nation," that forms the subject matter of this volume.

The Process of Nation Making

Nation making refers to both the production of a collective definition of "peoplehood" and the construction of individual "personhood" in terms of such a definition. This statement can be expanded initially by contrasting nation making with the more familiar if somewhat discredited concept of nation building. That is, nation making is first of all not nation building, at least not as the latter term is defined in *The International Encyclopedia of Social Sciences*.

Nation building was a central concern of the comparative study of recently independent former colonial states in Asia and Africa during the late 1950s and early 1960s (see, for example, Bendix 1969, Deutsch and Foltz 1963, Fallers 1974, Geertz 1963, and Pye 1962). The term *nation building* came to possess both a general and a restricted sense. In general, the term referred to the policies and projects by which newly independent governments would purposively effect the transition from tradition to modernity, "tradition" and "modernity" themselves conceived as Weberian ideal types; hence the title of an important collection of papers from 1963: *Old Societies and New States: The Quest for Modernity in Asia and Africa.* This quest or transition entailed a total and massive effort of social "engineering" (a characteristic architectonic metaphor) in which all the elements of a modern state were assembled. These elements included the administrative, legal, extractive, and coercive organizations recognized by Max Weber as the core of any state. The crucial element for establishing a *modern* state, however, is the erection of "an 'independent political apparatus' distinct from the ruler, and which indeed the ruler has a duty to maintain" (Tivey 1981, 3; see Breuilly 1985). Thus, in its more general sense, nation building implied and encompassed "(modern) state building."

In its more restricted sense, the term *nation building* referred to the self-conscious production and dissemination of national consciousness and sentiment—of a felt sense of national identity. This task was to be undertaken by a small minority of intellectuals and state officials. Nation building in this sense effectively denoted the cultural and psychological dimensions of the transition to modernity ("state building" proper, then, denoted the social, political, and economic dimensions). Accordingly, students of nation building focused their attention on cultural and educational policies in the new states. Anthropologically inclined investigators, in particular, examined the various ways in which the construction of identity was implemented and communicated through schooling, mass media, child socialization, and the iconography and ceremonies of the nation-state (see, for example, the papers by Marriott and LeVine in Geertz 1963).

It is this same concern with the pragmatics of identity formation that pervades the recent revival of anthropological interest in nationhood (Foster 1991) as well as the concept of nation making that I will outline. The current revival, however, has rejected two related key presuppositions of the earlier work on nation building. First, the analytical framework of "modernization" has been abandoned. It is no longer assumed that the formation of national identity occurs within the constraints of an inexorable historical (evolutionary) process in which traditional communities must yield, often painfully, to modern forms of social life (of which the nation-state is the form par excellence). This process was represented as a teleology of "progress" or "rationalization," or sometimes as one of "acculturation," mediated by elites, to a modern world culture originating in the West. But whatever its representation, the process of "transition" from traditional to modern forms of society no longer enters into discussions of national identity formation as an idealized description of historical change. How could it, given the "disconcerting realization" that programs of national development and modernization have generated "massive civil war, repressive authoritarianism by military coteries fortified by Western weaponry, and gruesome interracial and interethnic bloodshed roused by fundamental religious bigotry and inflamed by flagrant misuse of mass media" (Tambiah 1988, 2)?

Second, current anthropological approaches to the construction of national identities dispense with the unstated assumption that nation building, in both senses of the term, is exclusively the worry of newly independent colonial states or "transitional societies." On the contrary, recent work in the "old" states of Europe—not to mention active separatist movements—makes it clear that the construction and maintenance of national identities is now and always has been a live, contested issue (see, for example, Grillo 1980, Llobera 1990, and Tonkin, McDonald, and Chapman 1989). Social historians, moreover, have sensitized scholars to the dangers of assuming that the formation of European national identities was a smooth, automatic process predicated upon the "ethnic homogeneity" of European territorial states. As Massimo d'Azeglio, the former prime minister of Piedmont, is supposed to have put it in 1861, "We have made Italy: now we have to make Italians."[4] Thus the process of turning peasants into Frenchmen (Weber 1976), for example, is not wholly unlike that of turning tribespeople into Papua New Guineans (but see LiPuma's and Kelly's cautions in this volume about overdrawing the similarity).

Despite these major differences, current anthropological discussions of nations and nationalism bear one important resemblance to the discourse of nation building. I say important inasmuch as this particular resemblance suggests a motivation for the current work. All the current discussions treat "the nation" as fabricated—an actively made and remade cultural product. Consider the two dominant tropes of contemporary talk about nations: imagination (Anderson 1983) and invention (Hobsbawm and Ranger 1983). Both tropes direct attention to the processes and means by which interested agents create and circulate images and ideals of nationhood, and hence definitions of collective and personal identity. Both tropes, moreover, communicate a notion of fabrication without an implication of falsehood or spuriousness. That is, "the nation" is no less real because it is imagined or invented. By the same token, "the nation" is no more real because its images and ideals often assert for it a primordial or natural existence. It is precisely the reality of "the nation" that is struggled over and variously achieved in the confrontation of multiple images and inventions.

Certainly, some writers operating within the paradigm of modernization criticized a "static view of cultures" that stresses continuity in the transmission of "basic values" (Pye 1962, 42). Nevertheless, the present preoccupation with nations as contingent products cannot be traced genealogically to the earlier concern with nations as the goals of nation-building policies. Rather, this preoccupation derives from and sustains recent shifts in anthropological thinking about culture (Fox 1990). It is the new orthodoxy that culture be treated as the changing outcome of "practice"—interested activity that is not reducible to rational calculation or policy planning (Ortner 1984, 1989). The production and reproduction of collectively held dispositions—the work of making culture—is taken to be problematic, the site of often fierce contests among a plurality of agents and agencies with a plurality of intentions. "Culture" no longer conjures up associations with timeless and inert traditions, passed on from generation to generation in the manner of a family heirloom. It is this shift in thinking about culture within the fields of anthropology, history, and cultural studies that informs the chapters in this volume and their diverse approaches to nation making.

The concept of nation making posits "the nation" as *an imaginative construct that constitutes persons as legitimate subjects of and in a territorial state.* "The nation" is always a contested construct, precisely because "the nation" is never singular: multiple constructs invariably compete with each other for unquestioned and widespread acceptance. Produced by a variety of agents (especially state agents) with a variety of interests (sometimes contradictory), these constructs circulate in heterogeneous forms, both discursive and nondiscursive: official policy documents, letters to the editor, school textbooks, public monuments, state ceremonies, poems, advertisements, product logos, coin and currency.

The last few listed items hint at one important way in which *capitalist social relations* condition the dissemination of "the nation," namely, by rendering "nationality" a quality that can be acquired through the purchase and use of particular commodities, including money. More generally, "the nation" figures as a resource fought over in contests between local populations and state representatives to control the material and legal means—land, minerals, labor, tariff schedules, tax codes—for participation in the global capitalist economy. Consider, for instance, the claims made by various state agencies (military, economic, judicial) to define "the national interest." Or consider the attempt by various agents, not only state ones, to package "the nation" as a commodity attractive to foreigners such as investors and tourists. Let me cite one such striking example, a six-page advertising foldout purchased from *The Economist* by the National Productivity Board of Singapore. The first page claims that "It's time you hired the best worker in the world." Subsequent pages portray individual archetypes of these workers in glossy black-and-white photographs beneath the captions: "He's Malay," "She's Indian," "He's Eurasian," and "She's Chinese." The final page concludes: "But above all they are Singaporean."

In addition to competition among multiple versions, "the nation" often competes with (as well as provokes) other imaginative constructs that define other collective and personal identities, constructs such as "ethnicity" and "race." It is an open and empirical question whether any particular construct of the nation opposes, subsumes, or aligns with constructs of a different kind. Accordingly, the process of constituting subjects as "nationals"—the process of situating national identity with respect to other identities—unfolds neither automatically nor in exactly the same way everywhere. The chapters in this volume highlight different aspects of this rough and uneven process as it has occurred historically and is now occurring in the former colonies of the southwestern Pacific.

The key terms I have just highlighted invite and require elaboration in order to specify further the import of "nation making." Although I will discuss them separately and in turn, it is the coimplication of the terms that I stress. For instance, I discuss "the nation" with respect to its use as a construct in challenging or legitimating the exercise of state power, on the one hand, and defining persons as the subjects of state power, on the other. Balibar's (1990, 331) remark is apposite: "In reality, the idea of nations without a state, or nations 'before' the state, is thus a contradiction in terms, because a state always is implied in the historic framework of a national formation." It is the problematic inseparability of nation and state, itself a contingent historical construction and by no means a necessary conjunction, that I seek to foreground (see Jourdan this volume and Kelly this volume).

Similarly, the spread—if not origin—of the nation-state as a form of polity is intimately bound up with the global expansion and development of capitalism. (This is one of the few points of agreement between otherwise widely disparate approaches to the vexing question of origins [Anderson 1983; Gellner 1983; Hobsbawm 1972].) Every contemporary nation-state of Melanesia is a product of colonization organized within a global economy of dominant centers and subordinate peripheries. The historical diffusion of the nation-state to Melanesia as well as its mixed fortunes in the wake of decolonization can only be apprehended within this framework. Capitalism, as LiPuma argues in his thematic essay, is a background condition against which "the nation" is being made throughout the South Pacific.

Imaginative Construct

To treat "the nation" as an imaginative construct is to say plainly that "the nation" is an ideal, an ideal promulgated through a variety of discursive and nondiscursive means. Saying this, in turn, opens up a field of inquiry. What kind of ideal is "the nation"? Who produces such ideals? How do such ideals circulate? How do they gain currency and secure acceptance?

Benedict Anderson's essay *Imagined Communities* has become the starting point for addressing all such questions. Anderson argues that "the nation" ideally describes a definite kind of moral community, one imagined by its members ("the people") to exist as a particular type of polity. This polity is inherently limited; not only does it have putatively inelastic territorial borders, it "cannot be imagined except in the midst of an irremediable plurality of other nations" (Anderson 1986, 659). At the same time, it extends backward and forward into past and future through infinite linear time. This sort of polity is, moreover, sovereign (the part of Anderson's definition most commonly overlooked in a rush to exploit the poetic possibilities of the trope of "imagination"). It "contains" within its borders a space over which an autonomous authority— the state in "nation-state"—uniformly exercises itself. Accordingly, members of the community defined as "the nation" coexist as subjects of the authority of a single state.

There are at least two ways, both of which appear in this volume, of apprehending the generic kind of imaginative construct that Anderson identifies as "the nation." The first involves thinking about "the nation" as a *narrative* or *story* that articulates the relation of a people to a state (see Bhabha 1990). As Layoun (1992) points out, this metaphorical equation makes it possible to bring to bear upon constructs of "the nation" considerations drawn from the analysis of literary narratives: voice, time, space, emplotment, strategies of closure and containment, and so forth. That is, it becomes possible to grasp how

> the national narrative seeks to construct its history or to posit a narrative past (usually as continuous and uninterrupted) in an assertion of legitimacy and precedent for the practices of a narrative present. And this narrative of nationalism postulates a narrative future or constructs a telos, presumably one deriving from the structure and content of the narrative—and the nation—itself. (Layoun 1992, 411)

In other words, the means for constructing the peculiar sense of "homogeneous, empty time" that Anderson sees as necessary for imagining "the nation" can be disclosed through the workings of narrative performance. Indeed, this is Anderson's point in suggesting that the realist novel encodes and imparts the sense of time (more specifically, of simultaneity) implied by the construct of nationhood (see also Anderson 1986).

Furthermore, thinking of "nations" as narratives or stories makes visible the rhetorical effect of nation making, that is, the effect of persuasive narratives to render their contents as unquestionably true. This effect is not guaranteed, however, and not only because narratives often exhibit internal contradictions. Narratives vary in their plausibility depending upon who performs them; they also remain vulnerable to challenges posed by other, competing narrators or narratives. The protest "Whose story is this, anyway?" potentially subverts any effort at realizing what Williams (1985, 213) calls "the persuasive unitary sense" of a national narrative—the implication that "the nation" as narrated defines "the whole people" as a collective individual or cohesive totality. (This competition between narratives is emphasized most in the chapters by Rutz and Kaplan in this volume.)

A similar notion of competing definitions is central to a second (and, some would say, complementary) way of thinking about the nation as an imaginative construct, namely, treating the nation as a product of nationalist *ideology*. Fox advocates this approach in taking the term *nationalist ideologies* to denote "the production of conceptions of people-hood" or "ideologies of common ('national') culture" (1990, 3). Nationalist ideologies, for Fox, are invariably multiple and usually contradictory. It is as the contingent outcome of their confrontation with each other that a "national culture" emerges:

> Struggles among nationalist ideologies—contests over ideas as well as conflicts between people—may propel one nationalist ideology into dominance and leave others by the wayside. A national culture is always "temporary" because, whether antique or recent, its character and puissance are matters of historical practice; they are plastic constructions, not cultural givens. (Fox 1990, 4)

This approach directs attention both toward the specific agents and agencies involved in the production of nationalist ideologies *and* toward the political and economic conditions of this production. The production of national culture is, then, a "a fluid process rooted in power, domination and human interests" (Fox 1990, 10).

What Fox's argument tells us about nation making is that we must conceive the process as one of attempting to establish the hegemony of a particular imaginative construct. Because hegemony is a process and not a condition (Williams 1977), we need to see nation making as ongoing and open-ended. We must, moreover, dispense with any lingering supposition that nation making can be conceived as a matter of cultural forms and not of material conditions. Rather, both cultural forms and material conditions must be conceived as resources for and outcomes of the practice of nation making.

For Example: Imagining or Inventing Australia

Let me briefly interrupt this exegesis of "nation making" with a concrete and current instance of competing national narratives and constructions of the national past-future.[5] I write these words in Canberra in 1992 on the day after Paul Keating returned to Australia from Indonesia and Papua New Guinea (PNG), thus completing his first official overseas trip as prime minister. Keating's visit to PNG coincided with Anzac Day, a state holiday proclaimed to commemorate Australian war dead and especially to remember the anniversary of the landing at Gallipoli during World War I. Gallipoli, and the Anzac legend surrounding it, dominates the collective memory of Australian military activities (see Inglis 1989; Kapferer 1988).

In Australia, Anzac Day 1992 was celebrated in almost all major cities by parades of marching war veterans and crowds of flag-waving spectators. The event was enlarged by the participation of veterans from the Gulf War. In PNG, Keating marked the occasion with a public address made during the Anzac Day ceremonies in Port Moresby, the national capital. Here are some edited excerpts from his speech (printed in full in today's edition of *The Australian* [27 April 1992]), a speech remarkable enough to justify the length of the excerpts:

> Gallipoli and the history of the Australian nation are indissoluble. It is inscribed in legend. The spirit of Anzac became the canon of Australian life; the ideals to which we aspired, the values by which we lived. We will continue to hold the memory of those who served and died as inextinguishable and sacred. We will continue to remind ourselves "Lest We Forget."
>
> Legends bind nations together. They define us to ourselves. But they should not stifle us. The world moves on. Our country must move with it. Today I think we should remember that.
>
> Today we would do well to remember the two great dramas which were played out 50 years ago . . . we should also remember the battle fought out in Canberra and London and Washington—for in large part it was that battle which made success here in Papua New Guinea possible. In that battle John Curtin defied those people Australia had never defied. He insisted to his counterparts in London and Washington—his friends, our friends—that Australian troops then serving in the Middle East should return home and defend Australia.
>
> John Curtin was right. Just as he was right when he declared that in the hour of crisis after the fall of Singapore, Australia looked to the United States—free, he said, "of any pangs as to our traditional links of kinship with the United Kingdom." "We know that Austra-

lia can go and Britain still hold on," he said. "We are therefore determined that Australia shall not go." In doing this he took the Anzac legend to mean that Australia came first—that whatever the claims of Empire on the loyalty of those who died in the Great War, the pre-eminent claim had been Australia's.

The Australians who served here in Papua New Guinea fought and died not in defence of the old world but the new world. Their world. They died in defence of Australia and the civilisation and values which had grown up there.

That is why it might be said that, for Australians, the battles in Papua New Guinea were the most important ever fought.

On the following day, Keating traveled from Port Moresby to the nearby mountain village of Kokoda, the site of intense combat between Australian and Japanese troops during World War II. His brief speech resumed the themes of the previous day (*The Australian*, 27 April 1992):

It was here that young Australian men fought for the first time against the prospect of the invasion of their country, of Australia.

This was the first and only time we have fought against an enemy to prevent the invasion of Australia, to save the way of life we had built for ourselves.

These young men believed in Australia. And we need to give Australians, all Australians, particularly young Australians, something to believe in.

And everything we see here, there can be no deeper spiritual basis for the meaning of the Australian nation than the blood that was spilt on this very knoll, this very plateau in defence of the liberty of Australia.

Keating dramatically underscored his message by laying wreaths at the base of three monuments to Allied and Japanese soldiers and "native carriers" killed at Kokoda. At a fourth monument, dedicated to individual acts of heroism by Australian soldiers, Keating stepped forward, knelt, and kissed the cement base of the stone memorial. A small picture of the kneeling prime minister, lips pressed to the ground, appears on the front page of today's *The Australian*.

The import of Keating's words and actions was lost on no one.[6] Indeed, *The Australian's* lead article, titled "Keating Sparks Outrage on

Anzac Legend and Flag," began as follows: "The Prime Minister urged Australians yesterday to redefine the Anzac legend in favor of nationalism rather than traditional ties . . ." Strong reactions came first of all from Bruce Ruxton, national vice president of the Returned Services League, who said "that it was 'the bottom of the bucket' using Anzacs as the background for republicanism" (*Canberra Times*, 27 April 1992). " 'Those thousands of Australians in the Bomana war cemetery would have got up and pushed him down one of the holes,' Mr Ruxton said." According to *The Australian*, "The Leader of the Opposition, Dr. Hewson, angrily criticised the comments, accusing Mr. Keating of trying to 'buy new friends in Asia by disowning old ones, by apologising for Australia's past and by committing his Government to changing our flag.' "

In his speeches, Keating challenged a dominant national narrative by seizing upon one of its internal contradictions, namely, that the Australian nation was born at Gallipoli—in dutiful service of the British Empire. The challenge he put to his audience—obviously not the Papua New Guineans in attendance—was to rethink the national past-future. As Renan would surely point out, Keating urged Australians to "forget" Gallipoli (that is, to remember it differently) and to "remember" Kokoda (that is, to remember it differently as well). The apparently innocuous claim that the World War II battles in Papua and New Guinea (to avoid Keating's anachronism) "were the most important ever fought" in fact establishes a new chronology for the Australian nation. Gallipoli, in this view, was merely a prelude to or foreshadowing of Kokoda; only at Kokoda was the passage effected from empire to nation-state, from old world order to new.

What is perhaps most remarkable about Keating's two speeches (and indeed much of Australian nation making) is their self-consciousness. Keating acknowledged the instrumental effects of national narratives and argued plainly that he wished to recast the narrative in order to produce a particular effect: renewed Australian nationalism. In doing so, moreover, he seemingly cribbed the argument made a week earlier in *The Weekend Australian* (18–19 April 1992) by Gregory Pemberton, a lecturer in politics at Macquarie University. In an article titled "The Conspiracy to Keep Secret Our Finest Hour," Pemberton spoke perceptively about the role of the state in nation making:

> A people's national memory is largely constructed by the State. The government normally has the greatest resources at its disposal to

shape how its citizens view their past, and it can promote certain events and values while suppressing or downplaying others.

Pemberton then continued by urging the prime minister to remind Australians about the "forgotten" military achievements in New Guinea, which Pemberton describes in some detail. "Perhaps the Prime Minister can redress this in New Guinea [*sic*] this Anzac Day."[7] The prime minister apparently heard Pemberton's demand that "Australians reclaim the past and dispense with much of the imperial historical baggage that has hindered the development of our sense of identity and direction."

Keating's new national narrative is not without its own internal contradictions. The story intended to demonstrate Australia's break with imperialism omits mention of the fact that Australian soldiers spilled their blood in an Australian colony, the Territory of Papua, and in a Mandated Trust Territory of the League of Nations, New Guinea. Indeed, Keating's anachronistic and ambiguous use of "Papua New Guinea" to name the location of the heroic World War II battles implicitly moves decolonization forward by more than thirty years. Likewise, the story that Hewson condemned as a ploy to make friends in Asia has the unfortunate feature of casting Asians, "the Japanese," as fearsome aggressors. These contradictions leave Keating's narrative itself vulnerable to challenges and open to further transformations.

Keating's narrative, moreover, must compete with other definitions of the nation, definitions that do not invoke military history in justification either of republicanism (and sui generis Australianness) or of loyalty to the monarch (and Anglo-Australianness). The most prominent of these definitions currently circulating within Australia is "multiculturalism" (see Castles et al. 1990; Gunew 1990). Consider the lyrics of the chorus to the popular song, "I am Australian," now marketed by its creator as "suitable for opening and closing TV transmissions and sporting events such as grand finals" (*The Australian Magazine*, 11–12 April 1992):[8]

We are one, but we are many
And from all the lands on earth we come
We share a dream and sing with one voice
I am
You are
We are Austral-ian

Versions (and visions) of contemporary Australia as a culturally diverse nation became part of official state policy (federal as well as local) during the mid-1970s, and today the discourse of multiculturalism underwrites such events as Carnivale 91, New South Wales's statewide multicultural festival. The premier of New South Wales sent the following message (published in a supplement to the *Sydney Morning Herald*, 23 September 1991) to mark the occasion:

> No other celebration in Australia has such a powerful and distinctive theme—the value and meaning of multiculturalism to Australian society. Carnivale is alive, vibrant and full of surprises.
>
> The remarkable community support and involvement of almost all members of the different ethnic communities is highly commendable.
>
> Carnivale is not only evidence of my Government's endorsement of the multicultural ideal; it represents substantial investment in the growth of our society and culture generally.

The centerpiece of Carnivale was a familiar display of ethnic foods, crafts, and music offered under the aegis of corporate sponsorship in various locales throughout Sydney. (The display recalled the advice of the Bicentennial Authority on how to be multicultural: "Plan to have a meal from a different culture at least once a month in 1988" [cited in Castles et al. 1990, 6].) Satellite events throughout Sydney's suburbs and the whole state of New South Wales included "An Aboriginal Event" in Redfern and, in Broken Hill, a "Workshop, international night, cabaret and bocce tournament celebrating Yugoslav culture and history in Broken Hill."

In short, in April 1992, alternative imaginative constructs of Australia fill the landscape that they compete to appropriate. These images and ideals are produced by politicians, patriotic entrepreneurs, and commercial advertisers. They circulate in the discursive forms of campaign speeches, newspaper articles, and song lyrics; they circulate in the nondiscursive forms of shish kebabs, boomerangs, war memorials, and ministerial genuflections. They function as resources in mobilizing committed voters, charitable donors, festivalgoers, and supermarket shoppers. Nation making in Australia, as everywhere else, intertwines cultural forms and material interests in a creative and contested process of identity formation.

**Persons as Legitimate Subjects of and in a
Territorial State**

I return now to the general concept of nation making. Fox's use of the
phrase "nationalist ideologies" to refer generally to the production of
conceptions of peoplehood is a deliberate exercise in lumping. He
prefers to obviate the analytical difficulties of distinguishing among
"nationalisms," "ethnicities," and "racial identities"—of splitting—by
emphasizing that all these terms refer to "cultural productions of public identity" (Fox 1990, 4). His point is that these identities "develop,
alter, and integrade in real life," and it is these fluid processes, rather
than some classificatory scheme of the analyst, that merit attention. By
this account, then, Fox might find the concept of nation making proposed here unacceptable, for we wish to preserve something of the
specificity—historical as well as categorical—of nationhood and nationality as particular kinds of collective and personal identities. Recognition of the novel and alien nature of "the nation" as a form of
identity is crucial to understanding important aspects of nation making
in postcolonial Melanesia (as LiPuma and Kelly rightly stress; see also
Jacobsen this volume).

Most important, we want to emphasize with Anderson that the imaginative construct of "the nation" always implies a possessive relationship
between "the people" and a territorial state. This relationship is double
inasmuch as it entails relations between irreducibly different "peoples" or
nation-states and between an individual person and his or her nation-
state. Relations between nation-states follow necessarily from the construction of the nation as inherently limited; some people are automatically and irrevocably excluded (recall Anderson's remark that the nation
must be imagined as existing amid a plurality of other nations). This
inherent limitation underwrites an unbreakable association between "the
people" and some definite territory, an association that establishes a
physical boundary separating the "inside" from the "outside" of the nation. As Balibar (1990, 348) puts it, "external frontiers have to be imagined constantly as a projection and protection of an internal collective
personality, which each person carries within him/herself and enables
him/her to inhabit the space of the state as a place where one has always
been—and where one will always be—at 'home.'" Indeed, state agencies work hard to bound and to police state space through a repertoire of

gatekeeping procedures: presentations of passports, exchange of currencies, customs inspections, and so forth. Similarly, some of the most difficult work performed by national narratives involves naturalizing this boundary or frontier—so patently arbitrary in most former colonial states—and thus rendering as given the tie between people and place.

Verdery (1992) has usefully called attention to the other dimension of the possessive relationship between "people" and state by proposing that we treat "nation" not simply as an ideological construct, but as one that ties subjects to the state. Her formulation, accordingly, highlights not only the contestation involved in all ideological construction, but also the fashion in which ideologies constitute subjectivities. "The nation" is thus an ideological device in terms of which subjection is legitimated, through which politically institutionalized power is presented or accounted for in terms of common interest and morality. Because nationalist ideologies or national narratives invariably differ, we must expect that state-subject relations will likewise vary, both between nation-states and historically within nation-states. How does the "nation" mediate the state-subject relationship? What kinds of variations in state-subject relations can be identified?

Verdery notes, as have many others, that "the nation" has been implicated in two very different formulations of the state-subject relationship, usually associated with Western Europe and Eastern Europe, respectively. On the one hand, there is the relationship known as *citizenship* which emphasizes common political participation as the basis of "the nation" and thus links subjects to the state through their political agency. On the other hand, there is the relationship known as *ethnicity,* which emphasizes common language, history, and culture as the basis of the nation and thus links subjects to the state through their ethnic similarity. Verdery then distinguishes a third state-subject relationship that socialist rule sought to institute. This relationship of *socialist paternalism* "emphasized a moral tie linking subjects to the state through their rights to a share in the redistributed social product" (1992, 8). It thus constituted the nation as a moral community and subjects as "dependents" of the state.

Verdery's delineation of three state-subject relationships demonstrates how broadly different imaginings of the nation alternatively legitimate state power and constitute subjects of state power. This double process of legitimation and constitution can be looked at from another angle. Each type of subject that Verdery identifies—citizen, coethnic, and dependent—is one subspecies of *Homo nationalis,* to use Balibar's term.[9] And *Homo nationalis*, like "the nation" itself, is largely a product of state agencies. State agencies, in other words, mediate the formation of collective and individual identities—nationality and personality—and in so doing assert their presence and power as a natural and normal condition of daily affairs. What are the mundane ways in which state activity imbricates "individual existence into the weft of a collective narrative" (Balibar 1990, 346) and thereby produces an imagined community of "nationals"? What are the routines and rituals of rule, legitimated as originating with "the people," that in turn produce and reproduce "the people," both collectively and individually?

In this regard, the concern of the earlier work on nation building with state-controlled practices of socialization is pertinent. The role of schooling is central (see Jourdan this volume). History textbooks disseminate the official national narrative; examinations measure individual conformity to appropriate standards of thought and behavior; everyday school performances—flag ceremonies, anthem singing, oaths of allegiance—enjoin the bodily enactment of nationality.[10] But formal schooling is perhaps only the most visible aspect of a whole project of moral regulation through which state agencies—Althusser's ideological state apparatuses—constitute subjects. As Cohn and Dirks argue (1988, 224), following Corrigan and Sayer (1985), state agencies constitute subjects through an extensive set of "officializing" procedures. The state creates and accumulates knowledge of "the people" by rendering "the people" as knowable subjects: subjects counted and classified in censuses; registered on birth certificates; issued with draft cards; and so forth. Moral regulation, in this sense, is all about the establishment of categorical identities. Individuals "are related to a focus of loyalty which entails a territory, a people and a legitimated system of rule"—the nation-state (Corrigan and Sayer 1987, 7). At the same time, these individuals are "quite specifically identified in terms of gender, race, age, residential, occupational, religious, and linguistic categories" (Corrigan and Sayer 1987, 7); they are constituted as individual subjects within the nation-state. When all this documentation and certification seem normal and neutral—by no means the case in postcolonial Melanesia (see Kelly this volume)—the institution of *Homo nationalis* happens as a self-legitimating occurrence.

italism and "the Nation"

The ways in which capitalism conditions the production and dissemination of imaginative constructs of the nation are both numerous and complex. This is as true in Melanesia as elsewhere. For example, constructions of "the nation," and hence "the national interest," clearly serve class interests, not in the least by deflecting attention from class conflicts that belie the putative solidarity of "the people." Different competing interests within the ruling class itself, moreover, often advance themselves through alternative definitions of the nation. Class analysis thus helps in locating the social situation of the agents and intentions behind the actual making of imaginative constructs of nationhood (for Melanesian examples, see Philibert 1986 and LiPuma and Meltzoff 1990).

There is another way, however, in which capitalism informs nation making that I want to mention here, mainly because of its bearing on issues of collective representation and the construction of subjects (or individual identity). In his chapter of this book, LiPuma raises a question about "how the epistemology of capitalism, embodied in its practices and objects, becomes embedded in the production of national culture." Put differently, I want to ask how the possessive relationship between persons and things in a world of commodities functions as the reference point for thinking about collective and personal identities. Let me begin by returning to the matter of constituting subjects.

The paradigmatic Western state-subject relationship constitutes "citizens" as autonomous, free agents. These citizens are "individuals" with inherent and equal rights who, by exercising their freedom, enter into social relations independent of the state (that is, into civil society). The state, somewhat paradoxically, protects the autonomy of this realm of social relations and forfeits its legitimacy to the extent that it violates this autonomy. In the realm of civil society, individual free choice—the capacity to enter into contractual relations—reigns supreme.

The sort of subject described by the term *citizen* is clearly well suited to the exigencies of social life in a world conditioned by capitalist economic practices; for the "citizen" is none other than the famous self-interested "individual" free to choose what exchanges (say, of wages for labor power) that he or she enters; free to purchase in the marketplace whatever consumer goods he or she chooses; free to allocate his or her productive resources as he or she chooses.[11] There is, in other words, a resonance or fit between the constitution of subjects engendered through capitalist economic practices and rhetoric, on the one hand, and the state-subject relationship of "citizenship," on the other. The subject in both cases is a "possessive individual" (Foster this volume), an individuated being who "is essentially the proprietor of his own person and capacities [especially the capacity to labor], for which he owes nothing to society" (MacPherson 1969, 263).

Consequently, the expansion of practices and discourses of possessive individualism through capitalism potentially enables various imaginings of "the nation" within the trope of possession: people belonging to a nation; a nation, state, or territory belonging to a people or (double-sided possession) belonging to *its* people. The way that states regulate and adjudicate possession through law and police force is mediated by the trope of possession itself: the nation-state has (possesses) laws. But ambiguities and possibilities abound in the operation of the trope of possession in relating subject and state—not only, but especially, in the Pacific. Consider, for example, Fiji's "people of the land" and Taukei, "owner's movement" (Rutz this volume). More generally, what form has the expansion of possessive relations taken in Melanesia, and with what consequences for the way in which "the nation" is imagined?

The spread and generalization of market relations is at once the spread and generalization of possessive individualism, necessarily so because the operation of market relations implies and requires an individual's proprietorship of himself or herself. Thus, to the extent Melanesian social life becomes progressively "commoditized"—reproduced through the production, exchange, and consumption of commodities—Melanesians engage in practices that constitute subjects as possessive individuals: earning a wage; paying rent, head taxes, or school fees; buying rice and tinned fish. This particular construction of the subject potentially competes and clashes with other constructions, realized in other practices, that posit subjects not as bounded, self-contained proprietary individuals but, rather, as "relational persons," nodes in a matrix of social relations (Strathern 1988; see Hirsch this volume). These latter constructions, long familiar to anthropologists of Melanesia from the work of Mauss and Leenhardt, (stereo)typically find their locus in practices of gift giving. Hence, the deep concern of anthropologists and Melanesians alike with the apparently radical differences between gifts and commodities is also a concern with fundamental definitions of personhood.

Some scholars directly implicate the commodity form in the imagination of the nation. Handler, in his studies of cultural politics in Quebec (1985, 1988), has made the Dumontian point that both possessive individualism and nationalism share the same "epistemology of 'entivity,' " the presupposition that an entity can be bounded by attributes or characteristics that it uniquely possesses. Nationalism accordingly posits the nation as a "collective individual" composed of individuals alike in the attributes they possess. Nationality itself, then, is a common possession of the individual subjects, tangibly in the form of the set of commodities and other material objects that constitute the "national culture." That is, the things of national culture comprise a unique collection, proprietorship of which, in turn, renders "the people" a distinctive collective individual.

Many commentators have noted, often unkindly, how this sort of objectification of national culture has become institutionalized throughout the South Pacific (Babadzan 1988; Keesing 1989). The representation and definition of "the nation" take the form of material exhibitions—of art, artifacts, songs and dance performances, ancient customs, house styles, and the like. The Pacific Arts Festival thus operates according to the same logic as Carnivale '91 or Seville Universal Expo '92, equating collective identities (national in one case, subnational or ethnic in the other) with objects, then vending these objects as consumer goods. Hence we see the suitability of this form of objectification to ideologies of "unity in diversity": diversity means not difference but, rather, stylistic variation (Facey this volume). The exhibited objects, moreover, are necessarily decontextualized. Consequently, as LiPuma (this volume) points out, "Objects that were once exclusively plural and immediately functional—that is to say imbued with meaning and hence valued by virtue of their local cultural specificity—are now given a singular and 'abstract' function as national symbols." "The nation" is thus realized in the form of commodities: "an assemblage of discontinuous, observable and thus reproducible material elements" (Babadzan 1988, 207). These material elements—possessed by "the people" but displayed or sold as commodities to the tourists—are the stuff people have when they have a national culture.

In short, capitalism conditions the imagination of the nation not only by conditioning the interests and resources of the agents responsible for producing "the nation" as an imaginative construct. The practices and rhetoric of capitalism also educate people into a particular way of thinking about and representing nations and nationals, collectivities and persons. In this view, each nation and each national exists as a generically similar entity; it is only with reference to the things that each possesses that specific differences emerge. Accordingly, the burden of nation making becomes the identification, inventory, and preservation of a national patrimony.

The Chapters in Brief

The chapters of this volume originated as papers presented during a working session on national cultures at the 1991 conference of the Association for Social Anthropology in Oceania. At that session, Edward LiPuma surveyed some of the general problems and issues invariably encountered in the study of nationalism and nation-states in Oceania, and in the study of nation making, in particular. Afterwards, contributors to the session were asked to read a revised version of LiPuma's paper and encouraged to address some of the issues and problems that he had formulated. LiPuma, in turn, read the revised papers of the various contributors and developed his own paper into a programmatic call for a nonreductionistic approach to nation-states, nationalism, and nation making in Oceania. That approach, outlined in part 1, the opening chapter of this volume, draws on concepts of European social theory such as those of civil society and the public sphere, concepts rarely, if ever, employed in studies of postcolonial Melanesian societies. On the one hand, LiPuma insists that nation making cannot be understood as a reflex of putatively more basic political and economic realities and interests (see also Kaplan this volume). On the other hand, he underscores how the nation-state as a political form is inseparable from Western culture and capitalism, that is, how the nation-state entails Western notions of the relationship between the individual, state, and civil society. His chapter therefore both extends certain points made in this introduction and provides a second, sometimes alternative, frame in which to read the subsequent ethnographic analyses.

LiPuma's holistic approach to nation making issues the methodological challenge of accounting for everything all at once—the task of squaring intensive local ethnography with a historical analysis of "large scale epochal transformations," for LiPuma delineates the way in which the process of nation making is doubly conditioned. The particular versions or inventions of the nation put forward by competing agents are "infiltrated by an increasingly internationalized Western capitalist culture," on the one hand, and "imbued with meaning, appropriated, and used by local communities," on the other. Nation making, in other words, responds simultaneously to global and local conditions. Nation making involves the uncertain attempt to define and bound a community less inclusive than the world but more inclusive than local communities of language, kinship, and so forth.

As LiPuma remarks, however, it is not necessary that all accounts of nation making do everything all at once, only that they recognize the intrinsic relationship between local, nation-state, and global processes. This recognition informs the organization of the volume. Accordingly, all the chapters register with different emphases the circumstances and effects of nation making in colonial and postcolonial Melanesia. LiPuma's chapter concentrates especially on the operation of world historical forces and phenomena, or more specifically, on the project of creating in Oceania modern states with a place in the global capitalist order. The other chapters vary noticeably among themselves in the attention they give to the instrumental means for disseminating images and ideals of nationhood and to the local receptions and interpretations of these images and ideals. The chapters in part 2 focus on the former, while the chapters in part 3 concentrate on the latter.

The chapters by Rutz and Kaplan form a complementary pair that together expose the various limitations operating upon the imagination and achievement of a democratic nation-state in Fiji. (Readers unfamiliar with the colonial history of Fiji will profit from reading Kaplan's chapter before Rutz's.) In treating "the nation" as a political narrative, Rutz explicates the rhetorical strategies through which a variety of agents have historically confronted each other in a struggle for legitimacy and empowerment. He shows how these agents—the former prime minister Ratu Mara, the Fijian Nationalist Party founder Sakeasi Butadroka, and the leader of the coups, Sitiveni Rabuka—all produced narratives that define the nation as a composite of three elements: "chiefs," "land," and "church." Since the colonial period, competing political narratives have reordered the hierarchical relations among these elements but never challenged the status of the elements as "given." Rutz shows, furthermore, how different rhetorical strategies have become unpersuasive over time, and he speculates that possible political narratives premised upon the interrelationship of chiefs, land, and church have been exhausted.

Kaplan also discloses the internal logic of political narratives, not-

ing for example the contradictions in official postindependence procla-
mations that attempted to represent Fiji Indians as integral to the Fijian
nation. But she focuses more on the periodic ritual performances that
sustain and/or transform such narratives. By contrasting the official rituals of the independent Fijian state (such as ceremonies for visiting dignitaries) with the unofficial rituals of one eccentric and visionary citizen
(such as the commemoration of a public monument), Kaplan demonstrates how different persons and/or groups or classes seek to establish
and routinize their versions of "the nation." In this view, ritual is not the
"symbolic" acting out of a narrative made real by other means, but the
very action by which people "create and implement narratives to control
or to empower, to contest the old or envision the new (or even envision
the old anew)." Juxtaposed, each set of rituals reveals the contradictions
and obfuscations of the other, as well as the marginal place of Fiji
Indians in narratives and practices of Fijian nationhood grounded in
"chiefly" rule and Methodist Christianity—the legacy of the colonial
state.

The chapters by Jourdan and Foster locate the processes of nation
making in sites other than political ideology and ritual politics. Jourdan
identifies three such overlapping sites: formal schooling, language policy, and popular culture. She treats the Solomon Islands as a case study
in how the state uses the first two means in order to disseminate ideals of
the nation—its history, geography, and shared language of Pijin. "The
nation," in other words, is used to produce legitimacy for the developing
state apparatus. This strategy is all the more important, Jourdan reminds
us, in situations—common in postcolonial Melanesia—in which the independent state itself functions as the Other in opposition to which local
populations define distinctive "ethnic" identities (see Howard 1989;
Jacobsen this volume). By contrast, popular culture develops more or
less beyond the reach of the state apparatus, spun out of the encounter
between Solomon Islanders and the images, objects, and practices circulating within the cultural and economic world system. Jourdan attributes
the "innocuous spread" and "binding power" of this emergent popular
culture throughout the Solomons to its "neutrality": "Not being anyone's culture that can be associated with an ethnic group, but being a
type of generic culture (Philibert 1986), it overcomes ethnic boundaries:
it allows for new shared meanings, symbols, and representations to
reach out on a wider scale."

Jourdan describes nation making as a process particularly visible in urban settings such as Honiara and Port Moresby. This visibility comes about inasmuch as urban areas bring together in one place people of an emergent middle class who are equipped with the knowledge and means to participate in a developing popular culture of consumerism. In my chapter, I treat print advertisements aimed at such urban populations as instruments for the dissemination of images of Papua New Guinea(ns). My discussion focuses as much on the form of the ads as on their content in order to emphasize how consumer practices in a capitalist economy enable definitions of personhood different from those grounded in social relations of kinship. That is, commodity consumption enables persons to define themselves as individual subjects with reference to a world of neutral objects—objects that could belong to anyone. By the same token, consumption enables persons to imagine themselves as related or not related to other persons through their shared or unshared consumption practices. Print advertisements that deploy imagery of "the nation" thus posit the possibility of consumer citizenship, placement in a national community acquired through the consumption of national commodities.

The chapters by Jourdan and Foster recall LiPuma's insistence about the need for intensive local ethnography in the study of nation making. It is one thing to note the importance of schooling in disseminating narratives of the nation; it is another thing to demonstrate how or if students actually engage these stories. Likewise, it is one thing to disclose the semiotic logic of the ad form; it is another thing to demonstrate how or if readers actually construe this logic. The chapters in part 3 of the volume address questions of this order, that is, questions about local appropriations of, resistance to, and indifference about images and ideals of the nation originating elsewhere. Jacobsen's chapter asks, moreover, to what extent there is a process of unmaking nations that opposes and subverts the work of nation making.

Hirsch takes up this question from the perspective of the Fuyuge, a group of people living in cutoff proximity to the sources of wealth that they perceive to be localized in nearby Port Moresby. His discussion focuses on two distinct ways in which Fuyuge attempt to overcome this separation by appropriating elements of metropolitan culture for local use. On the one hand, Fuyuge actively attempt to procure from Port Moresby large amounts of money and betel nut, objects they deem necessary ingredients of the rituals (*gab*) that produce a sense of cosmic order. On the other, Fuyuge use the names of locales in and around Port

Moresby to rename stretches of the local landscape. Hirsch argues that a "national culture" in Papua New Guinea emerges out of such variable attempts by peripheral populations to appropriate the same material and symbolic resources concentrated in urban centers. This "national culture" is immanent, an inner sense of belonging to some supralocal imagined community that derives from locally variable projects of cultural appropriation.

Facey similarly explores the issue of local appropriation through a case study of how a rural community receives and interprets images and narratives of the nation circulated via nationwide political processes. Specifically, she asks why, on the eve of Vanuatu's independence, the people of Nguna enthusiastically embraced the Vanuaaku Pati and its visions of the national future. The answer, Facey claims, lies in the Pati's rhetoric about *kastom* or "traditional culture," for the stance adopted by the Vanuaaku Pati was one of "*kastom* within Christianity," a reconciliation of "tradition" with introduced religion that fit well an Ngunese status quo grounded in a dual structure of chiefly titles and Presbyterian church leadership. The Ngunese case thus poses a useful counterpoint to the cases of Tanna (Vanuatu) (Lindstrom 1982) and Kwaio (Solomon Islands) (Keesing 1992) where definitions of *kastom* as non-Christian and non-Western underwrote confrontations between local populations and the newly independent state.

Jacobsen's discussion identifies sources of resistance to a "national culture" in PNG in addition to those of competing ideologies of *kastom*. He focuses instead on the relatively weak penetration of state political institutions into rural areas and argues furthermore that the social relations of capitalist production have not fundamentally threatened the economic autonomy of local communities in these areas. It is this very political and economic integrity of local communities that undoes the work of nation making. Writing from the perspective of the Dom people of Simbu Province, Jacobsen claims that local communities, far from being incorporated into the administrative machinery of the independent state, use this machinery in pursuit of their own ends. The attitude of the Dom toward national and provincial government recalls the Fuyuge perception of Port Moresby: "a source of wealth which can be tapped if only the right means are employed." The inability of weak state agencies and attenuated capitalist social relations to encompass Dom society signals for Jacobsen a novel outcome: the subversive transformation of the imported unitary nation-state into a variety of hybrid institutions, all of which bear the impress of indigenous ("primordial") social structures and cultural interests.

Several of the issues and problems raised in this introduction (and by LiPuma) run through Jacobsen's chapter: the radical foreignness of the nation-state to Melanesia; the inseparable connection between the spread of the nation-state and the global expansion of capitalism; and the historical contingency and potential decline of the nation-state as a viable form of polity. Kelly resumes the general discussion of these themes in his epilogue by relating the papers in this volume to the question of how one goes about writing an ethnography of nation making. In so doing, he derives from the chapters an approach that treats nations as narratives and pays attention to the ways in which agents, including the state, contend with each other to secure acceptance of particular narratives. He goes further, however, in arguing that just as ethnographers need not take "the nation" as given, so they need not regard "the state" as necessary, not even as necessary for providing the regulatory and coercive mechanisms that make world capitalist markets work. Indeed, he asks, given the notorious weakness of state institutions in Melanesia, what, if anything, makes for the integrity of the nation-state as a form of community poised somewhere between localities and world markets? Kelly concludes by calling for the situation of contemporary processes of nation making in Melanesia within the larger history of colonialism and capitalism in the Pacific. The effect of this strategy, he suggests, is of double significance for the ethnographic project: to reveal something about the tenacity, elasticity, and limits of a world historical form—the nation-state—by looking at how certain Pacific people use this form in combination with other more "experience near" forms, changing their lives in the process.

NOTES

1. The exception here is France, reluctant to remove itself both from the former condominium of the New Hebrides (Vanuatu) and now from New Caledonia (Kanaky), the only recognized colony remaining in the southwestern Pacific. (West Papua/Irian Jaya remains an unrecognized colony.)

2. "We, the people of Papua New Guinea, united in one nation, pay homage to the memory of our ancestors, the source of our strength and origin of our combined heritage, acknowledge the worthy customs and traditional wis-

doms of our people, which have come down to us from generation to generation, pledge ourselves to guard and pass on to those who come after us our noble traditions and the Christian principles that are ours now." On reconciling noble traditions with Christian principles, see Latukefu 1988.

3. The recent coups in Fiji and the present secessionist movement on Bougainville necessitate the qualification of this claim.

4. Quoted in Seton-Watson 1977, 107. Hobsbawm (1972, 393) notes in passing that "in 1860 the percentage of citizens of the newly united kingdom who actually spoke Italian at home, and not merely (when they knew it at all) used it as a language of literate culture or a *lingua franca* for communicating with Italians from other regions, probably did not exceed 2.5 per cent."

5. There is a large literature on the construction of Australian national identity (see Whitlock and Carter 1992). In particular, Richard White's *Inventing Australia* (1981) prefigures the flood of anthropological and historical writing on national invention and imagination unleashed by Anderson (1983) and Hobsbawm and Ranger (1983).

6. Keating's speeches came in the middle of an election campaign in which the prime minister has made an issue of designating Australia as a republic. Keating's campaign has focused in particular on the question of a new national flag—one without the famous Union Jack.

7. Note how Pemberton's use of the anachronistic "New Guinea" for "Papua New Guinea" establishes continuity between the World War II battle scene and the destination of the prime minister's visit. Both colonization and decolonization are erased from his narrative.

8. Next month, the song's author, Bruce Woodley, "will close a $1500-a-plate Prime Minister's dinner for 1000 people to sponsor the Olympic Games team. He'll sing *I Am Australian*, backed by a boys' choir, as he does in a big screen audio-visual presentation which is the centrepiece of the pitch to potential donors" (*The Australian Magazine*, 11–12 April 1992, 35).

9. "A social formation only reproduces itself as a nation to the extent that, through a network of apparatuses and daily practices, the individual is instituted as *homo nationalis* from cradle to grave, at the same time as he/she is instituted as *homo oeconomicus, politicus, religiosus* . . ." (Balibar 1990, 345).

10. Likewise, the annual (decennial, centenary, etc.) performances of state rituals not only display the nation to "the people" (as Keating said of legends), but also assert the power of the state to make the display (see Kaplan this volume).

11. I say "he or she." Pateman 1988 shows that this "individual" is always more-or-less explicitly masculine in gender.

REFERENCES

Anderson, Benedict. 1983. *Imagined Communities: Reflections on the Origin and Spread of Nationalism*. London: Verso.

————. 1986. Narrating the nation. *Times Literary Supplement* (June 13): 659.

Babadzan, Alain. 1988. *Kastom* and nation building in the South Pacific. In R. Guidieri, F. Pellizi, and S. J. Tambiah, eds., *Ethnicities and Nations: Processes of Interethnic Relations in Latin America, Southeast Asia, and the Pacific*, 199–228. Austin: University of Texas Press.

Balibar, Etienne. 1990. The nation form: History and ideology. *Review* 13:329–61.

Bendix, Reinhard. 1969. *Nation-Building and Citizenship*. Garden City, New York: Doubleday.

Bhabha, Homi, ed. 1990. *Nation and Narration*. New York: Routledge.

Breuilly, John. 1985. *Nationalism and the State*. Chicago: University of Chicago Press.

Castles, Stephen, et al. 1990. *Mistaken Identity: Multiculturalism and the Demise of Nationalism in Australia*, 2d ed. Sydney: Pluto Press.

Cohn, Bernard S., and Nicholas B. Dirks. 1988. Beyond the fringe: The nation state, colonialism, and the technologies of power. *Journal of Historical Sociology* 1:224–29.

Corrigan, Philip, and Derek Sayer. 1985. *The Great Arch: English State Formation as Cultural Revolution*. Oxford: Basil Blackwell.

————. 1987. From "the body politic" to "the national interest": English state formation in comparative and historical perspective; an argument concerning "politically organized subjection." Paper presented at Mellon Symposium on Historical Anthropology, May, at California Institute of Technology, Pasadena.

Deutsch, Karl W., and William J. Foltz, eds. 1963. *Nation-Building*. New York: Atherton Press.

Fallers, Lloyd A. 1974. *The Social Anthropology of the Nation-State*. Chicago: Aldine.

Ferguson, James, and Akhil Gupta, eds. 1992. *Space, Identity, and the Politics of Difference*. Theme Issue, *Cultural Anthropology*. 7:3–129.

Foster, Robert J. 1991. Making national cultures in the global ecumene. *Annual Review of Anthropology* 20:235–60.

Fox, Richard G. 1990. Introduction. In Richard G. Fox, ed., *Nationalist Ideologies and the Production of National Cultures*, 1–14. Washington: American Anthropological Association.

Geertz, Clifford, ed. 1963. *Old Societies and New States: The Quest for Modernity in Asia and Africa*. Glencoe, IL: Free Press.

Gellner, Ernest. 1983. *Nations and Nationalism*. Ithaca: Cornell University Press.

Grillo, R. D., ed. 1980. *"Nation" and "State" in Europe: Anthropological Perspectives*. London: Academic Press.

Gunew, Sneja. 1990. Denaturalizing cultural nationalisms: Multicultural readings of "Australia." In Homi Bhabha, ed., *Nation and Narration*, 99–120. New York: Routledge.

Handler, Richard. 1985. On having a culture: Nationalism and the preservation of Quebec's *patrimoine*. In George Stocking, Jr., ed., *Objects and Others:*

Essays on Museums and Material Culture, 192–217. Madison: University of Wisconsin Press.

———. 1988. *Nationalism and the Politics of Culture in Quebec*. Madison: University of Wisconsin Press.

Hobsbawm, Eric. 1972. Some reflections on nationalism. In T. Nossiter, A. Hanson, and S. Rokkan, eds., *Imagination and Precision in the Social Sciences*, 385–406. London: Faber and Faber.

Hobsbawm, Eric, and Terence Ranger, eds. 1983. *The Invention of Tradition*. Cambridge: Cambridge University Press.

Howard, Michael C., ed. 1989. *Ethnicity and Nation-Building in the Pacific*. Tokyo: United Nations University.

Inglis, Ken. 1989. Men, women, and war memorials: Anzac Australia. In J. Conway, S. Bourque, and J. Scott, eds., *Learning About Women: Gender, Politics, and Power*, 35–59. Ann Arbor: University of Michigan Press.

Jolly, Margaret, and Nicholas Thomas, eds. 1992. *The Politics of Tradition in the Pacific*. Special Issue, *Oceania* 62:241–354.

Kapferer, Bruce. 1988. *Legends of People, Myths of State: Violence, Intolerance, and Political Culture in Sri Lanka and Australia*. Washington: Smithsonian Institution Press.

Keesing, Roger M. 1989. Creating the past: Custom and identity in the contemporary Pacific. *The Contemporary Pacific* 1:19–42.

———. 1992. *Custom and Confrontation: The Kwaio Struggle for Cultural Autonomy*. Chicago: University of Chicago Press.

Keesing, Roger M., and Robert Tonkinson, eds. 1982. *Reinventing Traditional Culture: The Politics of Kastom in Island Melanesia*. Special Issue, *Mankind* 13:297–399.

Latukefu, Sione. 1988. Noble traditions and Christian principles as national ideology in Papua New Guinea: Do their philosophies complement or contradict each other? *Pacific Studies* 11:83–96.

Layoun, Mary. 1992. Telling spaces: Palestinian women and the engendering of national narratives. In A. Parker, et al., eds., *Nationalisms and Sexualities*, 407–23. New York: Routledge.

LeVine, Robert. 1963. Political socialization and culture change. In Clifford Geertz, ed., *Old Societies and New States*, 280–303. Glencoe, IL: Free Press.

Lindstrom, Lamont. 1982. *Leftamap kastom*: The political history of tradition on Tanna (Vanuatu). In R. Keesing and R. Tonkinson, eds., *Reinventing Traditional Culture*. Special Issue, *Mankind* 13:316–29.

———. 1990. *Pasin tumbuna*: Cultural traditions and national identity in Papua New Guinea. Paper presented at the meeting of the Association for Social Anthropology in Oceania, 23 March, Kauai.

Linnekin, Jocelyn. 1990. The politics of culture in the Pacific. In Jocelyn Linnekin and Lin Poyer, eds., *Cultural Identity and Ethnicity in the Pacific*, 149–73. Honolulu: University of Hawaii Press.

LiPuma, Edward, and Sarah K. Meltzoff. 1990. Ceremonies of independence and public culture in the Solomon Islands. *Public Culture* 3:77–92.

Llobera, Josep R. 1990. Catalan national identity: The dialects of past and present. *Critique of Anthropology* 10:11–38.

MacPherson, C. B. 1962. *The Political Theory of Possessive Individualism: Hobbes to Locke*. Oxford: Clarendon Press.

Marriott, McKim. 1963. Cultural policy in the new states. In Clifford Geertz, ed., *Old Societies and New States*, 27–56. Glencoe, IL: Free Press.

Ortner, Sherry B. 1984. Theory in anthropology since the sixties. *Comparative Studies in Society and History* 26:126–66.

————., ed. 1989. *Author Meets Critics: Reactions to "Theory in Anthropology Since the Sixties."* Ann Arbor: Program on the Comparative Study of Social Transformations, University of Michigan.

Pateman, Carol. 1988. *The Sexual Contract*. Stanford: Stanford University Press.

Philibert, Jean-Marc. 1986. The politics of tradition: Toward a generic culture in Vanuatu. *Mankind* 16:1–12.

Pye, Lucien. 1962. *Politics, Personality, and Nation-Building: Burma's Search for Identity*. New Haven: Yale University Press.

Seton-Watson, Hugh. 1977. *Nations and States: An Enquiry into the Origins of Nations and the Politics of Nationalism*. Boulder, CO: Westview Press.

Stocking Jr., George W., ed. 1985. *Objects and Others: Essays on Museums and Material Culture*. Madison: University of Wisconsin Press.

Strathern, Marilyn. 1988. *The Gender of the Gift: Problems with Women and Problems with Society in Melanesia*. Berkeley: University of California Press.

Tambiah, Stanley J. 1988. Foreword. In R. Guidieri, F. Pellizi, and S. J. Tambiah, eds., *Ethnicities and Nations: Processes of Interethnic Relations in Latin America, Southeast Asia, and the Pacific*, 1–6. Austin: University of Texas Press.

Thomas, Nicholas. 1992. Substantivization and anthropological discourse: The transformation of practices into institutions in neotraditional Pacific societies. In James W. Carrier, ed., *History and Tradition in Melanesian Anthropology*, 64–85. Berkeley: University of California Press.

Tivey, Leonard. 1981. Introduction. In L. Tivey, ed., *The Nation-State: The Formation of Modern Politics*, 1–12. Oxford: Martin Robertson.

Tonkin, Elizabeth, Mary McDonald, and Malcolm Chapman, eds. 1989. *History and Ethnicity*. London: Routledge.

Verdery, Katherine. 1992. Comment: Hobsbawm in the East. *Anthropology Today* 8:8–10.

Weber, Eugen. 1976. *Peasants into Frenchmen: The Modernization of Rural France, 1870–1914*. Stanford: Stanford University Press.

White, Richard. 1981. *Inventing Australia*. Sydney: Allen & Unwin.

Whitlock, Gillian, and David Carter, eds. 1992. *Images of Australia*. St. Lucia, Qld.: University of Queensland Press.

Williams, Raymond. 1977. *Marxism and Literature*. New York: Oxford University Press.

————. 1985. *Keywords: A Vocabulary of Culture and Society*. New York: Oxford University Press.

Part 1
Issues and Problems

Edward LiPuma

The Formation of Nation-States and National Cultures in Oceania

Issues and Problems

The rapid emergence of new nation-states from the ashes of colonial regimes—polities composed of linguistically and culturally diverse populations, tossed onto the world historical scene and placed in front of the relentless economic train of capitalism—raises issues that belong both to the realm of anthropological theory and nation-making politics. At the dawn of the 1970s, the major islands and peoples of Oceania were under colonial rule (the exception is Western Samoa, which received its independence in 1962). Ten years later, Fiji (1970), Tonga (1970), Papua New Guinea (1975), American Samoa (1977), Tuvalu (1978), and the Solomon Islands (1978) had been granted independence, with Vanuatu (1980) soon to follow. An independence movement had sprung up on Palau, and there was a strong rebellion against French rule on New Caledonia. If the 1970s were marked by the quest for independence, the 1980s and early 1990s have been the time of problematic nation making and forging of new identities. So increasingly, inevitably, an anthropology of Oceanic societies is inseparable from "nation-ness, the most universally legitimate value in the political life of our time" (Anderson 1983, 12).

Scholars and politicians, citizens and revolutionaries have recognized the significance and power of the notion of "the nation" and the depth of feeling that appeals to the motherland, fatherland, greater nation (e.g., greater Morocco, greater Serbia), or ancestral homeland (e.g., Israel, Zululand) can evoke—and every autonomous state and independence movement in modern times has defined itself in national terms and language. The nation-states and subnational movements of Oceania are no exception. Yet, the visibility of the nation-state notwithstanding, a focused theory of the nation and an articulate research

33

agenda is still very much in its infancy (see Foster 1991). It is the peculiar genius of nationalism to seem both so familiar as to require no special explanation and so multidimensional that every explanation seems to lack the depth and/or breadth needed to account for the fact that na-tionness is uniquely local, yet global. When the issue of nationhood is not elided, entering the analysis as a presupposition, it has usually been understood as derivative of something else seemingly more solid and less imagined. Hence, we have the nation as the result of the rise of industri-alization (Gellner 1983), the advent of the modern "public" state (Breuilly 1985), the manifestation of ethnicity (Smith 1986), the diffu-sion of European ideology (Kedourie 1985), the advancement of technol-ogy (for example, Anderson's [1983] print capitalism), and the need of the capitalist state to insure internal cohesion (Wallerstein 1991).

Even a first review of the Oceanic materials shows that these theo-ries are far too narrow to create an account of nationhood adequate to its object. A lesson of the emergence of Oceania's nation-states is the necessity of a holistic, rather than reductionistic, perspective. With this aim in mind, I have drawn on the tradition of European social theory and have sought to conceptualize the issues in a way that ignores disci-plinary boundaries and does not automatically privilege any one dimen-sion of social life (such as history, economy, or technology).

My point of departure—supported and amplified by the chapters in this volume—is that an understanding of nation-states requires the cre-ation of a holistic relational approach. Such an approach would have to be developed along several fronts. First, it must transcend the usual set of embedded oppositions that, implicitly as much as explicitly, have guided the discussion. The aim is to delineate the issues in ways that do not reproduce the dichotomies of material-economic versus symbolic-social; subjective versus objective; theoretical-scientific knowledge ver-sus indigenous-political knowledge; primordial versus invented tradi-tions; or the often-used oppositional model of state-society relations. Such an attempt always runs the risk of being grasped through those categories, and merged with those tendencies, which it seeks to over-come. It is all too easy to misread an account of the force of global capitalism on local political economies as an example of economic deter-minism, or to misconstrue an account of the imagination, imagery, and ideology of the nation as an allegiance to an ungrounded culturalism.[1] Nonetheless, it is clear from the history of nation making in Oceania that the embedded oppositions that have informed theories of the nation must give way to a more relational, holistic approach.

Second, a comprehensive viewpoint must include an awareness of encompassment—that sociohistorical process by which "autonomous" societies (or economic sectors) are progressively and sometimes simultaneously subsumed and enchanted by the political economy of capitalism, internationalized Western culture, and interstate organizations such as the United Nations. This awareness entails abandoning the assumption that individual "cultures" or the set of cultures that constitute the nation-state exist in a totalized state. It entails recognizing that there now exists an *intrinsic* (versus external) relationship between the structure of a culture and the encompassing forms such that specific societies—and indeed, nation-states—have no "ontological presence" other than that imagined, mapped, institutionalized, and fought for in the public political sphere by citizens in those societies and nation-states. This intersection between emerging nation-states and encompassing forms is power-infused, highly asymmetrical, and mutually dynamic (Abercrombie 1991). The nations of Oceania (like Nigeria, India, Indonesia, Brazil, Zaire, and many others before them) exist only by virtue of the totalizing project of first the colonial and now national state, as the project unfolds in the context of capitalism and internationalized Western culture.

Third, it is necessary to use a relational, as opposed to an essentialist, definition of nationalism and national identity. This is crucial because at the level of content—that is, in terms of held beliefs, concrete policies, and manifest conflicts—each nation has its own specific historically constructed character. Nationness is not and cannot be treated as a unitary phenomenon. What "the nation" is, and what it means to have a nationality, varies dramatically from one nation-state to another (for example, religion is a fundamental facet of Israeli nationality whereas ethnicity [e.g., Russian versus Ethiopian Jews] is self-consciously downplayed [Dominguez 1989], in contrast to other nations such as Japan, where ethnicity is fundamental and religion of comparatively minor importance [Twine 1991]). What we refer to as "the nation," nationhood, and nationalism, in different words, are numerous heterogeneous structures associated and linked by a historically entrenched and validated discursive form. So although "nationalisms are extremely varied phenomena," as Calhoun says, "they are joined by common involvement in the modern discourse of nationalism" (1993,

216). From such a relational view (implicitly invoked by Fox 1990, 3–4), nationalism or nationness is a genre of claims, understandings, and grounds for recognizing, promoting, and legitimizing peoplehood, identity, and sovereignty. Accordingly, the studies in this volume are not about nationalism (taken as singular and an essence) in Oceania; rather, they are an effort to draw out "family resemblances" among the nationalisms that are evolving mutually in Oceania. These family resemblances are created by commonalities of colonial history, position within global capitalism and internationalized culture, the necessity of confronting similar kinds of national problems, and the fact that discourses of nationalism often take shape in relationship and response to each other.

Fourth and finally, an adequate account must be self-reflexive, aware that the scientific project of writing about a nation-state is part of the production of that nation and a form or use of power (positive or negative) in relation to the present state. In this respect, a "scientific history" of a nation may be opposed by certain members of the bureaucracy and the populace, not because the history is transparently false, but because it discloses and reminds everyone of historical realities erased in the official, ideologized history. Spriggs (1992), for example, shows that it is not only possible to define alternative prehistories for Bougainville island (Papua New Guinea), but that each alternative has rather different implications with regard to the construction of Bougainvillean nationality, and thus each has its own political constituency.

The concept that animates all the chapters in this volume is that for the peoples of Oceania, nationness is an irreducible threshold between modes of life; the emergence of the nation-state redefines the structures and strategies of objectification and the construction of the subject. Being a "citizen" of a nation-state, as opposed and in addition to being a member of a region, culture, and kinship group, engenders new ways of thinking and experiencing. By placing the connections among culture, language, and identity in a larger, encompassing context, it transforms their meaning and the terms of their reproduction. It constitutes a transition from a world in which culture and language are the given, and therefore uncontested, ground of knowledge and contestation to a universe in which culture and language are themselves *the* objects of knowledge and contestation. The ground of practice becomes the interdynamic between capitalism, emerging forms of mediation (such as radio and newspapers), and localized cultures. This interrelationship gives rise to novel forms of self-reflection, critique, and emancipation (for example, women's movements), sometimes with contradictory effects. The enfolding of local cultures, organized around relations of kinship and community (such as intermarriage or regional alliances), within the nation-state defined by colonialism, capitalism, and against other nation-states, reconfigures the entire set of relations that define collective identity and so what it is to be a social person. What makes nationalism a uniquely contemporary and flexible concept is that it can accommodate capitalism and the modern state in their various forms, and can be fashioned out of, but also transcend and transform, an extraordinary variety of local cultures and regional identities. The emerging result is a social order and person essentially different from those engendered by local traditions but also very different from the British, French, and other Western models and images.

For the emerging nation-state, invention of a national culture is the most visible form of objectification; inculcation of an embodied sense of national identity becomes central to the very construction of the subject. The production of a national culture and identity is mediated by, and evolves in terms of, other social practices and processes. These include the development of mass media and a lingua franca; a reshaping of social geography through urban migration; the institutionalization of power or knowledge (e.g., department of health); the creation of a public, political sphere; the intervention of transformed images of the body (Foster 1993); and the emergence of distinct social fields (such as those of science, politics, education, and law), each endowed with its own structure, logic, and historical trajectory (Bourdieu 1985). These enormous transformations unfold against two powerful background conditions: the sense of community fostered by and within local cultures, and the rapid spread of global capitalism and internationalized Western culture. Even as the peoples of Oceania seek to differentiate and separate themselves from their colonial rulers in particular, and the metropolitan powers more generally, the objects, images, styles, tropes, and rituals that they use to construct national identity are increasingly inseparable from the worldwide flow of commodities and information technologies. The formation of nation-states in regions that would never have imagined nationhood or nationalism in the absence of Western intervention and power is deeply contradictory because, as Chatterjee (1984, 2–3) observes, it involves two rejections, both ambivalent: "rejection of the alien intruder and dominator who is nevertheless to be imitated and surpassed by his own standards and rejection of ancestral ways which are seen as obstacles to progress and yet also cherished as marks of identity." One result is that the narrative of the postcolonial nation tends to embrace two alternative themes, the first of liberating rationality as the nation-state shapes the means for people to transcend their "traditional" identities, the second the celebration of "custom" and the reawakening of primordial identities (LiPuma 1993).

That so much is involved in the invention and imagination of the nation, and its inseparable relation to the state form, means that analysis must transcend the received limits of anthropology. Certainly the analyses offered in this volume demonstrate that an adequate understanding of those structures and strategies used to objectify "the nation" and create national identity must consist of three aspects. The first defines the conditions and consequences of encompassment by capitalism, and the ways in which the peoples of an emerging nation appropriate, resist, and are infiltrated by an increasingly internationalized Western capitalist culture; the second aspect maps out the social mediations (e.g., the mass media) by which nations construct themselves, in particular the terms of representation and contestation; and the third grasps the ways in which these mediations are imbued with meaning, appropriated, and used by local communities. What makes theorization difficult is that an account adequate to its object must make a space for both the large-scale epochal transformations in these societies and be sensitive to the reality that these transformations are local and indeterminate. That is, the methodology must presuppose and take into account discursive changes in the foundations of social life and simultaneously center around intensive local ethnography that reveals the strategies and plurality of meanings inscribed in any event. This does not mandate, and I emphasize, that every account include a full analysis of all three aspects. It does imply that our analyses should start with the understanding that there is an *intrinsic* relationship among these aspects, even if all of them are not foregrounded simultaneously. It implies that an analysis of a specific aspect in a particular location should remain aware of the constitutive powers of the other moments. It implies that our analyses take into account the ways in which the backgrounded aspects enter into the meaning and trajectory of a given practice.

Most important, it states that our analyses of the mediating practices used to construct nationness must be located within the structures of capitalism and local cultures. To give an example, an analysis of the political messages broadcast on national radio (representation) and the distribution of the broadcasts should be grounded in the understanding of the conditions of capitalism and the appropriation of Western practices and epistemology embodied in such practices, and what meanings a culturally differentiated audience ascribes to such messages and what they do with them. In other words, we cannot be content with knowing how mass media contribute to the formation of nationness; we need to know how the penetration of capitalism, the character of appropriation and resistances by local communities, and the policies adopted by the state have entered into the very constitution and meaning of printing, radio, movies, television. To give another example, an ethnography of the nation needs to be mindful not only of how the development of a lingua franca, such as Pijin, or the creation of national rituals, such as an independence day ceremony, defines national culture and identity, but how that very use of Pijin and public ritual for this end are part and product of a sea change in relations of capital, power, and discourse. Thus, a science intent on giving an account of the emergence of the nation-state must be self-conscious about its search for a nonreductionistic paradigm, not least because the Euro-focused accounts at our disposal, such as those of Anderson (1983) and Gouldner (1976), present the rise of nationalism as an exfoliation of a material technology such as printing (Warner 1989, 5).[2]

The ethnography of national culture and identity is rather far from that to which students of Oceania have been accustomed. Indeed, it compels analysis to have a broader horizon and to deal with issues that were formerly the province of social theorists of Europe. It introduces a new inventory of concepts, such as civil society, the public sphere, and narrative into the discourses of Oceanists. In this light, my objective is to set out what I view as the critical issues and problems immanent in any account of the construction of national culture and identity.

The analysis that follows is more a set of questions than resolutions; my aim is to thematize rather than theorize, even if the former necessarily implies the latter. Within the compass of this analysis, I seek to thematize and set out the ethnographic ground and colonial background for three issues. The first issue is: how are the notion and institutions of the nation-state and of civil society fashioned in opposition and relation both to each other and, simultaneously, in opposition and relation to the more indigenous, local, and embedded structures of kinship, community, and region? This issue is critical if for no other reason than that the way in which the state encompasses specific local communities and regions, and the extent to which the needs and/or grievances of these local communities and regions can be resolved through the institutions of the state and civil society (e.g., the press), will affect the possibility of armed insurrection and attempted secession (as on Bougainville). The second issue is: how are national culture and identity shaped within, and mutually constitutive of, the public sphere? Put otherwise, how do publics come to be, how is their consent "educated" (to borrow a Gramscian phrase), and how does the dominant national discourse endeavor to shape and animate subjects or citizens? The final issue guiding the account is: what is tradition and history, or how does the imagined community come to imagine itself?

The Emergence of Capitalism

It is not my purpose here to offer a theory or method for the study of the emergence of capitalism in the Pacific, although I have outlined the ground for such an account in my research elsewhere (LiPuma and Meltzoff 1989). Here, I would like to identify without further comment some of the critical ways in which capitalism informs national culture and identity. That is, I would like to suggest some ways in which the encompassing voice of capitalism must enter even as an uninvited guest into an understanding of national culture and identity. This is important because so much of what passes as an analysis of the nation and identity is founded on the mistaken opposition between culture and production. The opposition has permitted those who focus on social and political economy to ignore the concept of "the nation" and those who focus on culture to treat "the nation" as separable from capitalism.[3] I would submit that the chapters of this volume strongly suggest that the emergence of the citizen, national identity, and forms for objectifying "the nation" are inseparable from a progressive materialization of history, whereby people increasingly identify history with object property (for example, cultural artifacts housed in a national museum) rather than with knowledge or social relations. This volume (exemplified in Foster's analysis) also suggests that there is a deep connection between the rise of the nation and the emergence of the possessive individual.

A crucial because submerged issue is how the epistemology of capitalism, embodied in its practices and objects, becomes embedded in the production of national culture. For example: how the adoption of Western practices, such as trials (Larcom 1990), leads to the adoption of

Westernized notions of the individual; or, how the association of the nation with commodities objectifies the nation in such a way as to imbue it with the properties of capitalist commodities (Foster this volume); or, how the "rational" standardization and rationalization of life promoted by bureaucracy informs people's view of the nation. The commodity—or, more precisely, the commodity form—is of critical import because it is a form of objectification that is stable, coherent, and significant across a wide range of contexts (Lukács 1971). It therefore provides a motivation and metaphor for a naturalization of the social, in this case the notion of nation. When linked and likened to a commodity, "the nation" appears to be "objective" rather then socially constituted; it appears as primordial rather than historical; it appears as "necessary" rather than contingent; and it appears as a unified, autonomous entity. So a goal of analysis is to grasp the ways and means whereby a people come to understand their national identity as a natural identity.

A second and related issue is how the advent of capitalism leads to the differentiation of fields—such as the artistic, legal, and economic fields—and the way in which these fields are placed in service of the construction of national culture and identity. Important areas for investigation here include the development of national education and health systems, the creation of museums and institutions to promote the arts, mapmaking and census taking, standardization of the legal system and business regulations, and the establishment of a national currency. All these are instrumental in the production of a collectively held disposition to see "persons as legitimate subjects of and in a territorial state" (see Foster's introduction, this volume). Jourdan's chapter, for example, argues that educational conformity and the promotion of Pijin as a national language are instruments in the creation of a Solomon Islands national consciousness. In the same way, we may ask how the emergence of national culture and national centers of power—especially the power to shape and represent the interconnections between the political economy and the public—redefine the conditions for the construction of meaning in local practice? To phrase this differently, how does the externalization of social life (in which the increase in subjective freedom is intrinsically linked to the decline in objective control) inform the social reproduction of local societies? These questions are central because the emergence of differentiated fields at the nation-state level is, paradoxically, linked to forms of resistance and resentment at the local level. At the local level—that is, within the sphere still dominated by and organized around kinship and community—people seek to preserve the indigenous value of moral and social wholeness.

Finally, an analysis of national identity must account for and locate class relations. Class relations inform the modes of objectification used in the construction of "the nation" and agents' willingness to endorse such objectification. More to the point, we need to analyze the social space in which class intersects with, and is mutually constitutive of, other forms of identity. The obvious example is the significant role the national elite and intelligentsia play in creating and mapping the terms for the making of a national identity. As a number of the chapters illustrate, the national elite are the first to engage in entrepreneurial capitalism and accumulate goods and wealth, even as they undertake the hard ideological labor and develop the government agencies required to shape and instill a national consciousness. Class relations may also be linked to ethnic, cultural, and regional identities, as when members of a specific culture or region make up a high percentage of the elite. The internal danger for the nation-states of postcolonial Melanesia is that class and ethnic or regional identities will become interchangeable and mutually reinforcing forms of social hierarchization and contestation.

From Colony to Nation

A combination of geopolitical competition, a concept of nation, and administrative ease led the colonial regimes to aggregate, sometimes arbitrarily, people and territory into larger polities than had existed before. The creation of a nation in the space that was once a colony produced polities that subsumed different and distinct cultures within a single political identity. As a result, the people of Oceania can no longer conceptualize cultural differences and identities as founding differences between types of subjects. It is no longer possible to live in apolitical coexistence. Rather, there now exist cultural and speech variations within that solitary encompassing unit called "the nation"; and, moreover, these social variations have political implications. There is thereby a reorganization of cultural space; the cultural Other is no longer external or foreign (see Jourdan this volume). The cultural Other has become internalized so that cultural or ethnic differences have to be accommodated within the framework of the national community. The internalization of the Other transforms the terms of cultural self-representation:

members of a culture represent other cultures in the public sphere (as being too aggressive, clannish, and so forth) in order to represent themselves; and they seek to represent themselves to others in order to represent others.

For example, if the present residents of Guadalcanal represent themselves as the true, autochthonous people of the island, then newcomers from other islands are foreigners who fundamentally lack political legitimacy. An even more telling illustration is the claim by "indigenous" peoples of Fiji to be the true authentic people (as opposed to the later-arriving Indian populace), and thus the one legitimate source of political power (Kaplan 1988; Kelly 1988; Rutz this volume). A more common, but no less important, example comes from Vanuatu, where an indigenous political party is seeking to secure its mandate by claiming that Vanuatu's expatriate citizens are interlopers and foreigners who lack legitimate rights to own local territory or wield political power (Facey this volume). Thus, the internalization of the Other makes the public political sphere a critical arena for redefining and reproducing culture—the similarities and differences that organize the relationships among races, ethnicities, cultures, and regions.

The form and content of the contemporary nation-state were imported into the Pacific thanks to, and as the offshoot of, occupation by European powers. As a result, what existed of civil society under the colonial administration was a form of public sphere and discourse whose function was to legitimize, underwrite, and otherwise locate the virtues of colonial rule. The nature of the virtues evolved over the course of colonial rule, beginning with the familiar notion of enlightenment and ending with preparation for nationhood. The major feature of the colonial public sphere was that it was highly constricted. On the one hand, the relationships among peoples from the regions and cultures of the colonial state were transitive: they were related insofar as they were all subjects of a colonial ruler and administration rather than as coeval citizens of a modern state. On the other hand, the records of the Western Pacific high commissioner, planter society, and the missionaries make it clear that the European populace was the sole public and that what counted as "public opinion" were the views of this white minority. So, while colonialism was the historically percipient training course in nationhood, it was hardly the best.

Nevertheless, colonialism did, in a restrictive sense, prepare the Pacific states for nationhood, once at least the colonized peoples accepted the intellectual and moral premises of modernity upon which nationalism rests. After it is deemed inevitable that capitalism will encompass all societies, and that the nation-state is indispensable to participation in global history, then imposition of colonial rule to "prepare" for this end gains a certain rationality—appearing retrospectively, even to many of those who opposed colonialism and struggled for independence (see, for example, the autobiography of Michael Somare), as a kind of objective, if sometimes harsh, training course in unavoidable nationhood. Subjectively, the concept that "the nation" should transcend community, that the interests of the nation must, at least on certain occasions, come before those of one's own kin and neighbors (*wantoks*) appears as the inevitable corollary.

It also appears as nearly impossible to attain because the demands of culture and community are insistent. Indeed, there exists a built-in contradiction: an internalized, unwavering national identity presupposes the existence of dispositions and attitudes that are themselves produced by a transcendent sense of nationness, meaning the subsumption of local culture and community. This implies that the cultural identity of nationality—being, for example, a Papua New Guinean—is more important than being an Enga or Orakaiva. It implies that conflict between groups is understood as part of the production of the national will and not as a threat to the unity of the nation-state. The production of a national identity that integrates the existing cultures or ethnic groups is critical because the discourse of the nation presupposes a one-to-one correspondence between state and nation, implying that the cultures that constitute the nation-state are, despite their ostensible and often self-proclaimed differences, joined at a historically deeper and culturally fundamental level. Jacobsen (this volume) makes the argument that the dynamics of community are so powerful, enduring, and penetrating that they are now undermining and will ultimately destroy the emerging nation-state.

The fate of a specific nation-state depends on whether it can incorporate within its body all the social groups that it desires to represent. The concern is whether the national culture and the terms for its production will be so hegemonic and inclined to privilege an elite urban tradition that they marginalize minority cultures, remote areas, and underclasses. Empirically, these are increasingly overlapping categories as minority cultures, situated in rural, economically undeveloped regions, are exporting their young and unskilled work force to clogged and increasingly stratified cites such as Honiara and Port Moresby (see May 1984; Meltzoff and LiPuma 1985). Crafting a national politics of inclusion is made all the more important by the democratic notion, now becoming widespread in Oceania, that to deny a culture or region recognition in the political or public sphere constitutes a form of oppression and that a politics of inclusion entails both the recognition of the unique identity of each culture or region and the equalization of rights and entitlements.[4] An explicit example is the Maori quest for political recognition on their own terms (rejection of multiculturalism on the grounds that it would dilute and efface Maori identity), even as they press the New Zealand state for equal rights and entitlements (Dominy 1990; Sinclair 1990).[5] Both these notions have been quickly adopted in Oceania, in part because they resemble the indigenous idea that every cultural and regional identity is distinctive (which was part of the indigenous, precontact politics of exclusion) and in part because most Oceanic societies are familiar with an egalitarian ethos and the notion of balanced reciprocity.

An important result in Oceania and elsewhere is that the discourse of ethnic groups or regions disenchanted with their nation-state tends to focus on the failure of the state to recognize their special needs (anything from a new road to greater local autonomy) and to offer them an equal portion of the state's attention and funds (for local improvements). Focusing on Southeast Asia, Tambiah (1989, 341) has noted that the politics of the newly independent states, framed initially in terms of "nation-state" ideologies and policies, have entered a new political phase dominated by competitions and conflicts of emerging "ethnic collectivities," which question nationalism and national culture. For the former colonies of Oceania, the imagination, installation, and reproduction of a national identity—an identity that transcends cultural, regional, and emerging class loyalties—depends on the emergence of a state sufficiently inclusive to encompass its diverse cultures, and sufficiently centralized to organize a program of ideological education. The quest is to expand the discourse and practice of nationhood beyond the rather narrow political terms of the colonial regimes to include cultural, historical, and social-relational terms of cohesion and collective identity.

Although we may speak of the nation-state in the singular, we need to recognize that in all of Oceania's emerging states, a key and contentious relation is precisely that between nation and state. The state, as each of the chapters makes clear in different ways, is both a means by which a nation objectifies its independence and establishes its place among nations, and the means by which specific classes or groups instill, impose, and sometimes force a particular definition of the nation on a diverse populace. Accordingly, the state aims to discharge its "modern" functions—regulating commerce, collecting taxes, administrating services, printing money, and so forth—and to do so in a way that (1) advances a specific view of just what the nation is, and (2) deals with the participatory interests of the different communities. The creation of an independent nation in that space that was once a colonial state engenders a special problem: how to transform an adversarial state that ignored, circumvented, and suppressed local interests into an institution and instrument of participatory nationhood.[6] The issue is whether these nation-states can fashion a state able and willing to accommodate a nation so diverse in language and culture.

What remains uncertain is the form and depth of nationhood that will evolve in Oceania, especially as these nations are caught in that dilemma of being either culturally homogeneous island states that are too small and economically strapped to function effectively in the global political economy (as in Micronesia)[7] or larger, more economically viable nations (such as Papua New Guinea) that must relentlessly struggle to overcome their internal cultural diversity. Will these nations become nations only in themselves—that is, will their integrity be a function of external forces—or will they be nations for themselves? Subjectively, will identity be hierarchical, with national identity first among equals, so that disputes between regions, ethnic groups, or an ethnic group and the state are never nation threatening? Will cultural, regional, and other forms of identity, no matter how differentiating, celebrated, and felt within the nation, always remain subordinated to the national identity? How will different levels and forms of identity—ethnic, regional, national, religious, and the like—be organized? And, how are they contextualized so that in certain situations, one form of identity takes precedence over others? From the vantage point of political action, what are the relations and conditions of equivalence in which differentiated groups align themselves against the nation and the "national interest"? Particularly important are the ways in which regional, cross-cultural (e.g., New Guinea Highlands) movements are organized. The larger question is: how will the emerging forms of equivalence at the national level modify or mute forms of local and regional identity? For example, will the equivalence relations created by going to the same school, traveling overseas, sharing a mutual interest in the success of the state, and enjoying a relatively high income (national elites) restrain the pull of cultural or ethnic identity? Will the equivalence relations that arise from working in the same occupation (for example, when workers play on the same company soccer team or join together in opposing management) moderate ethnic, cultural, and linguistic differences? Can the peoples of Oceania develop the ways and means to transform a colonial state into a nation-state?

Ethnicity, the State, and Civil Society

The transition from a colonial state to a nation-state is far from culturally neutral. The nation-state as a political form is quite inseparable from Western culture and capitalism because the concept, "nation state," is fundamentally founded on Western notions of the relationships among the individual, state, and civil society. So a critical issue becomes how and in what form newly formed states will shape a notion of civil society and how the notion that emerges informs the formation of national identities. By civil society, I mean a sphere of public interaction outside the state, made up above all by the familial-community sphere, sphere of associations, social movements, and forms of public communication. It implies the existence of associations that are independent of the sway of state power, and that can significantly determine and redirect the course of state policy (Taylor 1990, 98–99). Such associations constitute a realm of civil society that is deideologized in the sense that these associations are far enough removed from a state's control over power or knowledge to reach decisions and take action in a way that more effectively represents society (understood as the popular will). These associations include those that have a religious basis; corporate groups (such as cultural associations) that are funded by, and usually linked to, the government; and new social movements such as environmental and women's groups. The formation of civil society is a critical dimension of the emergence of "the nation" because civil society is the way in which a nation becomes a putative actor in relation to the state. This permits "the people" to press the claim that the role of government or state is to serve the "needs" of that nation—that is, to act politically as if the state is separate from and subordinate to the citizenry.

The Western conceptualization of civil society upon which the idea of the nation and its political life rests is itself based on two concepts.

These concepts are in everlasting and perpetual tension in that they are founded on a contradiction. I paraphrase Chatterjee (1990, 128–29), who notes that the first concept proclaims the sovereignty of the individual will. It insists that the state has no right to interfere in the arena of individual freedom of choice and contractual arrangements. The other concept is that there exists one solitary political community based on the determinate-bounded form of the nation-state. Here the state exercises a strong regulatory function over the workings of society and assumes the right to commit individuals to group actions (e.g., waging war) and to compel classes of individuals to perform the same action (e.g., carry a draft or identification card). The state assumes the right to sort people into categories of attribution (e.g., educated) and then attach (often changing) sets of rights, obligations, and privileges to these categories. There is an objectification of biography in the sense that the qualities of subjects are externalized from the community in the guise of certified impersonal knowledge. In so acting, the new nation-states of Oceania are claiming a right that could not and did not exist prior to colonialism—the authority to define the subjecthood of people outside the sphere of kinship and community, and to do so in terms of categorical identities that preempt and, in some cases, subvert local relational identities.

The problem for the new nation-states of Melanesia, particularly those such as Papua New Guinea and the Solomon Islands, which are famous for their cultural heterogeneity, is not only in trying to resolve the tensions between these concepts, but also in the reality that the entire notion of civil society is, as Chatterjee eloquently argues, Eurocentric in an important way: there is no space or allowance for "community." This concept of civil society has no space for regionalism, ethnicity, and the other factors that determine nation making in the Pacific. The narrative of the local community is not dissipated by the emergence of the imagined community; rather, it is projected into a larger space and thus acquires new purposes and powers. To put it comparatively, Oceania's nations cannot be an Australia (or a United States), where the idea of community has, right from the start, been preempted and subsumed by the capitalistic nation-state.[8] They cannot be a Japan, where the nation is coterminous with the community, Japan being composed of a single ethnic, linguistic people (with the exception of the tiny population of Ainu). Rather, the nations of Oceania must be an Indonesia or an India on a smaller scale. Here, the narrative of community and local culture remains decisive; it stands in opposition to both the centralized state and the formation of civil society. Historically, these nations have been unified only in themselves, that is, in opposition to a foreign power such as a colonial regime. Once the colonial regime has been dispatched and independence won, these nations must struggle to hold themselves together as the muted voice of local culture, community, and ethnicity reemerges. The secessionist movement in Bougainville, like other subnational movements from India to Indonesia, inaugurates the beginning of such devolution in the nation-states of Oceania.

The dynamic of community is subversive because it is the counterweight to the naturalization of the concepts of nationhood and national identity. The existence of a local culture, founded on its own concepts and conventions, provides a reminder that the nation-state is arbitrary. The discrepancy between local cultures and national culture, which was relatively narrow in the nascent European nation-states of the nineteenth century and is narrow in the advanced capitalist nations, is here as wide as it can be. So what is constructed as national culture always appears to be sociopolitically constituted in the sense that one group feels that another has imposed its desires upon it. What is more, the development of dispositions that correspond to nationness can never develop as fast as the nation itself, in part because the notion of nation was imported and imposed by an exogenous power and in part because local cultures are busy inculcating another more local and community-focused set of embodied dispositions. A consequence is that conflicting and mutually exclusive dispositions toward nationness coexist, not only in the same nation, but also in the same individual. This is especially true of elites. How else to make sense of a Melpa with whom I talked for hours in a Mt. Hagen hospital as he awaited surgery for a shotgun wound? Educated, intelligent, a high-ranking local administrator, he had gone home that weekend to be a warrior in an "intertribal" dispute. In his role as an administrator, he wanted the state to solve the dispute, knowing that nations are defined and held together by common law; nonetheless, as a clansman he is, in his own words, compelled to "help" his fellow clan members. In this case, the dispositions inculcated by clanship and community overpowered those inculcated by exposure to nationness.

By the same token, the "Melanesian Way," as it is called, is continually invoked, not because it represents a coherent tradition, but because it is an emerging, newly invented tradition that offers at least the semblance of an alternative, non-Western standpoint from which to launch a critique of modernity and the implications of the modern, capitalist, community-subsuming state. The invention of that Melanesian Way is an attempt to mark off an essential cultural difference—an inner space of sentiment, disposition, and belief outwardly manifest, for example, in the use of pidgin—which separates the postcolonial nation both from the colonizer of the past (especially Britain but also France, Australia, and the United States) and from the same dominating powers with which the former colonial nation-state must interact, for example, to obtain foreign aid and exchange.

The Social Construction of a Public Sphere

The formation of civil society and emergence of national public voices entail the formation of an articulated public sphere (Habermas 1964). This is a domain in which citizens, regardless of regional or cultural identity, can form public collective opinion. Mostly the public sphere as a domain of action concerns discussions and commentary about the actions and practices of the government. The public sphere thus mediates between the state and the various local societies that comprise the nation. In that regard, the public sphere is a zone of negotiation and contestation in which local cultures (often united into regions), modern interest groups (such as and especially multinational companies), and the state forge a notion of nationness. This raises a number of issues that begin with language itself (for language, like the commodity, combines an elevated level of cross-contextual salience with a high degree of coherence), and ways in which communication through mass media influences the nature of public political discourse.

What is the role of media and their forms of representation—such as a broadcast of political speeches, advertising, and local and international news—in the formation of a public, political sphere? Where do the modes of discourse used in such a public sphere come from—for example, are Western stylized forms such as classified advertisements tied to localized indigenous aims or functions? How are subversive voices conceptualized—as part of the formation of the general will or as antithetical to its formation? How are such voices dealt with? For example, are threats to the powers of the current leadership represented as national threats, and what is the power of this representational strategy? Clearly, a main struggle is over control of the nation's representation of itself—both to itself and to others. Such control centers around who (for example, class or ethnic groups) can exercise power and authority over representation; the dialogic strategies pursued or thrown into historical play; and the instruments of control (these may range from television to ancient manuscripts to the construction of presidential residences and public works) over the nation's self-representation. A salient example from this volume is Rutz's account of the forms of ideological discourse implicated in Fijian nationalism. He shows that Fijian chiefs staked out a "royalist" rhetorical position within "tradition" by locating the epicenter of Fijian nationhood in the colonial narrative, thereby binding the Fijian nation to the historical powers and actions of the queen of Great Britain.

A connected issue is the extent to which the state's technologies of power are used to preempt and control the space of public discourse, especially the means used to suppress or discredit voices that hold that regional interests transcend and should override the "interests" of the nation (as contested). For example, in the early days of secessionist movement on Bougainville, the Papua New Guinea state maneuvered the national press into portraying the situation as an "atomistic law and order problem" (Layton 1992, 305), rather than an insurrection with deep community support. Important here are the means and strategies that a society uses to appease nondominant groups (e.g., Fijian Indians), sectors, and factions without compromising the interests and trajectory of the dominant ones. What role does the state play in defining and orchestrating these forms of appeasement?

A critical institution here is the mass media and their functional control. There are two dimensions to this issue. The first is the extent to which history is made and portrayed in the mass media and in national educational institutions so that normative positions appear to be the result of political consensus rather than of contestation. For example, the presence of foreign companies in extractive industries (mining, fishing, and forestry) usually is depicted by national politicians and the companies (for example, in radio messages) as though this corporate presence is an uncontested realization of the nation's will and interests. The second dimension is the extent to which that power to set and impose normativity is misrecognized as such. An analysis of the nation-state needs to discover the extent to which the transforming of contestation into consensus is the expression of hegemonic power.[9]

A second crucial facet of the making of the public sphere is the emergence and effects of the various fields. The issue is how the differentiation of fields created by the advent of capitalism is bound to the production of a national culture and identity. In particular, how is the formation of a sphere of cultural production and presentation tied to this process? There are here two critical and articulated moments. The first is the emergence of national representational forms, usually with the dual intention of symbolizing the nation and indexically differentiating a region or culture. For example, the various groups that participate in the Goroka show, such as Melpa from Mt. Hagen, use body decoration that identifies them as Papua New Guineans, as possessing a commonality with all the other participants so adorned. Simultaneously, the forms employed—the colors, plumes, wigs, and such—distinguish them as Highlanders and further as Melpa.

The second moment concerns the ways that the nation learns to appropriate and appreciate art and other forms of culture as instruments of national culture and identity. On the one hand, this means the emergence of new art forms or, more precisely, social relations of art—for example, a poster competition for schoolchildren defined within an educational field in which the creation of national identity and unity is understood as an educational goal. The educational field, its goals, plus the enlistment of children in such a project—itself a projection of Western educational values as filtered through the missions—have no precedent for societies founded on kinship, community, and alliance. On the other hand, this means that indigenous forms of artistic production, such as a sewn plank canoe, Gobi board, or kina shell, are given new meanings and functions. Objects that were once exclusively plural and immediately functional—that is to say, imbued with meaning and hence valued by virtue of their local cultural specificity—are now given a singular and "abstract" function as national symbols. Canoes are not Malaitan canoes used to transport warriors, but Solomon Islands canoes used to represent, codify, and construct a common past.

Politicians, educators, administrators, doctors, and other educated voices know from their exposure to nationalism that a common past is essential, and—as recent shows, festivals, and celebrations underscore—the field of artistic production and presentation is a privileged means of cultural redemption. It permits the construction of *a* singular cultural heritage by providing the idiom for the projection of a common image. Not surprisingly, attempts to produce a national culture by extracting artistic works and ritual ceremonies from in situ, and further, by trying to simplify the aesthetic field to appeal to a foreign, mostly Western, world audience (for example, by underplaying carvings of ancestors with long, protruding penises or by emphasizing the commonalities rather than the differences in artistic meaning) have drawn fire. Critics argue that such rituals and artwork lack authentic meaning outside their proper local place and time (see Facey's discussion of Vanuatu's National Arts Festival in this volume). The dilemma of nation making is that the debasement of village-based art and ritual is (at least) the partial prerequisite for constructing a nationally and internationally recognizable national culture.

A third facet in the making of a public sphere is the use of language and its contributions to the creation of identity. More precisely, the issue in Oceania is the use of languages—from English and French to the various pidgins and indigenous languages—to construct identities. Throughout Oceania, this attempt has led to a linguistic hierarchy that reflects the hierarchy of political identities (see Jourdan this volume). In Papua New Guinea, the Solomon Islands, and other former British and Australian colonies, English is the language used to identify with and operate in the international sphere. English is the instrumental and symbolic means of access to world capitalism and internationalized culture. There are local newspapers in English; it is the language of government and schooling, plus the major idiom of internationally attended events, including somewhat ironically, independence day speech making. English is the externally directed language.

Pidgin, by contrast, is the language of national identity, discourse, and solidarity. It is the critical driving language of the culturally diverse cities—appearing everywhere from newspapers to the workplace—the informal language of students, and the language used in the construction of national culture. At informal gatherings of the national elite, pidgin is spoken and expected, however fluent speakers may be in English. Finally, there are culturally specific languages: more than sixty in the Solomons and seven hundred in Papua New Guinea. These many indigenous languages are a hallmark of cultural differentiation, village lifeways, and the voice of community. Ideologically, people understand them as repositories of tradition. And while most people are fluent in pidgin, much smaller numbers know either English or the indigenous languages. A crucial issue here is how access to different languages, and so sources of information, generates a segmented and stratified public (or should we say publics?).

The Appropriation and Redefinition of History

The quest for a national identity that is naturalized is based on the search for a fundamental "givenness" outside of history that founds history. Rather than understanding the grouping of cultures and/or islands that compose the nation as indeterminately mapped by the contours of colonial policy, the nation is grasped as a primordial entity whose integrity antedates its name, its people's consciousness of it, or its unification. A principal aspect of this construction is the creation and reinterpretation of history via a periodization of history. Thus, we can talk about a precolonial, colonial, and postindependence Solomon Islands. The periodization is part of a larger set of representations. Our subject is the organized set of historical practices and modes of knowledge that generate the representations of national consciousness and identity.

Said another way, a nation cannot recover the primordial origin or incontestable founding that it attributes to itself ideologically because the origin or founding is based on the substantialization and naturalization of racial, territorial, linguistic, cultural, or religious commonalities; yet, it must hold also that this beginning before history is the transcendental source of the history that follows and, in the history that follows, contingent historical events are transformed into a necessary evolution. This is nowhere more true than in historical accounts. So "A history of the Solomon Islands during the age of Spanish exploration" assumes that there was a Solomon Islands based on the territorial, linguistic, and other commonalities of its inhabitants, although we recognize that the possibility of a Solomon Islands, as much as the possibility of a United States or an Australia, is the result of historical events that had not yet transpired in the sixteenth century.

So the nation seeks to imagine itself before itself, thus to represent the nation as a community on a par with indigenous cultural or ethnic communities. Independence day is itself the memorialization and celebration of that moment of consciousness when the virtual nation imagined as always being became the actual nation-state. For Oceania's nation-states, this is a difficult aspect of nation making, precisely because they did not struggle for independence as much as it was thrust upon them by increasingly reluctant and declining colonial powers. As a consequence, these nation-states must perform great historical labor to invent and reconstruct the moment of self-consciousness. So, for example, the Marching Rule rebellion on Malaita island (in the Solomon Islands) is reinterpreted as a stab at national independence rather than a rebellion triggered by how specific Malaitans were treated by colonial authorities. In sum, the nation is imagined as both historical, because it goes back to the advent of history, and also as ahistorical, because there is posited a transfixed, inalienable national being or essence or character that is immune to the forces of historical change.

A key point is the extent to which traditional forms of oneness that are quasi-kinship identities, such as identity based on territoriality, can be appropriated and deployed as a metaphor of nationhood. Is it possible, to put it crudely, for people to apprehend their nation as a local, territorial group? Or, more precisely, can the local group be used as a metaphor by which people can conceptualize the nature of the nation? Because all Papua New Guineans occupy the same territory, must they have a unitary identity? To so extend the terms of territorial identity is to grasp the nation's territory as primal, as existing prior to actual nationhood. This is crucial not only as a term of knowledge—what the boundaries of the nation are—and a term of identity—those whose ancestors come from this land share a common identity—but also as a term of contestation, a claim to the territory of another nation on the ground that this territory is part of the primordial heritage.

In the empowering politics of nation making, tradition (heritage, custom) is the ideologized form of history. What we call tradition acquires a historical shape and dynamic by virtue of the way the dominant (and usually competing) power factions harness discursive concepts to promote a particular interested version of national history, and the way in which subordinate (and usually competing) factions develop counterhegemonic alternatives (or traditions). For example, in the Solomons, the local elite (including expatriates), the former colonial power, and the state (administered by the elite and funded by the former colonial power) draw on the cultural concepts of common kinship and working together to promote the vision of a "traditionally" united Solomon Islands, whereas leaders of factions from islands dissatisfied with the present state of affairs stress the degree to which the contemporary union is a product of past colonialism. But there is even more to it than this, for the local elite also articulate the legacy of colonialism to remind Britain of its responsibility while those who argue, for example, for an independent New Georgia, erase its own precolonial tradition of internal warfare and domination (which is why subordinate cultures on that island

and Malaita especially welcomed British pacification).[10] The logic of
tradition thus has two dialectical moments. The first is the simplification
of political space where differences (such as those between different,
antagonistic ethnic groups) are subordinated to a common identity and a
unified interest (for example, "we are all New Georgians desiring independence"). The second moment is an enlargement and increasing complexity of political space. In Oceania, as elsewhere, the second moment
typically has flowered after independence when the narrative of community and local culture reasserts itself. So ethnic, regional, and cultural
differences that were subordinated to the independence movement reappear, though now recontextualized within the nation-state.

Theoretically, the Oceanic case material implies that we cannot
grasp tradition as a bounded object because the signifiers of tradition
bear no "fixed" meanings; there is no necessary or permanent tie between structure and discourse (Keesing 1982), only a struggle between
discourses, dominant and subordinate, to organize time and space by
controlling the definition, use, and cultural production of signs. Recall
that the collective term imposed by the colonizer, *kanak*, has far tran-
scended its historical origins, so that what began as a derisive term for
the indigenous peoples of New Caledonia was reappropriated by them as
a signifier of identity (Jourdan this volume). If the chapters of this
volume make one point clear, it is that there is a constant struggle to
"fix" tradition; this occurs precisely because in the life of a nation, the
significance and cohesion of tradition is at best temporary and variable
from one class or ethnic group to another. There do exist points where
tradition is momentarily pinned down or captured, some of which, like
uprisings, occur spontaneously, while others, such as independence day
rituals, have their meanings choreographed as much as that is possible
(though unanticipated events and the fact that public rituals symbolically
invite counterhegemonic action often turn even the best-planned ritual
into a contestation of traditions).

The Production of a National Popular Culture and Identity

The construction of a national culture can never be anything less than a
struggle to incorporate Western statecraft, rational modes of economic
organization and practice, modern technology, and science, and at the
same time define a mode of cultural life that is distinct from the West and

thereby ensures a measure of identity rooted in "tradition." This is a difficult project because Western practices embody Western epistemology and because all nations must participate in the capitalist world system. Though the problem of constructing a national culture and identity in the face of Westernization is general, its solution is culturally specific, as examples from Japan (Twine 1991) and India (Chatterjee 1989) testify.

The problem of forming a national culture is one of constructing a degree of sameness within a universe of difference. The assumption that this sameness exists naturally is itself an objectification and result of a culturally undifferentiating, because racially inspired, viewpoint of colonialism and colonists. With few exceptions, colonialists saw every Papua New Guinean or Solomon Islander as fundamentally the same. If my interviews with district officers have an underlying theme, it is that, based on racial and environmental determinism, they saw similarity beneath even profound cultural differences. Nonetheless, the continuation and refinement of this colonial objectification is an unavoidable condition and consequence of nationhood.

The blending of distinct cultural traditions to invent a national culture always begins by presupposing the existence of a national culture which, existing in a primordial state, needs to be uncovered and made known. National culture thus presupposes the "object" that it is responsible for creating. Nonetheless, the construction of *a* national culture from the mosaic of indigenous cultures entails a politics of heritage. Some "traditional" practices are consecrated as constructive of unity and are located in the modern, invented category of "custom" (*kastam*; e.g., respect for tradition itself). Other practices, such as head-hunting or pervasive intercultural distrust, are marginalized and treated as though they were fragments of a now distant and nearly extinct way of life. Still other practices are redefined as signs of cultural or ethnic identity. Among the Maisin women of northeastern Papua New Guinea, for example, facial tattooing, once connected to puberty rituals, has acquired new significance as a marker of cultural or ethnic identity and as a sign of the Maisin's commercial success as producers of marketable art (Barker and Tietjen 1990).

Jourdan's chapter especially illustrates how in the Solomons a binding national culture is being forged from a popular culture, derived in part from an internationalized Western culture; a lingua franca that derives its "meaning as language" by virtue of its counterposition both to English, the colonial language, and to the many mutually unintelligible local languages; and, finally, a tradition created in the form of preserved custom (*kastom*). We could map a similar set of relations, though in a more antagonistic and oppositional context, for indigenous peoples of New Caledonia. Both these examples underline the dialectical relationship between the forms of cultural objectification (such as the Kanak 1975 festival, "Melanesia 2000") that are put into historical play, and the construction and internalization of an embodied collective national and political identity.

The construction of a national culture also implicates the spatial dimension of cultural production and social identity. There exists a real tension between the spatial distribution of cultural or regional identities (for example, being an Enga from the Highlands), a distribution critical to their semiautonomous reproduction, and the organization of social space within the national political economy. Throughout Oceania there exists a dialectic of place and social person, specifically in the way that owning, living, and working on land is inseparable from the formation of persons' kinship or cultural identity (for the New Guinea Highlands, Strathern 1972, Wagner 1972, LiPuma 1988, and others have documented this dialectic). The result is that the reorganization of space, instigated first by colonialism and then by encompassment within a nation, has led to an elaborated cultural politics.[11]

The politics of space is epitomized by, but by no means confined to, the new and rapidly expanding urban centers of Oceania. An instructive example is the cultural geography of Honiara. Based on the practical structures of community and region, the city has become organized into quarters that correspond to the various island groups (Malaitan, New Georgian, and others). These quarters are further subdivided into the cultural groups (e.g., Kwaio) from the particular island, with members of the same clan usually living in the same or adjacent houses. But there is more here than a compression of geography. There exists a cultural politics of bounding and defining space in which parts of the city are named and thereby constituted (signified), a connection drawn between a particular type of people and a specific place or ground, and thus a means of tying the "telling" (hence creation) of history to a specific, named locale. This understanding of space is inscribed in people's accounts and explanations of city life.

At the same time, the political economy and the state create another structure of social space in which the members of different cultural groups are continually thrown together. To have a job in the modern sector (for example, working for Solomon-Taiyo or Burns Philp), attend school or sporting events, negotiate the bureaucracy (for example, to obtain a driver's license), attend church service, or just walk on the street requires multicultural interaction and creates a space for that interaction. In addition, the elite not only work in a multicultural setting, but almost invariably live in one of the nonethnically and non-racially defined parts of the city. This is epitomized by the high rate of intermarriage among elites from different islands and cultural groups, not to mention those who have married Europeans. One result is that the association here is between social class and place rather than between culture and place. The production of a national culture is thus inseparable from the production of social relations to organize the interface between cultural groups and also between social identity defined by cultural or regional affiliation and identity founded on wealth, access to state power, education, membership in private clubs, and the other forms of symbolic capital instrumental in mapping class distinctions.

While redefinition of cultural space is most dramatic in cities such as Honiara, the reconfiguration of space occurs on the local level as well. Although there is considerable variation, the peoples of Oceania conceptualize their world as grounded in an intrinsic relationship between people and things, and the relationship is never stronger than in the connection between people and place. As Hirsch (this volume) illustrates, capitalism and the central market-oriented state constitute faceless, impersonal, and abstract forces that "disconnect the primordial merging of persons and things," thus sundering the basis for the wholeness, identity, and historical continuity of local rural communities. Hirsch's point carries us even further, for it highlights the conundrum of encompassment within a nation-state. Should local cultures surrender to the forces of capitalism and take advantage of state-fostered opportunities for economic advancement, then they also must surrender their cultural image of what it is to be a person. Should local cultures resist the forces of capitalism and the nation-state, and in so doing hold on to their notion of the person, then these cultures will remain part of the economic backwater, denied political power and invariably taken advantage of. Caught in a vise from which there can be no release, a variety of mediating, mitigating strategies have been devised by the peoples of Oceania. So Hirsch suggests that cultures in Oceania may try to partake in national culture and simultaneously seek to maintain the wholeness that founds their forms of identity.

The formation of a transcendent national culture is being institution-alized. Critical avenues of institutionalization include the educational system; the establishment of museums with an accompanying literature on archeology, oral history, and contemporary regional artwork; and the holding of shows, such as the Goroka or Hagen show. Each of these selectively parses the past and then recontextualizes it, thus placing the past in the service of the future. Institutional mechanisms are evolving for defining, refitting, and inventing *kastom* to meet the needs of nation-hood. It follows that public, semisystematized forms of knowledge— such as those that focus on a nation's history and prehistory or how to appeal to people through mass media advertising—are, along with the study of history and mass media, vital areas of anthropological study. Such semisystematized forms of knowledge or how-to ideology also in-clude the art of guerilla tactics and resistance and the way that institu-tions (such as universities) enter and inform public discourse. A signifi-cant issue here is how the state serves to shape, guarantee, and enforce shared meanings with respect to nationness.

A critical way of imagining, instilling, and reproducing a collective identity is the invention of rituals that mark the moments of national political passage (such as an independence day celebration), and repre-sent the nation as a nation among nations (for example, welcoming ceremonies for visiting dignitaries). For the nation-states of Oceania, we may ask with Kaplan (this volume) in what way are the rituals shaped in opposition to a colonial heritage; how do the rites help to create and consecrate the very concepts encoded in their performance, then repre-sent these rites and ceremonies as embodying a normative model of how citizens (as opposed to clan members) should behave? How does ritual not only define what are important events and words, but also instill them so deeply in collective memory that these events, words, and ritu-als themselves become a ground, referent, and source of legitimization for subsequent cultural constructions?

Conclusion

This chapter is much more a set of themes, problems, questions, and uncertainties than a theory of national culture and identity in Oceania. My aim has been to pose the issue of nationhood and its construction in a such a way as to escape reductionistic and deterministic viewpoints, both of which often are accompanied by implicit but telling Eurocentric biases. Even a first review of the Oceanic material is enough to reject unidimensional theories that view nationhood as a result of the "breakdown of tradition," the rise of industrialism, the advent of the modern public state, the result of a certain type of economic policy, or simply an exported European ideology. The use of history, the elaboration of customs, and the reformulations of identity throughout Oceania also call into question theories that want to oppose primordial (i.e., real) and invented traditions (see, e.g., Gellner 1983; Hobsbawm 1990). A review of the emergence of nation-states, nationalism, and national identities underscores several observations.

First, it is necessary to use a relational notion of "the nation" and national identity because what a nation is and how national identity is defined and inculcated vary from one nation-state to another. Even within the circumscribed space of Oceania, the nationalism of Papua New Guinea is certainly not that of Fiji or Vanuatu. Each of these nations, though they have much in common, has its own historically constructed character and trajectory. The conclusion is that nationness is not and cannot be treated as a unitary phenomenon. What is called nationhood and nationalism are heterogeneous structures associated and linked by a historically entrenched and validated discursive form. From such a relational view, nationalism or nationness is a genre of claims, understandings, and terms for recognizing, promoting, and legitimizing peoplehood, identity, and sovereignty.

Second, an understanding of the emergence of national culture and identity is concerned with more than imagined communities and the reshaping of people's experience. For the imagined community to become possible as a mode of knowledge, empowerment, and human experience, there must come into being a horizon that transcends and seeks to preempt local culture and community. For kinspeople to become "citizens," they must be enveloped in a new social space. This space in which national culture and identity are articulated is the historical condition of nation and statehood; it is given and accepted as progress—as the condition for true participation in a world historical order where nations have a say and cultural or ethnic communities, such as the Kurds and Armenians, do not. The creation of this new space hinges on the production of new persons endowed with strong individualism and bundled into larger social entities (e.g., class, region) by virtue of categorical identities as opposed and in addition to relational identities.

Third, a nonreductionistic analysis of the institutions and practices that mediate the production of nationness must be done against that background of the conditions and consequences of the encompassment of Oceania by global capitalism, internationalized culture, and Western forms of polity. This entails abandoning the notion that individual "cultures" or the set of cultures that compose a nation-state exist in a totalized state. The evidence shows that there is now an *intrinsic* (versus external) interrelation between the structures of a given culture, the other cultures or ethnicities of that nation-state, and the encompassing forms. So, the limits of the nation-state, its regions, and its cultures exist only as they are imagined, institutionalized, and contested in the public sphere. Simultaneously, it is necessary to examine the social mediations, from mass media to the arts, through which nations construct themselves, especially how these mediations are imbued with meaning, appropriated, and used by local communities.

Fourth, the construction of national culture is a study in the culture of empowered consensus, such consensus being no more than the name for a type of contestation. Moreover, the evidence from first years of national independence seems to indicate that local cultures and relational identities remain powerful in the face of the florescence of "the nation" and national identity because they are becoming historically embodied in the formation of the nation itself as a critical term of contestation.

Fifth, the investigation of national culture and politics is inseparable from an account of the formation of the public sphere. Of special significance are the ways in which the forms of communication that appear in the public sphere represent and mediate the gap between people's experience of direct interpersonal relations (the life-world, to borrow a phrase from Habermas) and experience of the large-scale, seemingly autonomous, political system that began with colonialism and has carried over into independence. At issue is how an imagined national community and felt national identity become rooted in, and are reproduced by, practical, everyday life. The analyses in this volume suggest that this occurs in three ways: (1) through the uniformity and ubiquity of the commodity and the use of national languages; (2) through the centralizing powers and control exercised by the state; and (3) through the representation of oneness and differences (in particular, historical events that become imbued with so much talismanic force that they function as shards of instant history, operating at a precognitive level, able to tap great reserves of emotion).

Another way to state these conclusions is to say that there is something about modernity and capitalism that is inseparable from the development of nationness. Research in postcolonial Melanesia presents the opportunity of shaping a clear and nonreductionist account of that relationship. What is required is a fruitful combination of ethnography, historical analysis, and theory that goes beyond the conventional limits of ethnography, history, or anthropology, not to mention political science and economics.

NOTES

1. It is equally as important to avoid the forms of romanticism, so prevalent in anthropology, that think that because indigenous societies resist, appropriate, and transform the forms of economy and polity that have been thrust upon them, these societies have magically retained their precolonial, cultural integrity—as though capitalism were not an imposed economy and the narrative of the nation not a derivative discourse (see Chatterjee 1984). The passion with which certain anthropologists push the argument that local cultures "domesticate" capitalism is an attempt to preserve the traditional anthropological object—culture in its totalized, non-Western form.

2. My comparison of Europe and Oceania is based on two years of field research in Papua New Guinea, three months in the Solomon Islands, and three years of historical-anthropological study in Spain on the character and implications of Galician nationalism. Although the making of nations in Europe was (and in most cases continues to be) contested and problematic (one has merely to recall the Basque independence movements), the nature of the European nation-making process was (is) fundamentally different from that of Oceania, black Africa, and much of Southeast Asia. Because most accounts of nation making have been written by and about Europeans, this point has been hidden. Politically, this is a consequence of European chauvinism, which assumes that what is true for Europe must be true for the rest of the world. This ethnocentrism masks the fact that what similarities may exist between nation making in France and Fiji or, more appropriately, New Caledonia and Vanuatu, are a result of hegemony: that is, a result of the uninvited forced imposition of the European model on the Third World. Theoretically and ethnographically, there exist a host of fundamental differences between the creation of the nation in Europe and in Oceania. Not least is that the making of the nation in Europe was advanced by an essentially internal dynamic, whereas the nations of Oceania would never exist in the absence of external, colonial domination. Many of the cultures of Irian Jaya on the island of New Guinea, for example, are only distantly related to each other (cultures on the north and south parts of the island are about as similar as, say, Spaniards are to Hungarians), and they have absolutely nothing in common, culturally, linguistically, or religiously, with the Javanese or other Indonesians. It is as if some foreign

power were to have conquered Europe and North Africa and decided to include the region from Germany through Chad in the same nation, no matter the vast differences. Contrast this with Weber's (1976) study of French nation building. Despite the fact that Weber's work emphasizes differences over similarities, these peasants did indeed become "Frenchmen" because they were all part of a capitalist economy; the vast majority were Catholic; there was a powerful, existing state apparatus; and language differences were important, though certainly solvable. The commonalities are obscured by the fact that Weber has no real notion of the structures and structuring power of capitalism, culture, and language (so much so that neither capitalism nor culture even appears in his index). While it is certainly true that nation making in Europe was (is) contested, nonetheless, the nature of similarity in Europe is much greater and of a different order than exists in Oceania.

3. For the New Guinea Highlands especially, there are a number of Marxist accounts that touch upon issues of nationhood and national identity, but the Marxist accounts see nationalism and nationhood as epiphenomena of the system of colonialist-capitalist production. Their view is that statehood precedes nationhood, and that people's belief in nationality can be grasped in terms of the state's functional need to ensure order and internal cohesion (see, for example, Amarshi, Good, and Mortimer 1979). For a recent and paradigmatic account about how this form of Marxism deals with the embarrassing issue of nations and national identity, see Wallerstein 1991. He maintains that not only nationalism, but also racism and ethnicity, are functional consequences of the system of capitalist production and expansion. I would argue that only an interpretation of Marx that refuses to separate production from culture can come to terms with nationalism and other forms of sociopolitical classification (see, for example, Postone 1993).

4. For a detailed discussion of the politics of recognition within the Western tradition, see the working paper by the political philosopher Charles Taylor (1992).

5. Recent work by Dominy and Sinclair on Maori women illustrates the problematic nature of the assertion of women's rights within the context of an assertion of Maori ethnic identity. The claim from the standpoint of the women's movement is that all people, regardless of gender, should be treated with equal respect. The individual, protected by society's procedural norms (such as due process and antidiscrimination codes), should have and exercise the right of self-determination. The foundations for this claim are a civil society based on individual rights and individually defined life goals. Women, for instance, should not be confined to the domestic sphere through the creation of substantive goals by society (for example, that women should aim for procreation and child care) and their sociolegal embodiment (such as denying women educational and employment opportunities). This idea of civil society based on individual freedom and rights is part and parcel of a liberal European tradition. It is no accident, then, that the improvement in the status of Maori women is linked to that of Pakeha women—women of European descent—and to an advancement of *this* liberal conception of civil society. But the whole notion of Maoritanga, or Maori sover-

eignty, is founded on a collective goal. For Maori activists, it is axiomatic that the survival of Maori culture and identity is a social good, and that this good should be pursued, even if doing so requires abridging individual rights. On this view, the right of non-Maori to purchase—and in some instances retain— "traditional" Maori land should be denied, whether this is a true expression and exercise of individual interests or rights. The concept is that there exists a collective definition of what it is to be Maori, that this definition entails certain specific goals (control over land), and that the satisfaction of these goals is just, even if other New Zealanders deny the validity of the goals on the grounds that they compromise the fundamental principle of individual rights (freedom of choice and sexual preference). The struggle for Maori women is that they must use and find ways to reconcile practically these two incompatible views of society: an individual-rights view that forms the basis of their feminism, and a collective-goods view that forms the basis of their claim for Maori sovereignty. This is both a cause of disunity and the subtext of the double contestation over women's rights and Maori sovereignty. Moreover, this is an expression of a contradiction between a Western conception of civil society that proclaims the sovereignty of the individual and a narrative of community based on the sovereignty of the group. Taylor 1992 gives a critical analysis of these two views of society.

6. One has only to recall the British administration's reaction to Marching Rule in the Solomon Islands, especially the prosecution and jailing of its leaders, and that administration's unwillingness to take indigenous desires seriously, to realize the extent to which the colonial state had a mission almost diametrically opposite to that of the modern independent state. One consequence of this unwillingness is that the role of the state in civil society must be invented anew in each nation.

7. It is important to recognize that the notion of total political sovereignty, even for the smallest territorial entities and national minorities, is itself a modern phenomenon. Although little research has been done on this subject, Eley (1981, 95) suggests that it was the triumph of Wilsonian principles in the aftermath of World War I that made full political sovereignty a leading demand.

8. It is for this reason that Australia and the United States have historically tried to eliminate, contain, and otherwise circumscribe Aborigines and Native Americans, respectively.

9. A related question is: what is it to remember one's "culture" and to possess a historical consciousness of that culture in a epoch when the visual and aural media are taking the place of memory? More, how can local artists who desire to represent their culture bypass the conventions of written history and transform their oral history into a national narrative?

10. For a more detailed account see LiPuma and Meltzoff 1990.

11. Within colonialism, this appeared locally in the way, for example, members of different clans would reside on the same, because now neutralized, mission station; it appeared in the creation of the national high schools that gave rise to many of the modern-day elite.

REFERENCES

Abercrombie, Thomas. 1991. To be Indian, to be Bolivian: "Ethnic" and "national" discourses of identity. In Greg Urban and Joel Sherzer, eds., *Nation-States and Indians in Latin-America*, 95–130. Austin: University of Texas Press.

Amarshi, Azeem, Kenneth Good, and Rex Mortimer. 1979. *Development and Dependency: The Political Economy of Papua New Guinea*. Melbourne: Oxford University Press.

Anderson, Benedict. 1983. *Imagined Communities: Reflections on the Origin and Spread of Nationalism*. London: Verso.

Balibar, Etienne. 1990. The nation form: History and ideology. *Review* 13: 329–61.

Barker, John, and A. M. Tietjen. 1990. Women's facial tattooing among the Maisin of Oro Province, Papua New Guinea: The changing significance of an ancient custom. *Oceania* 60:217–34.

Bourdieu, Pierre. 1985. The social space and the genesis of groups. *Social Science Information* 24:195–220.

Breuilly, John. 1985. *Nationalism and the State*. Chicago: University of Chicago Press.

Calhoun, Craig. 1993. Nationalism and ethnicity. *Annual Review of Sociology* 19:211–39.

Chatterjee, Partha. 1984. *Nationalist Thought and the Colonial World: A Derivative Discourse?* Avon, U.K.: Zed Books Ltd.

———. 1989. Colonialism, nationalism, and colonialized women: The contest in India. *American Ethnologist* 16:622–33.

———. 1990. A response to Taylor's "Modes of Civil Society." *Public Culture* 3:119–34.

———. 1993. *The Nation and its Fragments*. Princeton: Princeton University Press.

Cohen, Jean L., and Andrew Arato. 1992. *Civil Society and Political Theory*. Cambridge: MIT Press.

Dominguez, Virginia. 1989. *People as Subject, People as Object: Selfhood and Peoplehood in Contemporary Israel*. Madison: University of Wisconsin Press.

Dominy, Michelle. 1990. Maori sovereignty: A feminist invention of tradition. In Jocelyn Linnekin and Lin Poyer, eds., *Cultural Identity and Ethnicity in the Pacific*, 237–57. Honolulu: University of Hawaii Press.

Eley, Geoff. 1981. Nationalism and social history. *Social History* 6:83–107.

Foster, Robert J. 1991. Making national cultures in the global ecumene. *Annual Review of Anthropology* 20:235–60.

———. 1993. Bodies, commodities, and the nation-state in Papua New Guinea. Paper presented at the University of Chicago, Department of Anthropology Conference on Culturalism, Nationalism, and Transnationalism, 1–2 November.

Fox, Richard G. 1990. Introduction. In Richard G. Fox, ed., *Nationalist Ideolo-*

gies and the Production of National Cultures, 1–14. Washington: American Anthropological Association.

Gellner, Ernest. 1983. *Nations and Nationalism*. Ithaca: Cornell University Press.

Gouldner, Alvin. 1976. *The Dialectic of Ideology and Technology: The Origins, Grammar, and Future of Ideology*. New York: Oxford University Press.

Habermas, Jürgen. 1974 [1964]. The public sphere: An encyclopedia article. *New German Critique* 3:49–55.

Hobsbawm, Eric. 1990. *Nations and Nationalism Since 1780*. Cambridge: Cambridge University Press.

Kapferer, Bruce. 1988. *Legends of People, Myths of State: Violence, Intolerance, and Political Culture in Sri Lanka and Australia*. Washington: Smithsonian Institution Press.

Kaplan, Martha. 1988. The coups in Fiji: Colonial contradictions and the post colonial crisis. *Critique of Anthropology* 8:93–116.

———. 1990. Meaning, agency and colonial history: Navosavakadua and the Tuka Movement in Fiji. *American Ethnologist* 17:3–22.

Kedourie, Elie. 1985 [1960]. *Nationalism*, 3d ed. London: Hutchinson.

Keesing, Roger M. 1982. *Kastom* in Melanesia: An overview. In Roger Keesing and Robert Tonkinson, eds., *Reinventing Traditional Culture: The Politics of Kastom in Island Melanesia*. Special Issue, *Mankind* 13:297–301.

Kelly, John D. 1988. Political discourse in Fiji from the Pacific romance to the coups. *Journal of Historical Sociology* 1:399–422.

Larcom, Joan. 1990. Custom by decree: Legitimation crisis in Vanuatu. In Jocelyn Linnekin and Lin Poyer, eds., *Cultural Identity and Ethnicity in the Pacific*, 175–90. Honolulu: University of Hawaii Press.

Layne, Linda. 1989. The dialogics of tribal self-representation in Jordan. *American Ethnologist* 16:24–39.

Layton, Suzanna. 1992. Fuzzy-wuzzy devils: Mass media and the Bougainville crisis. *The Contemporary Pacific* 4:299–324.

LiPuma, Edward. 1988. *The Gift of Kinship: Structure and Practice in Maring Social Organization*. Cambridge: Cambridge University Press.

———. 1993. National histories and primordial identities in the making of the nation-state. Paper presented at the University of Chicago, Department of Anthropology Conference on Culturalism, Nationalism, and Transnationalism, 1–2 November.

LiPuma, Edward, and Sarah K. Meltzoff. 1989. Towards a theory of culture and class: An Iberian example. *American Ethnologist* 16:313–34.

———. 1990. Ceremonies of independence and public culture in the Solomon Islands. *Public Culture* 3:77–92.

Lukács, Georg. 1971. *History and Class Consciousness: Studies in Marxist Dialectics*. Cambridge: MIT Press.

May, R. J., ed. 1984. *Social Stratification in Papua New Guinea*. Working paper no. 5, Department of Social and Political Change, Research School of Pacific Studies, Australian National University.

Meltzoff, Sarah, and Edward LiPuma. 1985. *Worker Experience and National Development in the Solomon Islands*. Manila: ICLARM/Rockefeller.

Postone, Moishe. 1993. *Time, Labor, and Social Domination: A Reinterpretation of Marx's Critical Theory*. Cambridge: Cambridge University Press.

Sinclair, Karen. 1990. Tangi: Funeral rituals and the construction of Maori identity. In Jocelyn Linnekin and Lin Poyer, eds., *Cultural Identity and Ethnicity in the Pacific*, 219–36. Honolulu: University of Hawaii Press.

Smith, Anthony D. 1986. *The Ethnic Origins of Nations*. Oxford: Basil Blackwell.

Spriggs, Matthew. 1992. Alternative prehistories for Bougainville: Regional, national, or micronational. *The Contemporary Pacific* 4:269–98.

Strathern, Andrew. 1972. *One Father, One Blood: Descent and Group Structure among the Melpa People*. London: Tavistock.

Tambiah, Stanley J. 1989. Ethnic conflict in the world today. *American Ethnologist* 3:335–49.

Taylor, Charles. 1990. Modes of civil society. *Public Culture* 3:95–118.

———. 1992. *The Politics of Recognition*. Working paper no. 50, Center for Psychosocial Studies, Chicago.

Twine, Nanette. 1991. *Language and the Modern State: The Reform of Written Japanese*. London: Routledge.

Wagner, Roy. 1972. *Habu: The Innovation of Meaning in Daribi Religion*. Chicago: University of Chicago Press.

Wallerstein, Immanuel. 1991. The construction of peoplehood: Racism, nationalism, and ethnicity. In E. Balibar and I. Wallerstein, eds., *Race, Nation, Class*, 71–85. London: Verso.

Warner, Michael. 1989. *The Cultural Mediation of the Print Medium*. Working paper no. 27, Center for Psychosocial Studies, Chicago.

Weber, Eugen. 1976. *Peasants into Frenchmen: The Modernization of Rural France, 1870–1914*. Stanford: Stanford University Press.

Part 2
Instruments and Narratives of "the Nation"

Henry J. Rutz

Occupying the Headwaters of Tradition: Rhetorical Strategies of Nation Making in Fiji

Dialogic Wholes and Rhetorical Strategies

In *Imagined Communities*, Benedict Anderson (1983, 19) concludes that "nationalism has to be understood by aligning it, not with self-consciously held political ideologies, but with the large cultural systems that preceded it, out of which—as well as against which—it came into being." He has in mind the religious and dynastic realms that preceded the rise of nationalism in Europe at the end of the eighteenth century, which "marks not only the dawn of the age of nationalism but the dusk of the religious modes of thought" (19). Once nations are created in the time-space of eighteenth-century Europe, however, they become capable of being transplanted to a variety of social terrains and merge with a wide variety of political and ideological constellations (14), not to mention diverse time-space concepts.

For Anderson, nations are linguistic and cultural facts as much as anything else. While he insists that capitalist development and democracy have much to do with the emergence of nation-states, his main assertion is that a nation is a narrative of "an imagined *political* community," sovereign and limited (1983, 15, emphasis added). "How is the nation imagined?" he asks.

This chapter pursues "the nation" into the time-space of one of its social terrains, namely, the colonial and independent state of Fiji.[1] Following Anderson's lead, I ask how the Fijian nation, as opposed to the nation-state of Fiji, is imagined as a particular kind of political community. Rather than focusing on the nation as a cultural artifact, however, by abstracting a cultural system from a particular political constellation, the emphasis throughout is on a narrative of nation making that presumes a connection between cultural artifact and ideological construction.

Rhetorical strategy framed by a political regime is one form of agency by which the nation is made. A contest of rhetorical strategies rests on the further presumption that agents know what they are about, whatever the outcome.

In brief, the Fijian narrative of nation, like so many others in Melanesia, is a contest about "tradition." Tradition, in the first instance, has been deployed as a rhetorical device to legitimize claims of a single "racial" community—Fijians—against those of an "alien" community—Indians—to govern the sovereign state of Fiji. But in the light of recent military coups that settled the question of legitimacy by force, at least for the time being, "tradition" has become a rhetorical battleground for a contest of nation making within the Fijian community. Events run ahead of ideology, expanding the field of rhetorical possibilities in the projects of Fijian leaders (see, for example, Rutz and Balkan 1992). A Fijian image of "the nation" is assured for all the citizens of Fiji, but which one? To establish this level of analysis within a larger field of political ideology and action, I use the phrase *rhetorical strategy*, by which I mean a tactic that captures "tradition" in a way that is persuasive and compelling to a constituency predisposed on other grounds to contend the legitimacy of the nation.[2]

The idea I have in mind is captured by the political philosopher J. G. A. Pocock (1971, 247–48) in a conclusive comment on the practice of dynastic politics in ancient China (emphasis added):

> But Mo Tzu was in the strict sense a radical: that is, he was adopting the posture appropriate to a rebel in a traditional society, which is that of a reactionary. The appropriate location for his image of antiquity was the remotest accessible past, since there the presumption of continuity with the *traditional present* would be hardest to apply and, once he had occupied the headwaters of tradition, he would be in a position to maintain that the stream had been diverted from its proper course. Instances of this radical strategy, the advocacy of return to the roots or sources, abound in the history of argument within systems of authority.

Like that of Mo Tzu, the rhetorical strategies of Fijians constitute so many attempts to occupy the headwaters of tradition—a return to roots or sources as a form of advocacy of a particular system of authority.[3] And the notion of the "traditional present" captures the point succinctly that, whatever contests are waged, however much the headwaters are diverted, the result is a victory for tradition. By showing how rhetorical strategies of nation making appear to be bound into a dialogic whole—a kind of cultural system—a question arises about how or to what extent such strategies generate possibilities that transcend the system in place, supplanting one form of authority for another.

In Fiji, the imagined political community of the European "nation" appeared for one brief historical moment prior to independence in 1970, thereafter struggled for seventeen years to surmount the colonial legacy of racial political communities, only to succumb in 1987 to a narrow, triumphant, but no less creatively imagined, Fijian nation.[4] This chapter focuses on a narrative of nation that ultimately triumphed over a fledgling European-style image during the military coups of 1987 (Lal 1990).

A Brief Interlude

To understand the depth of island xenophobia in the rhetoric of tradition, listen first to the words of Fiji's two principal nation makers at that historical moment when the old European rhetoric of nation-states was being transplanted to Fiji. A. D. Patel (1968, 5), the leader of the Indian political community, delivered these words to a receptive audience of fellow Indians on the eve of independence:

> Imperialism everywhere has been the greatest enemy and antagonist of nationalism. In every country which was under imperial rule people were never described even as people, they were always described as peoples. . . . People who have awakened nationally and have national consciousness now realize that religion is immaterial, race is immaterial, even your way of life is immaterial—what is most important is a sense of political solidarity, a sense of unity, a sense of oneness. . . . So after all is said and done, it is a question of the mind, not a question of the colour. . . . It is the same thing with our nation, covered with the ignorance of racialism and sectarianism. Remove the cover, and the nation is there.

And listen, also, to then Chief Minister Ratu Mara (1968, 1), a high chief and leader of the Fijian community, as he delivered these comments at the same historical moment to an audience of Fijian partisans:

This is the first mass party political conference representing the towns and villages of the nation assembled to discuss and debate the issues that confront us. The Alliance is and will be the political force expressing the will of the people—the citizens of Fiji—not the Fijians alone, not the Indians alone, not the Europeans, part-Europeans, Chinese or any smaller group alone, but THE CITIZENS OF FIJI. . . . our first loyalty is to this nation and not to any other. . . . So this party must build a national awareness that puts Fiji first in the minds and hearts of our people.

The new citizens of a "sovereign democratic state" of Fiji (preamble to the 1970 constitution) were engaged for a brief historical moment in a discourse of eighteenth-century European nation building, one which aspired to surmount the colonial rhetoric and reality of different kinds of people—primarily Indian and Fijian.[5] They were exhorted by political leaders of their respective racial communities to imagine "one people" who live in "multi-racial harmony." Both kinds of people—Fijians and Indians—would subordinate cultural difference and racial politics to the common secular goals of an encompassing capitalist development.[6]

For seventeen years, from independence in 1970 to the military coups of 1987, a discourse was framed by a dialogic that ranged across a wide terrain between two points on a horizon. An Indian assimilationist rhetoric presumed that a sovereign state would be the condition for a new kind of imagining, a nation to which A. D. Patel, anticipating much recent thinking about nation making, referred as "a state of mind." Indians imagined a newly created "citizen" living in a civil society that subordinated the status of religion, race, and particularist culture to national solidarity. Indians would have full political rights, buttressed by the institution of common roll (one person, one vote). In contrast, a Fijian rhetoric of accommodation presumed that the nation would be imagined as "mutual respect" between different racial communities, re-inforced by a narrative of "multiracial" harmony and the institution of communal roll (voting by racial community for persons of the same race).[7]

The military coups of 1987 put an end to the making of a national culture for the citizens of Fiji. Indians lost their political rights when a segment of the Fijian community seized the state apparatus in order to govern, as they said, in perpetuity in their own land (Dean and Ritova 1988, 105). The restoration of Fijian power, and with it a new constitution, brought to a halt the brief experiment of transplanting an eighteenth century nation-state in the time-space of Fiji.[8] More to the point, the coups took away the Other against which Fijian identity had been dialectically shaped by racial politics during the colonial and independence periods. The military guaranteed Fijian control of the state in the foreseeable future, even as the new constitution enshrined "tradition" as the resolution of a crisis of legitimation. Henceforth, the contest over "the nation" would be de-centered, resurfacing within the Fijian community itself.

The Cultural System of the Fijian Nation

Whenever political discourse was framed by racial politics, Fijians had no trouble imagining themselves—and had been encouraged by a century of colonial intervention to think of themselves—as a tightly knit political community whose identity rested on rhetorical traditions of "chiefs," "land," and "church." There were always contested narratives, to be sure, but as long as Indians were perceived to be a threat to the survival of a Fijian community qua political community, *different* rhetorical traditions were concealed in the interest of a "revealed" cultural system.[9]

My initial argument is that political rhetoric remained for decades within the cultural system as constructed during the colonial period (see Kaplan this volume). The key that unlocks the unity of terms as disparate as *chiefs, land,* and *church* is the ontology of "tradition."[10] It is the ontology of tradition that shapes political discourse about the Fijian nation, so much so that Fijians incorporate events, persons, and institutions into a single narrative about "the Fijian way of life" (*vakavanua*), which places supreme value on codes of conduct understood to be reproduced as tradition. The making of the Fijian nation was an exploration of beginnings within the possibilities offered by a cultural system that emphasized social hierarchy and "mutual respect" between chiefs and people. The Fijian term for "mutual respect," *veidokai*, denotes a reciprocity that must be understood within a framework of hierarchy and beliefs about divine chiefship. The citizens of Fiji—Indians and Fijians alike—are obliged to "Fear the Lord and Respect the Chiefs" in the motto written *in Fijian* on the national flag of the sovereign state of Fiji. The word for Fijian commoners is "land people" (*taukei*), which is associated with the idea of original settlers as opposed to those who came later—the chiefs. Usurpations are a common theme in the traditions of tributary states, and Fiji is no exception. The juxtaposition of origin and usurpation constitutes an enduring tension that might be termed mutuality within hierarchy. There is a continuous flow of morally attached products of the land to chiefs and reverse flows that display the chiefs' "generosity" to the land people. The result is "mutual love" (*veilomani*) and "mutual service" (*veiqaravi*), a particular historical variant of divine kingship. Tacked onto tradition is the ever-present theme of the "civilizing" process accompanying conversion to Christianity by missionaries and later colonization by Great Britain. What makes tradition a cultural system is a perceived unity of key symbols despite disparate beginnings for each.[11] Fijian political events are highly ritualized occasions for reaffirming the ontology of tradition by concealing contradictions in secular and sacred sources of legitimacy and real-time historical conflicts between land people and chiefs.

Briefly, the cultural system of the Fijian nation came into being during a century of colonial rule as an amalgam of original "cultural" logic that links chiefs (sea people) and commoners (land people) into a polysemic social hierarchy (Sahlins 1976, 1985), "encompassing" Christianity (Kaplan 1990; Rutz and Balkan 1992), "invented" property rights and customs of the land (France 1969), and modern native bureaucratic-administrative institutions (Spate 1959; Belshaw 1964, 1965).

The indigenous cultural logic that opposes land to sea, commoners to chiefs, and interior to coastal regions through complex permutations is crucial for understanding the vision of a tributary state at the political center of the Fijian nation.[12] Most Fijians today see themselves less as citizens of a democratic nation-state than as supporters of a local chief who holds rank in a hierarchy of chiefs from village to "nation."[13] The "land" not only is a metaphor for complex relations between chiefs and commoners, it also is part of a living Fijian tradition of communal property rights and corporate kin groups invented in part during the colonial era as a reactive pattern to incursions of money and the market. "Land" is viewed by Fijians as their contribution, analogous to the "labor" of Indians and "capital" of Europeans, to the development and modernization of Fiji. The institutionalization of "chiefs" and "land" by means of a colonial native bureaucratic-administrative apparatus, which extended from village to central government, guaranteed that the Fijian nation was to be a political and legal entity, not merely a cultural one.[14]

To "chiefs" and "land" was added "church." The diffusion of Methodism in particular, and Christianity in general—by means of print-Methodism, church discipline, and its own hierarchical bureaucratic organization extending from village to nationwide conference—added immensely to a pan-Fijian national consciousness over and above narrow tributary and dialect divisions. By the middle of the last century, Methodism's dissent from divine kingship and its hold over the flock of commoners had allied itself, uneasily, with chiefly establishment, giving shape to the time-space of pan-Fijian consciousness a generation before the islands were ceded to Britain.

In sum, by independence, Fijians had evolved, over the course of a century, a strong sense of an imagined political community, one that differed in important and antipathetic ways from the "deep horizontal comradeship" of anonymous contemporaries that Anderson (1983, 13) claims as that form of imagining peculiar to the modern European nation-state.[15] The historically contingent relations among "chiefs," "land," and "church," which from a vantage point outside Fijian political discourse gave "tradition" a peculiarly recent and modern shape, were imagined by Fijians as "in place" and immemorial. There is a dialogical whole—to borrow a phrase from Kelly (1988)—to Fijian political discourse about "the nation," one that frames a general ontology of "tradition." Meanings shifted with political and economic circumstances, but the apprehension of the present as a continuation of the past remained a constant feature of Fijian political discourse during the entire colonial encounter. Tradition gained in strength after independence as a consequence of new democratic rules of political competition between Indians and Fijians, who separately formed political parties to contest control of the state in national elections.

A rhetoric of tradition was the counterpart of a hybrid cultural system that absorbed a colonial legacy in the process of resistance and reaction, overriding all other interests and discontents within the Fijian community. Ratu Mara, paramount chief, leader of the chiefly Alliance Party, and prime minister during the entire period of independence, and major architect of normalization following the 1987 military coups, spoke about it this way when he addressed the Council of Chiefs in 1988, as reported in a May 5 *Fiji Times* article:

> [W]e share fully the concern which has been expressed about the divisive and debilitating forces that have created disharmony and disillusionment within the indigenous Fijian community. There

have been too many instances of an unfortunate lack of respect for, and sensitivity to, traditional Fijian institutions and ethical values. . . . Nevertheless, these individual rights and freedoms must be exercised responsibly and with sensitivity in full recognition of the over-riding importance that the indigenous Fijians attach to their communal values of duty and loyalty to the unity and harmony of their community and of obedience to, and respect for, their traditional chiefly authority.

Those familiar with Fijian ritual and rhetoric will recognize the code words used by and for Establishment hierarchy: *duty*, *loyalty*, and *respect*—values that express noblesse oblige in a tributary state. The threat to unity and harmony is code for democracy that would threaten the paramountcy of chiefs in the political economy and national culture of the independent state of Fiji.

Rhetorical Political Strategies of the Fijian Nation

The framing of Fijian nationalism by a dialogic of "tradition" has been documented by many scholars, but less attention has been paid to the dialectic of rhetorical strategies that link "tradition" to "the nation" as the latter's source of legitimacy, that is, the politics of Fijian nation making.

"Tradition" is a political idea (Pocock 1971), one way in which to implicate the "past" in the political projects of the "present." There are a variety of ways in which to implicate the "past," including the perception of a discontinuity or disjunction with the "present" (for example, the project of modernity). But whatever the historical facts, "tradition" as a political idea embodies two suppositions. First, the present is authorized by the past. Current political dialogue appeals to continuity between past and present in order to establish its truths. Second, a political discourse centered on "tradition" will conceive of rhetorical strategies that legitimize current beliefs in terms of their beginnings—a ceaseless search for the traditional present.[16] The authorization of Fijian narratives of nation is first and foremost about beginnings—whose interests are served by what origins—and the contest for a dominant narrative of nation that lends legitimacy to current imaginings.

These truths are precisely the trajectory to which Pocock (1971, 241) refers as "the abridgement of tradition by ideology" that is the

subject here. There are numerous rhetorical tactics, but if we are looking for paradigmatic strategies, there are only three, each a different
construction of the Fijian nation within the dialogic whole of "chiefs,"
"land," and "church." The rhetorical dynamics of the dialogic whole are
revealing. Each strategy maintains an appearance of remaining within
the bounds of a cultural system, while the sequence and timing of strategies are important for an understanding of the capacity of each to sustain
this appearance.

But the abridgement of tradition by ideology derives its power only
in part from rhetoric. The passion for rhetoric comes from the nature of
the events themselves. The Fijian nation is a highly emotional historical
object shaped by reaction and resistance as well as complicity and conversion to Christianity, democracy, and capitalism. The strategies are so
many variations in a game of sleight of hand, in which it is necessary to
maintain the appearance of remaining within the dialogic whole of the
Fijian nation while departing sufficiently to take advantage of shifting
political alliances and the quick chance for material gain. The very success of a rhetorical strategy depends upon a blurring of the distinction
between reproduction and transformation of a cultural system.

The Royalist Strategy

The first rhetorical "tradition," which I shall term the *royalist strategy*,
was promulgated by Ratu Sir Kamisese Mara, the paramount chief of
Lau, leader of the governing Alliance Party, and first prime minister of
independent Fiji. Under his guidance, this strategy was enshrined in the
1970 constitution as a protection against threats to an established "Fijian
way of life" posed by market rationality and political democracy. The
royalist strategy locates the tradition of a Fijian nation in the near past of
a colonial narrative that irrevocably ties the destiny of the Fijian people
to that of the British monarchy through the agency of their chiefs.[17]

The royalist strategy holds, paradoxically, that traditional chiefly
authority is "authorized" by the acceptance of the queen of England as
the Tui Viti (the chief of all Fijians). Ratu Mara and the paramount
chiefs of Fiji have been the most vocal and consistent advocates of the
connection between the chiefs and the Crown.

The narrative focuses on two historical events. The first is the Deed
of Cession in 1874, when the paramount chief of Bau and twelve other
paramount chiefs of petty tributary states ceded the islands to the queen.

A key article of the Deed of Cession is the statement "that the rights and interests of the said Tui Viti and other high chiefs the ceding parties hereto shall be recognized so far as is and shall be consistent with British Sovereignty and Colonial form of government."

This may seem a far cry from a stipulation of specific obligations, but in succeeding decades the Fijian chiefly and communal construction of this clause has come to mean that the chiefs engaged in an act of generosity in exchange for paramountcy in their own land. The claim is that there is a special relationship between the chiefs and the Crown that takes precedence over the Crown's obligations toward immigrant "races." Time and again, chiefs have used the Deed of Cession to authorize themselves as the protectors of native landowners against Indian claims for more land.[18]

The second historical point of origin for the royalist strategy is 10 October 1970, the date of Fiji's independence from Britain as a sovereign democratic state and member of the commonwealth. The constitution of 1970 calls for the British queen to be the executive authority and the governor-general to be her representative. It affirmed the allegiance to her of Fiji's people, as recalled in the *Fiji Times* article "The Question of Crown Links," 2 April 1988. The 1970 constitution also enshrined the special relationship between chiefs and Crown in guarantees that both "chiefs" and "land" would persist and be institutionalized as a separate political entity within the new nation-state.

In Ratu Mara's rhetorical strategy for holding power in the new nation-state (he was its first and only prime minister for the first seventeen years of independence), the link between the chiefs and the Crown was the linchpin of his ideology. He has stated publicly on numerous occasions that the chiefs owe their legitimacy to the Crown because of the Deed of Cession.[19] The Great Council of Chiefs, one of the invented traditions of the Fijian nation, "could not have the same influence with the people without the authority of the Crown" (Inder 1987, 7).

The 1987 coup afforded the Great Council of Chiefs the luxury of imagining a new state based on a constitution whose cultural roots would be the Fijian nation. One of their first pronouncements—as reported on the front page of the *Fiji Times*, 22 May 1987—was that the ties to the Crown be retained. When Fiji became a republic, breaking its ties with the Crown as a result of the second coup, Ratu Mara nevertheless returned to this rhetorical claim. By means of international diplomacy, he sought ways in which the ties could remain despite the attenuation of the queen of England as head of state.[20]

The reasons are not hard to find. The hierarchical and ritual politics of the Fijian nation are completely compatible with the traditions and ceremonies that legitimize the British Crown and help maintain social order. The *Fiji Times* of 30 December 1987 reprinted a story from *The Economist* on the constitutional crisis in Fiji, in which that magazine found it easy to see why in tradition-minded societies a monarch sits higher in public esteem than a commoner as head of state. The story quotes Sir Ian Gilmour in *The Body Politic* to the effect that "Legitimacy, the acceptance by the governed of the political system, is far better aided by an ancient monarchy set above the political battle than by a transient president, who has gained his position through that battle. . . . modern societies still need myth and ritual." Prior to the second coup and declaration of a republic, Fiji Supreme Court Judge Mr. Justice Rooney, in clarifying the position of the queen as the head of state of Fiji, had offered the following opinion in a *Fiji Times* article on 15 August 1987: "Apart from her place as the Queen of Fiji under the Constitution, Her majesty is the fountain of all honour and dignity and she can confer upon any of her subjects any title of dignity at Her pleasure. In general she exercises this power on the advice of her ministers." Ratu Mara would have found much comfort in Mr. Justice Rooney's added assurance that "the Queen reigns but does not rule over her subjects."

By attempting to occupy the headwaters of tradition in the flow of colonial history, Ratu Mara forcibly displaced the notion that tradition was lodged solely in immemorial custom, the timeless cultural logic of opposition between sea and land people (Sahlins 1976). Like Mo Tzu, he was in the strict sense a radical. By occupying the headwaters of colonial history, he could stake out his claim to be a rebel in traditional society, which became the stance of a reactionary in the new democracy. This strategy represents the ritual encompassment of a foreign monarch by an indigenous elite. The effect is to shift legitimacy of the nation from an origin in culture to one in history. The fate of the royalist strategy, however, is informed by Pocock's (1971, 242) observation that "The more precisely society is imagined as a series of concrete human actions in time, the more likely it is that tradition becomes desacralized." Ultimately, Ratu Mara suffered the fate of desacralization and lost the election, precipitating the 1987 coup that restored Fijians to power "in their own land." By desacralizing tradition, the royalist strategy opened the door to new rhetorical possibilities.

The Strategy of Betrayal of the Land

The second strategy, which I shall call the *strategy of betrayal of the land*, can only be understood as a reading and interpretation of the first. It is the strategy of disgruntled and discontented commoners, promulgated by Sakeasi Butadroka, an urban medium-level civil servant, founder and leader of the Fijian Nationalist Party. Premdas (1980) has given a percipient account of its rhetorical claims.

In brief, Butadroka argued that there was a double betrayal of land people by chiefs. The Deed of Cession of the islands to Queen Victoria in 1874 was the origin of Fijian poverty, not power. Butadroka claimed that the land was not the chiefs' to give. In effect, the Deed of Cession was a theft, a historical contravention of the sacred trust and immemorial custom between chiefs and land people.

The narrative then uses the first betrayal to make the rhetorical claim of a second historical contravention and betrayal at the time of independence in 1970. The queen, Butadroka claimed, should have returned the land to Fijians, the rightful owners. Instead, she returned the land to a new category of people, the citizens of the state of Fiji. The implication was clear: Indians had become a part of the land. While Ratu Mara's ancestor participated in the first betrayal, Ratu Mara himself was a major architect of the 1970 constitution that, to Butadroka, was an instrument for divesting ordinary Fijians of land, their ontological reality as a nation. For that reason, the chiefs had twice fallen from their pedestal and thereby forfeited the right to lead.

Ratu Mara had shifted the leadership claims of the chiefs from the ontology of immemorial custom to the historical event of the Deed of Cession and the ritual power of the British monarchy. Ironically, the chiefly claims of "tradition" were displaced from one enduring structure to another, from the "custom of the land" and the "custom of chiefs" (*vakavanua* and *vakaturaga*, respectively) to the custom of the Crown. Chiefly power suddenly rested on the act of independence with retention of ties to the Crown.

Butadroka countered with a brilliant rhetorical flourish. He claimed that independence for Fijians lay in the future, not the past. Fijians had to free themselves from democracy, which had linked their destiny to that of the Indians.[21] *Democracy* and *equality* are terms in the Western ontology of tradition. These, he said, have been the major obstacle to the true independence of Fiji. Citizen rights, equality, and the inclusion of the Bill of Human Rights (in the 1970 constitution) were the cause of the drawbacks (Premdas 1980, 35). Here is what Butadroka and the Fijian Nationalist Party said in a submission to the governor-general (himself a paramount chief) in 1977:

> Your Excellency, the Fijian Nationalists see the political standing and position of the Fijian race in the wake of the western concept of democracy as gloomy and uncertain. (Premdas 1980, 35)

> Sir, the Fijian Nationalist cannot accept the equality of all the races . . . in his native Fiji. Equality of rights is not a simple concept. It has to involve a recognized and accepted inequality of rights due to history. The right of ownership is crucial here. (Premdas 1980, 36)

Premdas notes that Fijian Nationalists saw both the chiefs and Britain as an impediment to the expression and realization of the Fijian nation, at the heart of which were the land people or commoners. They opposed the chiefly system and called for the retirement of chiefs from politics. As for the Crown, it had come to Fiji not as a civilizing force and protector of tradition, but, rather, as an economic exploiter.

This rhetorical strategy shares with the first an ideological locus in two events of colonial history: first, the 1874 Deed of Cession, wherein chiefs ceded the islands to Britain; second, the 1970 constitution, which enshrined Indian political rights and a democratic competition for power between racial communities. The strategy of betrayal holds that the land was not the chiefs' to cede and that Britain was obligated to return the land to Fijians at independence. This populist imagining of history as betrayal of the people, which exploits the sentiments of ordinary Fijians who became increasingly disenchanted and discontented with chiefly politics beginning in the late 1970s, returns both land and power to Fijian commoners.[22]

The radicalism of this strategy lies in its challenge to a cultural system premised on hierarchy and the apparent possibility it holds for a democratic populist rhetoric about government for the people. But the real headwater of tradition in the strategy of betrayal is the idea of "original settlers" that excludes immigrants from political power. Radical within the dialogic whole, the strategy of betrayal is a reactionary formation against the contingent events of colonial history that in due time brought democracy, capitalism, and Indians to Fiji. Of the rhetorical possibilities, the strategy of betrayal holds out the least possibility of transformation and, in its exclusionism, can result only in a virulent strain of nationalism and island xenophobia.

The royalist strategy and the strategy of betrayal offer alternative— and incompatible—visions of the Fijian nation. It is important to note that this is a departure from a cultural system of structured oppositions between land people and chiefs that draws strength from a morality of mutual duty and obligation. Nevertheless, the dialectic has taken shape within a dialogic whole of "chiefs," "land," and "church." The rhetorical claims of both, insofar as they are motivated by power and based on secular origins of recent "tradition," are rational and modern: both use unique events in the real-time of the "past" to make rhetorical claims for political projects in the "present." Neither political rhetoric bursts the boundaries of signification imposed by the cultural system. The rhetorical claims are those of "land" against "chiefs," not those of class struggle or of responsibilities of citizenship within a civil society that includes different kinds of people.

The Strategy of Divine Intervention

The third strategy emerged in the political crisis of 1987.[23] As an ideological articulation of beginnings of a Fijian nation, its rhetoric brilliantly exploits the terrain of *religion* to subordinate the other two terms (and political constituencies) of the dialogic whole. As in the other rhetorical strategies, it stands both inside and outside the cultural system as constituted, exploiting the last of the logical possibilities of the cultural system and at the same time moving beyond its apparent boundaries.

The promulgator is none other than the Fijian coup leader, Col. Sitiveni Rabuka, who claimed the headwaters of tradition when he asserted that Christianity turned Fiji "from cannibal land into Paradise" (Dean and Ritova 1988, 11). He placed the apparent beginnings of the Fijian nation within a broader narrative of the "civilizing" process begun in 1835 with the arrival of the first Methodist missionaries.[24] This source, however, is only apparent. The real source lies beyond the time-space of history and culture, in an imaginative and timeless covenant with God and the Fijian people. In this covenant, "chiefs" and "land" are authorized by "church." Fiji, he claimed, is a land "God has given Fijians" (Dean and Ritova 1988, 11). The problem was that a God-given treasure had come under threat of an "immigrant race." The solution, he offered, was "for Fijians to determine their own destiny in their own land" (17).

As Pocock (1971, 243) would have it, "What stands outside tradition is charismatic; where time itself is envisaged as the continuity of tradition, the charismatic may stand outside time and become the sacred." Charisma arrived on 14 May 1987, in the person of Colonel Rabuka, who led the successful military coup against an alien political ontology (Enlightenment democracy) and restored Fijians to power "in their own land."[25] A Methodist lay preacher and self-styled religious fundamentalist, Rabuka was a man of words as well as action. Appearing at Fijian village meetings around the country, he spoke of his belief that the first coup was a mission given him by God: "If this land is run by Christians, or Fijians who are Christians, everything will be in place" (Dean and Ritova 1988, 36). In Rabuka's imagination, the Fijian nation is divinely ordained by the Fijian conversion to Christianity.

The power of his rhetorical claims derives from their capacity to encompass the other two strategies while at the same time undermining them by selecting a sacred point of origin for "tradition" outside culture or history. He encompasses the Fijian nationalists' vision of the nation as a political idea that the "land" embodies "tradition" (*vanua* and *vakavanua*, respectively). He encompasses, also, Ratu Mara's view that chiefly usurpation makes royalists the custodians of a people imagined as inseparable from their land (*vakaturaga*). Furthermore, Rabuka made the rhetorical claim that at independence the British queen should have returned the gift of sovereignty to chiefs and of land to commoners, reciprocating an act of "generosity" made a century earlier. In sum, he encompasses some of the claims of both by agreeing with the claim made by the strategy of betrayal that history was a betrayal of tradition, yet agreeing with the royalist claim that tradition authorized the "chiefly system."

The really radical departure from previous rhetorical strategies—and therefore in this society the most reactionary against modernism—was the claim that legitimacy of both "chiefs" and "land" resided in spirituality, or in this case, revealed Christianity. Rabuka returned to the Deed of Cession for the true source of motivated interest in the original gift of land by chiefs. They were "desirous of securing the promotion of civilization and Christianity" (Dean and Ritova 1988, 36). Only after he established the original intention did he turn to how tradition authorized the nation. The chiefs, he claimed, were not wrong in their motivation and remained the true source of inherited learning and revealed knowledge. The betrayal was the queen's, when she returned sovereignty in 1970 to all the people of Fiji when it should have been to the chiefs.

The strategy of divine intervention amounted to the statement that, viewed in its proper perspective, the 1987 coup was the correction of an error made in 1874 (Cession) and compounded in 1970 (independence). History was made whole again, discontinuity became continuity, and the rhetorical traditions of "chiefs," "land," and "church" became the longed-for reality of the Fijian nation in control of the state. The royalist strategy was "correct" when it asserted the primacy of chiefly knowledge. The strategy of betrayal was also "correct" in pointing out an "error" made by the Crown when it mistakenly associated the land of Fiji with the people of Fiji rather than the Fijian people. The winning strategy, however, was to link motivation to its true source—the civilizing process of Christianity—and to sacralize the bond between chiefs and commoners, between the Fijian people and the land God had given them.

A prayer, delivered at a political meeting prior to the coup and attended by Rabuka, captures the essence of the third rhetorical strategy: "Save us and save our land. You saved the Israelites when their land was taken from them by foreigners. Dear God, please answer our prayer and do the same for us" (Dean and Ritova 1988). When Rabuka declared Fiji a republic following his second coup in September 1987, severing ties to the queen, he observed a symbolic correspondence between the Jewish Day of Atonement and the declaration of the republic. He set the course of the Fijian nation, he said, the way God had determined, atoning for the sin committed on 10 October 1970—the false day of Fijian independence.

The strategy of divine intervention was at once the most radical and most reactionary of the possibilities given by the dialogic whole. And it was realized only by the most extreme legitimation crisis of the Fijian nation. Its radical stance derived from the claim that tradition within the dialogic whole was located in a time out of time, surely the winning strategy for occupying the headwaters of tradition to claim that others had diverted the stream from its proper course. But in defeating the claims of other strategies that located tradition in foreign monarchy or original settlership, the strategy of divine intervention was the most reactionary. It took least account of historically contingent events such as Methodism's alignment with Establishment hierarchy, the reliance of chiefs on the project of modernity, and capitalist development of the land.

Conclusion

In Fiji, the nation as imagined on the eve of independence is dead. The making of a single national culture by Fijians and Indians is stillborn. Following the 1987 restoration of Fijian control of the state, the subsequent loss of Indian political rights in the 1990 constitution, the enshrinement of Fijian supremacy under the guise of a political democracy, and the shadow of the Fijian military in the political life of the country, the lived reality is a nation made in the image of "the Fijian way of life."

At that historical moment when the chiefdom encompassed the sovereign democratic state, one might have expected the triumph of a single narrative of the Fijian nation, melding nation and state. But nothing could be further from the true state of affairs, which is a further testing of the veneer of an "original cultural logic" by the corrosive effects of internal squabbles, not to mention the strains placed on politics by the realities of a solid Fijian working and middle class that shares much with its Indian counterpart.

The aftermath of independence in 1970 was an inflow of foreign capital, a rural exodus to the new wage and salary jobs concentrated in the capital city, and the rapid rise in consumption and the life-styles of a global middle class. The 1987 coups managed to cripple the middle class, but only temporarily. Capitalist work-discipline and a consumer culture are a part of the permanent political landscape that cut across racial communities, categories, and interests. The strategy of betrayal that articulated a radical Fijian nationalism has great appeal among urban workers and rural landowners. It already was in place by the mid-1970s, contesting the royalist narrative that kept land in the hands of powerful chiefs and ensured a flow of tribute from the bottom. The strategy of divine intervention following the electoral loss of the chiefs was a reaction to the speed at which the advance of the market had eroded the old bases of political competition.

The concept of a dialogic whole, based as it is upon discursive rules of language that are always subject to invasion by a wider field of possibilities, raises the question of competing and more encompassing dialogics. The dialogic of the market and its locus in the middle class is one among several alternative possibilities that are partially realized. This dialogic is a local extension of global economic integration. Another is a dialogic of international human rights and is backed by the force of world powers. The 1990 constitution ensures civil liberties and incorporates a notion of limited political competition *only* as a result of international pressures stemming from a dialogic of human rights.[26] A third alternative dialogic exists among Indians in Fiji, who are half the population. The coup did not erase their own narratives of nation, however silent and subordinate these are at the moment (Kelly 1988). The realpolitik of the republican era may, over time, result in a new dialogic whole that once again encompasses "tradition," bursting the limits of present political discourse. From recent history, we know that this will not happen quietly or without resistance. The tortured construction of Fijian culture and identity during the colonial era must be counted among those reactionary social formations in the history of capitalism.

If "the nation" is a narrative about collective identity within the framework of a state, it is also about that identity vis-à-vis other states. The focus of this chapter was on the internal dialogic of a Fijian nation. But it would be a mistake to conclude that Fijian nationalist discourse can disregard an encompassing world capitalism and democratic rhetoric, any more than to view it as free from a political ontology whose origin is in eighteenth-century European history and was engaged at the moment of independence in 1970.

ACKNOWLEDGMENTS

The ideas in this chapter were greatly improved by the editorial comments of John Kelly and Robert Foster. I have benefited also from numerous conversations with Michael Howard and Kostas Gounis. Colleagues at the Sociology Department Seminar of Bogazici University in Istanbul offered many comments that I have incorporated into the body of the chapter. Pete Taylor's close reading helped clarify and refine several points in the argument. I have relied on several insights of Nicholas Thomas, who reviewed an earlier version.

NOTES

1. The Fiji Islands were ceded to Great Britain in 1874 and remained a British crown colony until independence in 1970. *Fiji* refers to the colonial and sovereign state. In Fiji, different kinds of people are referred to as *races*, which form *communities*. *Fijian* refers to citizens of Fiji who also are deemed indigenous to the place. *Indian* refers to citizens of Fiji who are descendants of migrants from India. As of 31 December 1988, Fiji's population was 718,119. Of the total, 342,965 were Fijians, 340,121 were Indians (nearly all of whom were Fiji-born), and 35,033 were non-Fijian/non-Indians (most of whom were Fiji-born) (Garrett 1990, 110.)

2. Contested narratives of nation that deploy tradition as a legitimizing force are part of the political landscape that includes, but is not limited to, party ideologies.

3. The main argument of this chapter owes much to Pocock's seminal essay on rhetorical strategies of tradition. He argues that an essential feature of every society is *tradition*—the "handing on of formed ways of action and the images that transmit them" (1971, 234). Pocock is interested in traditions that rely on beginnings in order to maintain systems of authority.

4. On the tendency for new nation-states in Melanesia to be reshaped in terms of ethnic collectivities that question nationalism and national culture, see LiPuma (this volume). His contention that the narrative of community remains decisive and stands in opposition to both a centralized state and the formation of civil society would appear to apply to Fiji.

5. See Jourdan (this volume) for the point that the new nation-states of Melanesia defend, rather than contend, the previous colonial space. They do, however, contend what *kinds* of people will occupy that space, Fiji being a prime example.

6. Fiji's economic integration into an evolving global economy, from the standpoint of the labor process, began when Indians were brought to labor in sugar plantations owned by Australians during the last third of the nineteenth century. Full-blown capitalism in the form of absorption of large numbers of Fijians into labor markets appeared with policies of localization and heavy foreign investment at the time of independence.

7. For a really imaginative narrative of the nation of Fiji that synthesizes all the disparate elements of colonial history, see Kaplan (this volume). Perhaps only something this fanciful could achieve a synthesis in the face of overwhelming political realities that confront the people of Fiji.

8. For a concept of time underlying the Fijian narrative of nation, see Rutz and Balkan 1992 and Rutz 1984. For a concept of space, see France 1969.

9. This system is powerfully expressed in daily and periodic ritual such as kava ceremonies and the welcoming of chiefs. Iteration of a "Fijian way of life" is key to an understanding of the salience of a single cultural object.

10. It is ironic that orthodox Fijian rhetorical tradition leaves little social or political space open to militarism in the construction of the nation. War and

warriors are prominent themes in Fijian daily discourse. The *bati* (warriors) of a chief take a special place in myth and legend. Coincidentally, Lt. Col. Sitiveni Rabuka, prime minister since 1992, is from a clan that is *bati* to the chiefly clan of Cakaudrove. The late governor-general, Ratu Sir Penaia Ganilau, stood as paramount chief to the warrior Rabuka. British overlords contributed to the fierce reputation of Fijian warriors by portraying them as the world's finest jungle fighters in the Solomon Islands campaign during World War II. In the 1950s, a Fiji contingent led by a young Ratu Penaia fought in Malaysia. More recently, Fijians have been eager to enlist for duty as UN peacekeepers in Lebanon and Sinai, where Colonel Rabuka acquired his reputation as a fearless leader who earned the loyalty of his troops.

11. In his reviewer's report on this volume, Nicholas Thomas noted that "the Fijian idea of *vakavanua*, unlike the English word *tradition,* is not primarily grounded in the past . . . *vakavanua* is good because it is intrinsically good, not because it has been done for generations and is validated by time. Hence the 'invention of tradition issue' simply does not arise."

12. Sahlins (1976, 1985), following Hocart (1929, 1970 [1936]), argues convincingly that the time-space of a tributary mode of production is imbued with a politics of ritual and cosmology, and that its history is conceived differently from that of modern nation-states.

13. The institutionalization of rhetorical tradition, while not the main focus of this essay, is important for understanding how a "nonfanciful" nation is imagined. British overlords instituted a single hierarchy of paramount chiefs in place of petty warring chiefdoms. A novel institution, the Great Council of Chiefs, by and by was buttressed by a fully modern bureaucratic-administrative apparatus of provinces, provincial councils and chiefs, districts, district councils and chiefs, and villages, village meetings, and chiefs. Property rights to land were determined by a Native Lands Commission, and in 1940 all native lands were entrusted to a centralized Native Lands Trust Board. All these and more were enshrined in the 1970 constitution.

14. The Report of the Commission of Enquiry into the Natural Resources and Population Trends of the Colony of Fiji 1959 (Burns, Watson, and Peacock 1960), while commenting on the extraordinary situation in which the Fijian Administration had the power to collect its own taxes from Fijians within the larger structure of the central government, also noted "the tendency to regard the Fijian Administration as an almost independent government" (31). Its response to the chiefs' claim that "the absorption of the Fijian Administration into a multi-racial local government organization would mean consequent loss of racial identity, custom and culture to the Fijian" (31) was the following: "We consider that customs and culture are of their essence changeable, and that those which are truly alive and viable will survive" (31).

15. The land area of Fiji is barely 7,000 square miles and the population under a million. The web of kinship and associated rituals facilitates consociation and the replication of ritualized codes of collective and interpersonal conduct. These ties are further strengthened by the Fijian language. All these features

contribute to the diminution in Fiji of the classic time-space of the European nation-state as a population of anonymous contemporaries.

16. "Occupying the headwaters of tradition . . . to be in a position to maintain that the stream had been diverted from its proper course," as Pocock (1971, 247–48) would have it.

17. See LiPuma (this volume) for a further discussion of the quest for a national identity outside a history that founds history. LiPuma links the ceaseless struggle to fix tradition to the tendency for differences to reappear and become the basis of contests of narrative within the new nation-state.

18. Eighty-three percent of the total land area of Fiji remains in the hands of Fijians, mostly under a form of communal tenure.

19. In one important sense, this statement is factually correct. The Crown created a monolithic hierarchy of paramount chiefs out of the petty chiefdoms that shaped the politics of early contact and colonization. The chiefs of Fiji have been the Crown's most loyal subjects throughout the colonial era and since independence. All the governor-generals appointed by the queen as head of state have been paramount chiefs.

20. When Ratu Mara resumed the position of prime minister in the new Republic of Fiji, he went to London to attempt to regain links with the Crown that had been severed by the revocation of the 1970 constitution. Prior to his departure, he spoke as the paramount chief of Lau to his own people. On that occasion, he reassured his audience that the Deed of Cession had established the queen of England as the Tui Viti (highest chief of Fiji.) The revocation surely had not changed that! But Rabuka's hasty action had done just that, undermining royalist rhetoric in the process.

21. The strategy of betrayal rejected governance by chiefs, but it also rejected democratic processes on the grounds that democracy linked the destiny of Fijians to Indians in a new and unacceptable way—as political equals. The rhetoric was powerful, but no clear alternative form of government was proposed. On disloyal Fijians, see Kaplan (this volume).

22. Disenchantment surfaced in such forms of resistance as continuing squabbles over government-assisted development of native land (see Rutz 1987) and the appearance of the multiracial Labour party (see Howard 1991) in 1986. Both reflect the gradual but inexorable encompassment of Fijian everyday life by the market.

23. The crisis was precipitated by a national election victory in April of a coalition of the Indian-dominated National Federation Party and a new multiracial Labour party. The result was an end to seventeen years of Fijian and chiefly dominated Alliance Party government. There was a strong reaction among Fijians, followed by civil disturbances that were the occasion and excuse for Rabuka's military coup in May. The new government was ousted and the constitution revoked. Following Rabuka's second coup in September, there was a declaration of a republic in October and the promulgation of a new constitution in 1990. The new constitution, while bowing to international pressure by including guarantees of human rights and personal liberties for all citizens, di-

vests Indians of their political rights to govern. For the military viewpoint, see Dean and Ritova 1988; for the Labour party viewpoint, see Howard 1991.

24. Wesleyan Methodists had created a pan-Fijian consciousness by the mid-nineteenth century. They linked local circuits to a national congress that had ties to the international organization of the church. The idea of a Fijian nation can be traced to literacy and mass consumption of Methodist print media by the 1850s—several decades before the islands were ceded to Britain in 1874. For a more detailed description of the process of print Methodism and emergent nationalism, see Rutz and Balkan 1992. See also the connection between consuming images and nation making in the chapter by Foster in this volume.

25. There are two different ontologies of time in the strategy of divine intervention. The first is the origin of Fijianness in a time out of time, when God made Fiji for Fijians. The second is the "civilizing" process that begins with the coming of Wesleyan Methodist missionaries in the 1830s. Together they argue for the diversion of the headwaters of tradition in the rhetorical strategies of royalists and commoners.

26. One reason the new constitution was three years in the making is that early versions contained language and provisions contrary to democratic principles and human rights espoused by the inter*national* community. Fijian nationalist discourse was obliged to accommodate, at least in appearance, a worldwide discourse about the conformity of nations to universal human rights. A Fijian "democracy" that denies half the population (Indians) the political right to compete for who will govern mocks that which it names.

REFERENCES

Anderson, Benedict. 1983. *Imagined Communities: Reflections on the Origin and Spread of Nationalism*. New York: Verso.
Belshaw, Cyril S. 1964. *Under the Ivi Tree: Society and Economic Growth in Rural Fiji*. London: Routledge and Kegan Paul.
———. 1965. The effect of limited anthropological theory on problems of Fijian administration. In Roland W. Force, ed., *Induced Political Change in the Pacific*, 63–74. Honolulu: Bishop Museum Press.
Burns, Alan, T. Y. Watson, and A. T. Peacock. 1960. *Report of the Commission of Enquiry into the Natural Resources and Population Trends of the Colony of Fiji 1959*. Legislative Council of Fiji Paper No. 1 of 1960. London: The Crown Agents for Overseas Governments and Administrations.
Dean, Eddie, with Stan Ritova. 1988. *Rabuka: No Other Way*. Suva, Fiji: The Marketing Team International, Ltd.
Fiji. 1970. *The Constitution of Fiji*. Suva, Fiji: Government Printer.
France, Peter. 1969. *The Charter of the Land: Custom and Colonization in Fiji*. Melbourne: Oxford University Press.
Garrett, John. 1990. Uncertain sequel: The social and religious scene in Fiji

since the coups. In Brij Lal, ed., *As the Dust Settles: Impact and Implications of the Fiji Coups*. Special Issue, *Contemporary Pacific* 2:87–112.

Hocart, A. M. 1929. *Lau Islands, Fiji*. Honolulu: Bishop Museum Press.

——. 1970 [1936]. *Kings and Councillors: An Essay on the Comparative Anatomy of Human Society*. Rodney Needham, ed. Chicago: University of Chicago Press.

Howard, Michael C. 1991. *Fiji: Race and Politics in an Island State*. Vancouver: University of British Columbia Press.

Inder, Stuart. 1987. Ratu Mara: Man with a shattered vision. *Fiji Times*, December 2.

Kaplan, Martha. 1990. Christianity, people of the land, and chiefs in Fiji. In John Barker, ed., *Christianity in Oceania*, 189–207. Lanham, Md.: University Press of America.

Kelly, John D. 1988. Fiji Indians and political discourse in Fiji: From the Pacific romance to the coups. *Journal of Historical Sociology* 1:399–422.

Lal, Brij, ed. 1990. *As the Dust Settles: Impact and Implications of the Fiji Coups*. Special Issue, *Contemporary Pacific* 2:1–146.

Mara, Ratu K. K. T. 1968. Address of the President of the Alliance. Mimeograph.

Patel, A. D. 1968. Out of many races one nation. Speech to the 1968 annual convention of the Jaycees at Nadi. Suva, Fiji: National Federation Party Headquarters. Mimeograph.

Pocock, J. G. A. 1971. Time, institutions, and action: An essay on traditions and their understanding. In *Politics, Language and Time: Essays on Political Thought and History*, 233–72. New York: Atheneum.

Premdas, Ralph. 1980. Constitutional challenge: The rise of Fijian nationalism. *Pacific Perspective* 9:30–44.

Rutz, Henry J. 1984. Material affluence and social time in village Fiji. In Richard F. Salisbury and Elisabeth Tooker, eds., *Affluence and Cultural Survival*, 105–18. Washington: American Ethnological Society.

——. 1987. Capitalizing on culture: Moral ironies in urban Fiji. *Comparative Studies in Society and History* 29:533–57.

Rutz, Henry J., and Erol M. Balkan. 1992. Never on Sunday: Time-discipline and political crisis in Fiji. In Henry J. Rutz, ed., *The Politics of Time*, 62–85. Washington: American Anthropological Association.

Sahlins, Marshall. 1976. *Culture and Practical Reason*. Chicago: University of Chicago Press.

——. 1985. *Islands of History*. Chicago: University of Chicago Press.

Spate, O. H. K. 1959. *The Fijian People: Economic Problems and Prospects*. Legislative Council of Fiji Paper No. 13 of 1959. Suva, Fiji: Government Printer.

Martha Kaplan

Blood on the Grass and Dogs Will Speak: Ritual Politics and the Nation in Independent Fiji

If nation-states require narratives, stories of their past, present, and future, then surely rituals are quintessential moments of power in which such narratives are made and sustained, contested and overthrown, accommodated or transformed. Examining ritual efforts that failed to make a national community, rituals whose narratives failed to convince, this chapter considers the ritual requirements of nationhood.

In Fiji, from independence in 1970 to the present, there have been national rituals. But these national rituals have been an uneasy articulation of Fijian and Fiji Indian "customary" ceremony.[1] This chapter considers two ritual projects: the official national rituals of newly independent Fiji in the 1970s and 1980s, and an alternative series of rituals conducted by a visionary mystic Fiji citizen, who in the same decades sought to create a unified Fiji through media, prophecy, and his own forms of national ritual.

An Unusual Ritual: The Opening of the *Syria* Monument

The rituals of Harigyan Samalia, a Fiji Indian eccentric visionary mystic, will serve as our point of entry into these questions of ritual and nations.

In 1984, Samalia organized the building of the *Syria* Monument, a large stone structure erected at the bridge that spans the Rewa River and connects the town of Nausori to Fiji's capital city, Suva. The monument commemorates the *Syria*, a "coolie" ship carrying new Indian laborers to Fiji's plantations, which was wrecked on a Fiji reef in 1884, and the help given to the drowning Indians by Fijians who swam out to rescue them. The opening of the monument was attended by several members of parliament; the guest of honor was Ratu Sir George Cakobau, a high-ranking Fijian chief who was a former governor-general of Fiji. Throughout the course of the ceremony, Samalia made speeches of welcome in English, Hindi, and Fijian. The chief guest was garlanded, his wife was presented with a bouquet of flowers. Samalia then unveiled the monument and gave out medals and certificates to elderly Fiji Indian survivors of the indenture era and to Fijians who were descendants of those who swam out to save the drowning people.

But the opening of the *Syria* Monument was far from a typical national ritual in Fiji. The monument is not a civic, municipal project. It was not sponsored by a government ministry. It is the work of one person (and his organization, the Fiji Girmit Association), who raised the funds, mobilized the support, and organized the rituals to inaugurate the monument—and Samalia is not a typical person. Neither a politician nor a civic official, he was in the 1980s a keeper and maker of historical record, an advocate for (but not a typical member or representative of) the Fiji Indian community, and a prophet and visionary. Shortly before he inaugurated the *Syria* Monument, he had visited the Fijians of Drauniivi village to bring them a message from their ancestor Navosavakadua, a nineteenth-century Fijian prophet-leader of the Tuka movement (often described as a "millenarian movement" or "cargo cult"—see Burridge 1969; Worsley 1968; Kaplan 1988a, 1990a). In Drauniivi, Samalia was received with Fijian ceremonies normally reserved for a Fijian chief. He gave the people of Drauniivi a blue flag with a lamp on it, which he told them was Navosavakadua's flag. The lamp is, however, of the type lit by Hindus on the festival of Diwali. The same flag flew along with flags of Fiji and India at the opening of the *Syria* Monument. At the opening, and in Drauniivi, Samalia appeared in an unusual white uniform with a blue sash emblazoned with the lamp, the white uniform itself a variation on the uniform of governor-generals in the colonial era.

Most importantly, the "opening" of the *Syria* Monument unveiled key aspects of Samalia's cosmological vision. He said that the figurehead mounted atop on the monument was the actual figurehead from the original *Syria* boat (in fact, it is not). He claims that the figurehead represents both the Hindu goddess Lakshmi and the Fijian ancestor goddess Adi Sovanatabua, who will bring all the world's wealth to Fiji. He believes, as he has written in the text that became visible when the monument was unveiled, that "Fiji is the fatherland and India the motherland of the world" and, as he has proclaimed elsewhere, that Fiji is destined to be the home of the returning Messiah, the King of Kings.

This is not an ordinary or typical view in Fiji, among Hindu or Muslim Fiji Indians or Methodist Fijians. Indeed, most people in Fiji do not believe in Samalia's prophecies or share his cosmology. One of the issues to be explored in this chapter is how, given his eccentricity, Samalia manages to pull off his rituals to the extent he does. The chapter also inquires into the reason he feels he needs to do these rituals, to claim that Fiji is the fatherland and India the motherland of the world, that Hindu and Fijian goddesses are one and the same. The answers to these questions lead us squarely to the issue of ritual and "the nation" in postcolonial Fiji, for Samalia seeks to address, in his own eccentric way, a much more general failure of Fijians and Fiji Indians to form a coherent national narrative, in politics, myth, or ritual—the failure that led to the military coups of 1987. Here it is worth noting that Samalia prophesied the coups in 1984, saying that after the 1987 elections there would be a cloud of blood in Suva. Few took him too seriously because he also prophesied that flowers would sing and dogs would talk.

Nations, Narrative, and Ritual

Monuments and flags, rituals seeking to constitute or enact narratives of past, present, and future of a people, these are the stuff of the making of nations, the tangible vehicles for personal experience of national identity as a reality. As anthropologists make explicit the fact that for a very long time we have been studying complex situations of change, contact, and history making, we have started to analyze what is meant by "the nation" and to question whether the nation is an ideal, homogeneous, or inevitable form of polity (see Foster 1991). Current positions divide on whether there is some single defining characteristic to all nations or whether the rubric itself links fundamentally disparate sorts of polities (and here, mindful of Chatterjee 1986, I don't intend to suggest that there exists an ideal [Western] sort of nation and then other sinister or ineffectual variants upon it). My sense is simply that in a complex, dynamic, colonial, and postcolonial world, plural and competing forms of organization are juxtaposed under the single rubric. This is most powerfully obvious if we attend to the different narratives that make these nations real: we find nations self-represented, for example, in narratives of egalitarian antimonarchical revolt, in narratives of anticolonial movement, and—in the Republic of Fiji circa 1987—in narratives of the divine right of kings (see Rutz this volume).[2]

At least since Geertz's (1973) epistemological musing on culture and ethnography—that anthropologists tell versions of the stories people tell about themselves—anthropologists have found it highly productive to conceive of their project as seeking out a play of narratives or representations. This approach intersects with literary critical consideration of texts and context (Bhabha 1990; Eagleton, Jameson, and Said 1990; Williams 1977) and with study of "mentalities" (e.g., Darnton 1984). It can be traced into the "invention of tradition" literature, too. But these studies leave ambiguous what is real, whether representations make their own reality or have a social structural (as for Geertz) or political economic (as for Williams) ground. (See also LiPuma's comments [this volume] on the reductionism of much Eurocentric theorizing about nationalism.) In fact, scholars committed to such groundings have given us some of the most influential conceptions of the play and power of representations, notably Hobsbawm and Ranger's (1983) invented traditions[3] and Benedict Anderson's (1983) imagined communities. But if we don't accept a Parsonian separation of culture from social structure or a Marxist separation of imagined communities, invented traditions from "relations" of production, we need to understand how and by what agency and power proliferating narratives and other representations are ordered and limited.

I would not want to imply, as does certain of the invention of tradition literature, that a universal underlying maximizing interest constructs ideologies. Instead, we shall presume that subjectivities and interests are themselves established by routinized systems of representation (Sahlins 1976), and further that agency and relations of production, of kinship, and of political and social order in general use and remake available, culturally constituted materials. By this approach, the existence of one system or order—a social structure, an economy, or a totalizing cultural system—is not a given. Routinization and establishment of system in economic or other social relations is instead a historically observable and variable phenomenon. Rather than being given, structures are established.

In Fiji, as elsewhere, no narrative is eternal or uncontested. And if narratives of nations are plural and competing, the question becomes: how are they established and routinized? Or, to add some agency to the question, how do persons, groups, and/or classes make real their versions and visions of a nation? How do they constitute a nation? One way is through ritual. As I have been studying the painful and peculiar transition of Fiji from colony to nation, I have been especially interested in the role of ritual.[4]

By this approach, ritual is not superficial or "symbolic," just as narratives are not superstructural frosting on a political-economic cake. Instead, I take ritual to be those powerful moments in which people make things happen by appealing to some force, some defining cosmology (fate, history, manifest destiny, the gods, a constitution, dialectical materialism), which is claimed to be beyond the individual his or her self. Nor are rituals static and repetitive, traditional and unchanging. People are constantly creating new rituals. By so doing, they create and implement narratives to control or empower, to contest the old or envision the new (or even envision the old anew). Nor must rituals be the tools only of elites, nor always the collective expression of shared sentiment, nor necessarily the enactment of revolutionary anticipations. As Tambiah (1985, 166) has noted, rituals may take "opposite turnings: to the right when they begin to lose their semantic component and come to serve mainly the pragmatic interests of authority, privilege and sheer conservatism; and to the left when committed believers . . . strive to infuse purified meaning into traditional forms, as often happens during the effervescence of religious revival and reform." To illustrate this ritual dynamism, I think we can tell the story of Fiji's political history best if we pay attention to the ways in which Fijians and Fiji Indians have used ritual to make and unmake their nation.

Thus, this chapter will continue with a discussion of the articulation of indigenous Fijian chiefly ritual and colonial British rituals that shaped the colonial order. I will argue that the power of Fijian chiefs and colonial British authorities depended on a narrative of indigenous loyalty and aristocratic chiefly right, enacted in ritual. I then turn to the ritual history of Fiji Indians, a history of resistance and social transformation through ritual. Next a section on independent Fiji from 1970 to the present discusses unsuccessful attempts to create national rituals that incorporated British, Fijian, and Indian ceremony. Here I argue that rather than creating a whole and convincing narrative, such rituals merely juxtaposed segments from the various ritual practices. In a sense, Fiji Indian ritual was merely "tagged onto" an already whole Fijian-colonial ritual practice, parallel with the way the Fiji Indians were given a marginal political place in a Fijian postcolonial political hegemony.

The contradictions of 1970s national ritual are thrown into relief when compared with Samalia's attempts to create cohesive and coherent national rituals. Samalia's rituals proposed a narrative in which world history has ordained the coming together of Indians and Fijians, in Fiji, so that God can come to earth again. The chapter concludes with an analysis of the failure of Samalia's vision—not through internal illogic, but through the more powerful appeal of other narratives to the people of Fiji, especially to Christian-chiefly indigenous Fijians. In conclusion, I return to the broader theoretical question of the ritual requirements of nationhood.

Ritual and Colonial Fiji

Nineteenth-century indigenous Fijian kingdoms and the British Empire had a lot in common. Both were ritual polities. Both were ruled by high chiefs who were also gods, or at least very close to gods, in the case of Queen Victoria, head of the Church of England. Most important, both were very hierarchical. The British Empire's local and ongoing practice was a series of "routines and rituals of rule" (Corrigan and Sayer 1985): celebrations of the sovereign's birthday, the launching of ships and opening of monuments, village inspections, sanitation projects, the exchange and filing of sacred documents, daily teatimes (see, for example, Thomas 1990). Fijian chiefly power and British colonial power both relied on narratives, stories mapping time, space, and asymmetry of power between rulers and ruled. In their indigenous rituals and myths, Fijians told a story of the relationship between people of the land and chiefs, between indigenous, original Fijians and stranger, powerful Fijian chiefs who arrived later, to rule rightfully but never to own the land (Hocart 1969; Sahlins 1985). In their myths and rituals, the British told a story of a British Christian duty to civilize and protect "primitive," "uncivilized" indigenous people and of the desire of the uncivilized to be ruled by the civilized, so that they might advance eventually up an evolutionary ladder (see France 1969; Gordon 1879; Macnaught 1982).

Perhaps the first ritual political step in the making of colonial Fiji was the acceptance of Christianity by Fijian chief King Cakobau in 1854 (on Fijian Christianity, see Kaplan 1990b; Toren 1988). But if the entry of the chiefs into Christian ritual space and time opened the way, the most important ritual in the making of colonial Fiji was "cession" in 1874, the formal signing of a treaty (the Deed of Cession) that created this new polity, "Fiji," a "colony," where before it had not existed. Colonial historians carefully chronicled the moments when thirteen high chiefs, from the eastern and coastal kingdoms of Fiji, signed the document ceding the islands to Queen Victoria and her heirs and when the Union Jack was raised thereafter.[5] They celebrated the occasion annually.

From the British point of view, they were to rule, settle, and protect. The first colonial governor was a paternalist, amateur anthropologist, and reader of Lewis Henry Morgan determined to protect the Christian Fijians from settler exploitation. He set in motion projects to reserve 83 percent of Fiji's land for Fijians, which endures to this day, and a program of "indirect rule" that used local traditional chiefs as colonial officials. He created a new advisory council called the Great Council of Chiefs, to inform him on Fijian tradition, and to endorse his decisions about it. From a Fijian point of view, Fijians as a whole were constituted as people of the land in relation to British chiefs in the signing of the document, but perhaps the relation was most powerfully sealed not long after in a famous moment when King Cakobau of Bau made an offering of yams and kava root to the first colonial governor (Legge 1958, 206). Cession was known to Fijians as "the raising of the flag" (*vakarewa na kuila*) by the British. In oral and written histories, Fijians refer to it as a founding moment, the moment of the assertion of power on the part of the new rulers. And, in a happy coincidence, unusual in colonial encounters, the British did carry out one thing the Fijians expected: they came to rule, but not to seize the land (or at least no more than that which had already come into European settler and missionary hands; ultimately 17 percent of Fiji's land has come to be held by the Crown [now nationally owned] or privately).

The relationship between these leading Fijian chiefs and the British administration was a relatively happy one (see Rutz [this volume] on current versions of Fijian "royalist" political rhetorics). From the beginning of the colony, the British presented their authority in ways that incorporated and appropriated Fijian chiefly ceremony. Certain Fijians were participants in this appropriation, for example Cakobau's conversion, or the signing of the Deed of Cession.[6] In the early decades of this century, British and Fijian officials of the Native Administration would carefully codify ritual acknowledgment of rank due to officials and to traditional chiefs. They also decided who was not entitled to rituals of respect. Thus, for example, in 1917, G. V. Maxwell, a British official, and Ratu Lala Sukuna, a Fijian high chief who was also a colonial official, lectured a Fijian commoner called Apolosi Nawai for accepting whales' teeth in a ritual to which he wasn't entitled. Apolosi was an innovator who founded a Fijian-run produce company (see Macnaught 1982). Colonial officials hated him, one called him the "Rasputin of the Pacific" (Luke 1945). Maxwell told Apolosi that the rituals of *tama* [salutation of a chief] and *qaloqalovi* [presentation of whales' teeth to the arriving chief] could "properly be performed only in respect of the Governor [the *British* governor], the Vunivalu, and certain other high chiefs."[7]

Combining Fijian "custom" with British etiquette made public ceremony in colonial Fiji a truly weighty matter for the British.[8] For example, among the bright red, confidential records were numerous and voluminous files concerned with the visits of royalty and colonial and foreign dignitaries; everything was confidential, from security arrangements to floral arrangements. On these occasions, a careful calculus of status, self-representation, and welcome was observed. Only royalty and high colonial officials were entitled to "Fijian ceremonies of welcome." Then there was the question of which Fijians would get the honor of performing them. Colonial officials minuted one another on issues of suitability, and they consulted Fijian colleagues on "tradition." The Fijian officials they consulted frequently manipulated their participation toward their own dynastic and colonial interests, a story in itself.

A similar correspondence exists concerning the bestowal of local honors. Fiji already could make recommendations to the British queen and prime minister for the bestowal of knighthoods and the like, but in addition, the colonial administration decided in 1930 to begin to issue local honors, medals, and certificates to especially loyal, heroic, and meritorious members of the colony. Medals were ordered from the mint, and when their ribbons were not the right color, they were sent back. An interesting point to note concerning the local honors is that not until 1956 was a Fiji Indian honored. Even more interesting, the administration slipped up in actually presenting him his medal. They were so used to issuing the medals at the annual meetings of the Fijian Great Council of Chiefs that they made no provision for a special presentation for the Indian dairy farmer. In sum, colonial ritual in Fiji told the story of a British and Fijian relationship of British and Fijian aristocratic duty and the loyalty and service of indigenous commoners. Where, we may ask, did disloyal Fijians and the Fiji Indians stand, ritually?

Disloyal Fijians and Fiji Indians:
Resistance through Rituals

Much of Fiji's history was made in dramatic anticolonial ritual politics, whether indigenous Fijian political-religious movements such as those led by Navosavakadua or by Apolosi Nawai, or the Fiji Indian rituals of reversal of indenture days and their Gandhian devotional politics of the postindenture years which created a total transformation in their status and in the organization of Fiji's capitalism. Strikingly, Fijian and Fiji Indian anticolonial movements were highly separate phenomena. No common cause was struck between hinterland Fijians and the indentured and postindenture Indians. (It is equally striking that the far less successful Fijian movements have attracted the majority of anthropological interest as "millenarian" or "cargo" movements, while Indian rituals have only recently been discussed [see Brown 1984; Kelly 1988b].)

As to disloyal Fijians: during the 1870s through the 1890s Navosavakadua, an oracle priest, called upon Fijian gods and the Christian God to organize claims to autonomy by peoples of the northeast of Viti Levu island. Their local mobilization, the Tuka movement, directed earliest against eastern coastal chiefs and then against the colonial government those chiefs came to serve, became a British symbol of danger and disaffection. Colonial officials wrote a new law to deport Navosa and his people. Later, during the 1910s through the 1940s, Apolosi Nawai attempted to found a produce company that would cut out white intermediaries. He, too, claimed both Fijian and Christian sources of power and was seen as equally heathen and backsliding by colonial officials. Both Navosa and Apolosi challenged the colonial-chiefly narrative of Christianity and the colonial civilizing mission, a historical moment of transformation from darkness to light. Both were portrayed as unnatural, heathen, and backsliding (Kaplan 1988a). From a Fijian perspective, both spoke to a different story of power and time: the power of indigenes, the first, original people, as opposed to the power of the later, stranger kings (Kaplan 1990a).[9] But while these movements offered powerful explanatory cosmologies for some Fijians, they did not replace the colonial-chiefly hierarchies and the colonial narratives told in Methodist churches and colonial-chiefly rituals. Navosavakadua was deported in handcuffs; Apolosi Nawai was summoned to be lectured by G. V. Maxwell and later exiled as well.[10]

Among the Fiji Indians, ritual practice changed dramatically from indenture, which began in 1878, to postindenture days, following 1919 (see Kelly 1988a, 1991). Indenture itself was experienced by many in terms of the story of Ram, a Hindu god and king, exiled and oppressed by demons who stole his wife Sita. Far from India, laboring in oppressive conditions, constrained by the plantation system from constituting stable families, religious practice stressed the *bhakti* (devotional) version of Hinduism. In indenture days, the Hindu festival of Holi was the primary celebration. Holi, a ritual of inversion, dramatized the harsh hierarchies of the plantation system. With sprays of blood-red fluid, women bespattered men, and "coolie" laborers marked the oppressive sardars and overseers. Holi festivals climaxed in the burning of huge effigies, effigies of the Demon Ravan who tormented Ram. Read in colonial context, it was the immorality of the indenture system that was burned with the demonic image. Accounts of the Fiji indenture system (phrased as "a sorrowful story of Ram"; see Sanadhya 1991 [1914]) were crucial in the Indian nationalists' successful campaign to end by 1919 indenture of Indians throughout the empire.

In postindenture Fiji, devotional Hinduism continued to orient political and economic activities. Strikes of the 1920s were headed by holy men who led the Fiji Indians to refuse to work on plantations. The strikes drove the plantation system out of Fiji and forced change of the land-tenure rules to a system in which Indians rented land from Fijians and grew sugarcane, which they then sold to the mills. Ramayan mandalis (neighborhood associations that met to chant the Ramayan, the text that chronicles the story of Ram) were closely related to cane-harvesting groups as this new system of independent Indian small-holding farmers was arranged with the government and sugar company. In efforts for community uplift, groups built schools and temples. In the sixty years following the end of indenture, the Fiji Indians became the rural backbone of Fiji's sugarcane economy and the urban middle class (Kelly 1988b).

By the 1970s, public celebration of Holi had diminished. Instead, the festival of Diwali was the principal Hindu ritual. In India, Diwali celebrates households and prosperity, focused on Lakshmi, the goddess of wealth. In Fiji, Diwali was celebrated also as the night of the god Ram's return from exile. Families lit up their houses with beautiful little lamps and distributed sweets. In urban areas, there were joyous displays of neon. Up until 1987, Diwali in Fiji celebrated the Hindu devotion that uplifted a community (Kelly 1988b).

But while Fiji Indian ritual politics ended indenture and built a relatively prosperous largely Hindu community, it failed to break British political and legislative dominance. Marches and assemblies mirroring nationalist rallies in India were held to protest British rule in India. Fiji Indians looked forward to India's independence. The British colonial officials in Fiji were terrified of these events and sent spies to report on them. Moreover, the colonial British in Fiji could not see which way the wind was blowing. They truly never believed that one day India would be free. But on 15 August 1947, the Fiji Indian community celebrated Indian independence day. They carried banners portraying Mahatma Gandhi and Subhas Chandra Bose, leader of the separatist Indian army during World War II, who for a time sought to ally with the Japanese rather than fight for the imperial British (on Bose, see Gordon 1989). In the face of this challenge to their dominance, the colonial British developed a new rhetorical strategy (Kelly 1988b). Beginning in the 1920s, in response to Fiji Indian demands for electoral representation and independence, the British began to phrase their rights to colonial domination in terms of their duty to protect indigenous Fijian interests. In this strategy of divide and rule, the British drew upon old themes, of Fijian "primitiveness" and hence vulnerability, Fijian loyalty, and Fijian "customary" specialness. These differences sowed the seeds for the racial-political divisions that would plague independent Fiji.

National Ritual in Independent Fiji

Fiji's independence was a contested matter, insisted upon by Fiji Indians, feared by Fijians. Yet, after World War II, it became clear that a Labour government in Britain and a world insistence on decolonizing would create an independent Fiji. Constituted from the beginning as a community of diverse groups, independent Fiji did not institute an electoral system based on common roll (one person, one vote). Instead, independent Fiji's constitution created an elaborate system requiring that each citizen register as a Fijian, Indian, or General Elector (*race* is the local term). In its ritual self-definition, Fijian independence was celebrated as the making of a nation dependent on three communities. Ratu Sukuna, the famous Fijian high chief and colonial official, used the image of a three-legged stool to symbolize Fijian, Indian, and European interdependence (Sukuna 1983).

Fiji's 1970 independence ceremonies were specifically designed to stress this image of the three-legged stool, but they had a second message as well: to emphasize continuing links to the British Commonwealth. The national independence ceremonies centered on the capital city, Suva, and were planned by a committee consisting of British colonial officials and appointed European, Fijian, and Indian prominent persons. Prince Charles was the guest of honor who presided over the weeklong ceremonies in the capital while smaller celebrations were held in towns and outlying areas. In representing Fiji through new national rituals, for the first time Indian rituals were included as part of official ceremonial. In fact, there was a full-scale, self-conscious attempt to give equal time to Fijian and Indian ceremonies and entertainment. (British forms of ceremonies and entertainment got their full share, too.) Fijian ceremonies of welcome to a high chief were performed for Prince Charles, and then, as a South Asian Hindu practice, he was garlanded and given *arti*, the circling of a tray of incense in front of him, an Indian way of welcoming a stranger or worshiping a god. In addition to a plethora of British ceremonial (flower shows, review of troops, youth rallies, and such), traditional dances, songs, and entertainments were performed by Fijians, Indians, and members of some of Fiji's other, smaller ethnic communities. Even the amounts budgeted by the central planning committee for Fijian and Indian ceremonies were roughly equal (*Fiji Times*, 10 October 1970).

The importance and novelty of this balanced self-presentation was displayed in Prince Charles's carefully scripted remarks of thanks, which were prepared for him with significant help from the independence celebration local committee. He addressed his remarks to the "chiefs and people" of Fiji, a neat rhetorical trick that maintained respect for indigenous Fijian aristocracy but indicated that not all Fiji citizens were indigenous Fijians. As reported in the 10 October 1970 *Fiji Times*, his remarks continued:

> "Thank you for such a magnificent and touching welcome, and thank you also for the welcome that the Indian community have given me. I am told that it is a departure from tradition for a welcome of this kind to be combined with Fijian ceremonies, but this is a true indication of the future potential of this multiracial society and I wish all of its people success beyond measure.
>
> "One of the characteristics of the people of Fiji, which many remark upon, is their loyalty and affection for the Crown.

"Her Majesty the Queen greatly appreciates this, as have all previous sovereigns since Queen Victoria . . .

[He concluded with] "May God bless you all."

In intention, at least, independent Fiji's ritual was meant to create a nation that was a three-legged stool, drawing on Fijian, British, and Indian ceremonial to create a harmonious, balanced nation. Not surprisingly, these new national ceremonies did not draw on Fijian or Fiji Indian rituals of resistance. Instead, they looked to a theme common in both cultures, especially respect for a visitor, treated as though he or she is a god.

But, in so doing, the new ceremonies of Fiji as nation managed to subsume, to submerge, the narrative of the three-legged stool, of balance among communities, into another narrative: the long-standing, powerful, British colonial-Fijian story of the stranger king. Notice that independence itself was dramatized—not as egalitarian democratic overthrow of monarch or colonial hierarchy, but as an enduring hierarchical relationship between royalty and people. (The British flag was tactfully lowered one evening, and the new Fijian flag raised the next day.) Prince Charles's own presence, and his words—to the chiefs and peoples of Fiji— recreated the articulation between British and Fijian aristocratic projects. Note also that however well Indian ceremonies of respect for visitors fit in, however much attention was paid to equal time for the three communities, there was a crucial way in which Indians were left out of the story of the independence celebrations. The Fiji Indians have no chiefs. They have no aristocracy. They have no stranger kings. To the degree that the new rituals of nationhood continued to define power in Fiji in terms of chiefs and people, then only the Fijian community could offer those leaders with the right to power. So, the story told in Fiji's independence rituals was twofold: on the one hand, the explicitly intended narrative of the three-legged stool; on the other hand, the powerful, inescapable colonial-Fijian narrative of hierarchical relations and Fijian privilege. This uneasy juxtaposition of narratives was continued in the public rituals—and the political rhetoric—of independent Fiji throughout the 1970s and early 1980s.[11]

Thus, Fiji failed to live out the vision of communal diversity and interdependence proposed in the independence rituals. Ritual emphasis on "racial" distinctions and chiefly privilege were mirrored in political discourse. Each election from 1970 on became more "racially" polarized.

Fijian chiefly leaders, in particular, came to emphasize pro-indigenous Fijian rhetoric to maintain their position in the Fijian voting constituency in a rapidly changing nation. Indeed, ultimately independent Fiji's constitution itself had enshrined the "racial" categories of "Europeans," "Indians," and "Fijians," failing to weave a convincing narrative of interdependence, and the constitution gave disproportionate representation to Fijians in both the house and the senate. In the house, although there were more Fiji Indians than Fijians in the population, the two groups received equal numbers of representatives. In the senate, the Fijian Great Council of Chiefs had special rights to appoint members, and these members had the power to veto legislation that might affect Fijian affairs and land rights. In the ritual sphere as the years passed, the balance sought in the independence rituals diminished. Ongoing public ritual (for example, welcomes to visiting ambassadors or the opening of public buildings) became uneasy amalgams of lengthy Fijian chiefly rituals of welcome, the briefer presentation of flowers by a small girl (a feature of colonial British ceremony), and the Indian ceremonies of garlanding and *arti*. In percentage of time, personnel, and emphasis, indigenous Fijian ceremonies dominated "national" rituals.

In such Fijian-ritual preeminence lay the expectation that Fijians had ritual political preeminence in the nation. From independence in 1970 until 1987, Fiji's national leaders were high chiefs, Fijian paramountcy firmly established. Fijian chiefly ritual, used in Fijian national ritual, constituted a Fiji from the top down, a continuant of chiefly, Christian, colonial synthesis. Fiji was said to be a "three-legged stool," but it was to be the seat of power of indigenous Fijian chiefs. This confident synthesis was challenged by the Fiji Labour party, a coalition of Fiji Indians and indigenous Fijians seeking to define the nation as political-economic and democratic, enacting a theory of polity and power not based on divine kings, but on individuals, common roll electoral politics, and labor. The incipient crisis long threatening the "South Seas Paradise" crystallized in the military coups of 1987.

In 1987, the new Fiji Labour party, headed by a Fijian commoner, Timoci Bavadra, joined together with the National Federation party, the party of the Fiji Indians, to achieve a parliamentary majority. The head of the Labour party, this Fijian commoner, became prime minister, replacing the Fijian chief who had been prime minister since independence— but not for long. In less than a month, a Fijian lieutenant colonel, third in command of Fiji's almost completely Fijian army, staged a military coup.

He led a small group of armed men into Parliament, took the prime minister and his cabinet prisoner, and took over government and media. Although the prime minister and cabinet were released unharmed, the colonel handed over power to the Fijian chiefs who had lost the election and handed over the authority to endorse a new constitution to the Fijian Great Council of Chiefs (see Howard 1991; Kaplan 1988b; Kelly 1988a; Lal 1988). Ritually speaking, as well as politically, concerns of Fijians have become concerns of the nation as a whole. Chiefly succession disputes have an impact on national political issues. Celebration of the Sabbath, on Sundays, which is important to Christian Fijians, was made mandatory law for all of Fiji's population, including the roughly 50 percent Hindus and Muslims. In public ritual, following the coups, the Indian component of garlanding and *arti* was dropped out. Press releases from the colonel's ministry of information describe only Fijian participation in ceremonies of welcome to ambassadors. Only recently have I found one account of a public ceremony of welcome that included an Indian garlanding. In addition to simply ignoring Indian ritual, there have also been attempts to eradicate it, including the burning of four Indian religious buildings, plus temples, mosques, and a Sikh Gurudwara, by a Fijian Methodist youth fellowship group in 1989.

Now we step back in time, back from the coups of 1987, to the 1970s and early 1980s, to look at:

The Alternative Vision of Harigyan Samalia

In the 1970s and 1980s, in the face of the dominant Fijian chiefly national ritual discourse (but curiously intertwined with it), Samalia propounded his own vision of what a united Fiji might be, through newspaper articles and public rituals. What is extraordinary about Samalia is the way he drew eclectically upon a range of opposed narratives, communities, and ritual practices: the dominant Fijian-colonial chiefly ritual and the history of Fijian anticolonial ritual, the procolonial Indian Alliance and the history of Fiji Indian anticolonial rituals of resistance as well. He did all this to develop a cosmology that would include both Fijians and Indians, and all their gods.

As I have noted previously, Samalia is a well-known eccentric who was in the 1980s head of the Fiji-India Girmit (indenture) Association, a group dedicated to preserving the history of Fiji Indians. Samalia also had close ties to Fijians. He claims to have been raised in the Lau group of islands, a primarily Fijian area, and speaks fluent Fijian. He was also one of the few Fiji Indians to serve in the Fijian army. In 1984 he lived in a Fijian squatter settlement in Suva. He was a welcome figure in the ranks of the Indian Alliance (a small group of Indian politicians who collaborated with the chiefly Fijian party), participating in events sponsored by the Alliance party and receiving perks, such as representing Fiji at a conference on world peace in India. His name seems to have been adapted from the name of one of the coolie ships, the *Somalia*; he may have been born on it. His first name means "knower of Hari," that is, knower of Krishna, but he also stresses its similarity in sound to *Harijan*, Gandhi's name for the "untouchables," meaning "children of god."

As a visionary mystic with no single "natural" constituency in Fiji for his idiosyncratic positions, Samalia's notoriety has come largely from his skill in using public media. Through this means he has gained a hearing in several communities, though no sustained following has resulted from his attempt to unite Fijians and Fiji Indians with one cosmological history.

In 1983, he ran a paid advertisement in the *Fiji Times* (the quoted text reproduces his spelling, abbreviations, and syntax; my additions are in square brackets):

Warning to the World

Adolf Hitler is from Fiji, (Lord Krishna) na gone turaga ko Ratu Navosavakadua [Sir Navosavakadua the child chief], King of Fiji, King of Kings will be inform of Fijian, and will command the World.

[A section is skipped where he explains the reason for this ad. It is the text of a telegram to the mayor of Bonn, West Germany, concerning the removal of the name of Adolph Hitler from a still extant West German honors list.]

S. Harigyan Samalia Junior Counsellor delegated by the Supreme Counsellor on Earth 10/10/83. Fiji Times Newspaper p.2.

Fiji is a small Jerusalem in the South Pacific, Rarama kei vuravura [Fijian for "light of the world"], light of the world, ramnick deep [Hindi for "the place where the serpent Kaliya was thrown by the Hindu god Krishna"].

New book of god will be written in Fiji, the place of the living God, Fiji Fatherland will announce one religious body and the world will obey. India Motherland of the world will become a great empire. And coming of great man Netaji Subhas Chandra Bose.

Phone.
P.O. Box 3883 Samabula, Suva

When Samalia calls himself the "junior counsellor on earth," he means he is the prophet of the senior councillor, who is the King of Kings, who has been incarnated in forms including Krishna, Jesus, Navosavakadua, Subhas Chandra Bose, and Hitler. Navosa, as I have explained, was the important indigenous Fijian leader of an anticolonial ritual-political movement, who lived at Drauniivi. Subhas Chandra Bose was the Indian nationalist who formed an Indian army contingent to fight for Japan in World War II, an important hero to Indian nationalists in India and Fiji, who was pictured on banners along with Gandhi in the Fiji Indian celebration of Indian independence in 1947. Hitler, to Samalia, is not the Hitler of the concentration camps. He is seen simply as the enemy of Britain in colonial days. (It is not uncommon to read of anticolonial movements in the Pacific or other parts of the British Empire that used images of the German kaiser during World War I, or of Hitler, or of the Japanese emperor during World War II because they were thought of as being in opposition to the British Empire. See, for example, Dower 1986.) Samalia believes that Fiji is a sacred center, a little Jerusalem, product of India and Fiji. It is a little Jerusalem because, like Jerusalem, which is a holy city to multiple religions, he believes that Fiji is going to be the site of the return of the King of Kings. I interviewed Samalia in 1984, and he explained the relationships (I quote from my notes from this conversation):

The King of Kings began as Krishna of the Mahabarata, who, when he had finished his work in India, disappeared and changed his form. He sent a snake to Fiji [Degei, the Fijian ancestor god who takes the form of a snake], then went to Fiji himself and became incarnated as Navosavakadua; there he performed miracles, and was deported. . . . Navosa said to the people of Drauniivi, "Don't worry if I am gone for long. My flag will be raised." He pushed two stones into the ground, saying, "When the stones rise, it will be time." Those stones are now two feet above the ground. Then he went to Germany and became Hitler, he shaped the world; it was growing fast at that time. At another time he was incarnated as Jesus Christ. He returns each time in different forms. His next incarnation will be as a Fijian to found the new Kingdom on Maqo Island in the Lau Group. The living God will arise from earth, flowers will sing, dogs will speak like humans.

Thus, the King of Kings has been incarnated as Krishna, Jesus, Navosa, and Hitler. Samalia concentrates on the Navosavakadua story in part because I asked him, in part because he was then in process of announcing Navosa's imminent return.[12]

In March 1984, Samalia visited Drauniivi village, Navosavakadua's village in the 1880s, where he announced Navosa's imminent return. People in Drauniivi described the visit to me. He wrote in advance to tell them to build a flagpole. When he arrived, they performed Fijian ceremonies of welcome for him, including *qaloqalovi*. Their choir sang a hymn and they all prayed. Then he said, "I am going to raise the flag." He raised the flag in the center of the village, and one of my friends in Drauniivi told me:

> Many people said it was the Girmit (indenture) flag, the flag of an association or whatever, we don't know. But we just know, the lamp on it is bringing light to us . . . because of the lamp the light of God is with us.

In his speech at Drauniivi, Samalia told the people of his vision of India the motherland and Fiji the fatherland. He said that a red cloud in Suva portended bloodshed, that Prime Minister Ratu Mara's government would be changed, that Fijians would lose their land, that there would be blood on the grass.[13] About two thousand people attended the meeting, according to newspaper reports, more according to informants who were there.

At Drauniivi, Samalia, claiming to speak for Navosavakadua, raised a flag. This action evoked the way the British ritually constituted their rule when they raised their flag in 1874, and it recalls the anti-colonial flag raisings of Navosa and of Apolosi Nawai. Remarkably, he, a Fiji Indian, received the Fijian chiefly ritual of welcome from Fijians. Note that the rituals of welcome he received included *qaloqalovi*, the ceremony G. V. Maxwell had sought to regulate and restrict. We should also note his white uniform with gloves and a blue sash with the pink lamp of the Fiji Girmit Society on it. The white uniform is part of the British ritual apparatus, reminiscent of the uniform of the governor-general. But the lamp, the same lamp that appears on his flag, is a picture of a Diwali lamp, lit at the yearly Hindu festival, symbol of Fiji Indian devotion and prosperity. Samalia drew eclectically upon British, Fijian, and Fiji Indian ritual. But there was a meaning to the seemingly disparate juxtapositions. He had an underlying purpose, a story to tell.

That story was told most clearly by his work to establish the *Syria* Monument. Not all of Samalia's attempts to make a nation ritually were held on the fringes of political life, in the hinterlands at Drauniivi, or at the Girmit Society. He used newspapers, and he used the *Syria* Monument, to make his most public statement. As I noted at the beginning, the monument was built at Nausori, across the bridge from Fiji's capital city of Suva. Samalia convened the small crowd of politicians and dignitaries for the ritual under the patronage of Ratu Sir George Cakobau, former governor-general of Fiji and Vunivalu of Bau (and a descendant of King Cakobau). The occasion was the commemoration of the wreck of the "coolie" ship the *Syria* and the memorialization of Fijians who came to the aid of the drowning Indians. (No mention was made of Fijians who looted the ship.) Samalia unveiled a monument, which portrayed the female figurehead of the *Syria* and identified her as both Lakshmi (Hindu goddess) and Adi Sovanatabua (Fijian ancestral deity). Elderly Fiji Indian survivors of Girmit, and Fijians representing the kin groups who came to the aid of the ship, were given medals and certificates (on the model of the colonial medals and certificates I noted earlier). The certificates were headed: "India Fiji Bond of Relationship Syria Ship History," followed by a brief account of the shipwreck. The certificates mention India the motherland and Fiji the fatherland, but there is no mention of Navosavakadua or Hitler. Ratu Sukuna, the revered Fijian colonial official is quoted instead. But it is worth noting that Samalia still signed himself "Junior Counsellor delegated by the Supreme Counsellor on Earth and President General of the Fiji Girmit Council," and it was by that authority that the certificates and medals were issued and the ritual was performed.[14]

In this ritual, like his others, Samalia strove desperately to create a narrative of mutual cooperation, interdependence, and goodwill between Fijians and Indians, invoking in the rhetoric of Fiji the fatherland and India the motherland the gendered relations of marriage.[15] He strove to create a narrative, a history of the mutual interdependence of

Fiji's peoples. In this narrative, the presence of Indians in Fiji is not a historical accident or a jarring difficulty. Instead, Samalia turns historical contingency into historical necessity: in his narrative, the presence of Indians in Fiji is blessed and desirable. It is the necessary condition for the return of God to earth and the founding of the new Jerusalem. The wreck of the *Syria* becomes proof of this interdependence.[16]

But Samalia's narrative, his vision, failed to unite, to persuade, to create a nation of Fiji. Like most Hindu Fiji Indians, he argues that there is only one god, a rhetorical stance that some Fijians will accept, especially in public ritual contexts. However, he believes that the one god can have multiple manifestations or avatars (thus Jesus and Krishna, let alone Navosa and Hitler). Here he loses most Fijians, who strongly believe that the one god must be named Jesus Christ. In speaking to Fijians of Navosavakadua, Samalia loses his Indian audience and gets a polite but baffled hearing from only some Fijians. In fact, the Indian audience seems unconvinced by his insistence on tying together India and Fiji. Historically, Fijians and Indians have not frequently united, neither in political movements nor, more individually, in marriage. Thus the Fiji fatherland–India motherland imagery does not engage the Fiji Indians. They are looking to a wider world—specifically, planning to emigrate in many cases. The joining of India and Fiji seems the opposite of inevitable to them. Finally, the most demure of his rituals, with the most public potential, the *Syria* Monument affair—with its theme that cooperation, interdependence, and mutual service will lead to new prosperity—did not stand a chance against the forces interested in Fijian political paramountcy. He did not offer anything more concrete than a prospect of divine intervention to justify his alternative to the stronger assertion of Fijian political paramountcy. While Fijians readily accept arguments about impending benevolent divine intervention on their behalf, Samalia's vision of divinity contradicted the Christian version of the stranger-king narrative, the narrative of the relation of aristocracy and people, by not finishing with a privileged outcome for the "special" Fijian people. In his vision, Indians still would own what they own and the nation would be permanently plural and (in his marriage imagery) even more mixed.

At the meeting in Drauniivi, Samalia appears to have spoken freely about his apprehensions concerning "racial" tension in Fiji. In 1984, he was one of the few people openly speaking about impending violence, and certainly the most fearless. In fact, he predicted the coups when he told me in 1984 that

> 1987 would be the most dangerous election. The military was advanc-
> ing. Fijians were fighting with themselves. Chiefs failed to control
> the people, they were criticizing Indians. Chiefs used to command
> the Kai Colo [literally "hill people," here used to mean commoners
> and Fijians from the west of Viti Levu], but now the educated Kai
> Colo spoke back to the chiefs. Fijians newly in power thought they
> knew what to do, but Indians and Europeans too had sacrificed and
> should be respected. That was why he founded the Girmit organiza-
> tion so that Fijians would realize the truth about Indian sacrifices for
> Fiji. [From my field notes.]

Samalia described contradictions in racial relations in Fiji that he sought to resolve in his cosmological narrative. Only a visionary mystic such as he could speak so clearly of these contradictions. He identified with both Indians and Fijians and longed desperately to create a synthesis. He wanted Fijians to recognize and acknowledge the contributions of Indians to the making of Fiji.[17] But he did not seem to believe that they could or would do this, and thus instead saw a "cloud of blood in Suva" or "blood on the grass." Shrinking from this vision, ultimately reassured by belief in divinity in the world, he predicted that the coming crisis would give rise to the return of the syncretistic King of Kings, and dogs would speak and flowers would sing.

When the crisis Samalia foresaw came to pass, it was not his syncretistic King of Kings who came back to rule Fiji and the world. Instead, the Fijians who took power to prevent change in Fiji used chiefly Christianity as their main cosmological narrative. The colonel who seized power was a Methodist lay preacher and insisted on national observance of the Sunday Sabbath. In explaining his motives for the coups, he cited St. Paul to prove that it was wrong that a commoner Fijian or an Indian become prime minister: only chiefs should rule. And it was Methodist youth groups who burned temples and mosques. The new political order would dip as well into powerful ritual from Fijian nineteenth-century warfare, notably in an incident in which a *lovo* (earth oven for cooking cannibal victims) was dug and the Labour party leader threatened with it. Most powerful of all was the endorsement of Fiji's new post-coups, anti-Fiji Indian constitution by the Bosevakaturaga, the Fijian Great Council of Chiefs. In this replication of the rituals of cession and of independence, the authority of aristocracy to grant law and rights was reaffirmed, denying even the limited democracy in the alternative narrative of the three-legged stool.

Thus, the national rituals of the 1970s awkwardly juxtaposed Fijian, British, and Indian ceremonial, creating no convincing narrative of mutual substance, history, or interdependence. Samalia's rituals, newspaper ads, and speeches created a powerful synthetic narrative, but it too failed to convince—or to create—Fiji citizens. Both were supplanted by the powerful Fijian-colonial Christian synthesis of aristocracy and people, bound in loyalty, propounded by the leader of the coups and the chiefs whom the coups reinstated.

The Ritual Requirements of Nations

In conclusion, I return to the ritual requirements of nations. I have tried to stress in this chapter the practical nature of rituals and the power of rituals in political order and change. Rituals are unavoidable and central in social life, including the making of those polities, those social groups, that seem to us so real, so given, so pragmatic, those entities called nations. In fact, I agree with those who argue that nations require narratives, and I am suggesting that they also require rituals that enshrine particular narratives as the real or true ones. To clarify these points, and to suggest what I see demonstrated by this review of failed national rituals in Fiji, I return to two basic problems about nations raised earlier: first, is there an essential form to "the nation," and second, what is the ground of "the nation," and where do rituals fit in?

The matter of an essential form to "the nation" is a deep one in Western political theory, stretching back at least to the eighteenth-century writing of Locke, Rousseau, and Herder. Current anthropological debates seem to split between a camp seeking to find the general or universal features that all nations have in common, and others skeptical of finding an essential, common content to all nations and nationalism (see Foster 1991). On this question I side generally with the second camp. I do not think that nations and nationalisms are always egalitarian and democratic; the current Republic of Fiji is a clear instance of a nationalism insistent upon hierarchy and aristocracy. I also don't agree that nations and nationalism require fixed boundaries, or "entitivity," fixed individualism of nation and of citizen as some have argued (see Handler and Segal 1993). Again, Fiji's current republic is a clear counterexample: the corporality of the nation depends upon hierarchical connections between chiefs and people(s); it depends upon the denial of autonomous individuality to its version of "the people."

We might look instead to studies of nations that emphasize cultural difference. Kapferer (1988), for example, locates differences between nations in different "ontologies," then organizes the ontologies in a Dumontian typology, principally hierarchical group versus egalitarian individualist. Whether or not such typology is intrinsically constraining, the idea of an underlying ontology makes real contest difficult to understand. A theory that is alive to difference is far more convincing if we can also understand the real contests and history in the making of nations. In Fiji, it is precisely the problem which or what ontology will become the basis of national order. The potential limitation of a cultural approach is that it will reify or essentialize such outcomes. Further, even focus on struggle within a social-cultural universe might be misleading, involving the error Wolf (1982) identifies as the projection of bounded nation-society-cultureness onto parts of a world manifold.

Let us suppose instead that it is a world-level condition of possibility that makes nations the issue, capitalist postcoloniality that is the problem Fiji and other "new" nations struggle to deal with, that in a postimperial "united nations" world, bounded national order is forced upon all places that wish to be players on a world stage. Quite concretely, in Fiji's case, post-World War II United Nations resolutions and British Labour government platforms mandating decolonization made a partly reluctant population of Fiji into an independent nation.[18] To fill such a space, narratives are proposed that connect people to their rulers as one people, versus outside others, that create an "us versus them." National rituals are the place where these narratives of identity are made real. These narratives get made, ritually, when individuals or groups propose versions of relationships, group order, and history, past, present, and future, which they claim are not simply their own view or in their own interest, but instead are given, cosmologically, by gods, by tradition, or by principles of some sort.

Is the political-economic order of the capitalist "world system" the grounding of all nation-states, then? Surely there is no question that the world system creates pressures and limits. But the question can be rephrased: do these pressures and limits have intrinsic priority over other structures and systems, "ontologies," and the like? The tendency in "invented tradition" and "imagined community" literature is to envision the representation of tradition and nation functionally, serving interests of implicitly or explicitly political economic agents. Sahlins (1976) offers the best case against universalizing the capitalist senses of utility, money, and self-interest, but he grounds the alternative in totalized and totalizing cultural systems. I am not saying that cultures, ontologies, or nations are or are not totalized or totalizing systems, but that they are sometimes. That kind of systematicity is made and remade practically, when self-reproducing agents, relationships, and subjectivities fit together coherently. The important point to draw from Wolf's (1982) study of the world system is that it is not totalizing, but rather a loose integration of highly various modes, relations, and forces of production. Sahlins (1988) clarifies this point, demonstrating that a plurality of cosmologies drive, expand, and sometimes limit world relations of commodity production and exchange. So, if the world system decrees a nation-state form to regimes of law and order, it hasn't actually determined much about the content of those nation-states.

In the wake of collapsed colonial politics in independent Fiji, the chiefs sought to sustain their privileges while the Indians pressed for democracy. Nation-states mediate the interests of such groups with frameworks of law and administrative regulation. But what sort of regulation is routine? Should there be elections, and who should vote? Should land and/or labor be for sale, and under what conditions and restrictions? In Fiji, land reservation and even the overturning of elections have been justified by a narrative of Fijian autochthony and paramountcy. Myths may or may not ever have been social charters, but national narratives are charters for routine regulation. But what, in turn, routinizes such a national narrative? Surely, it is ritual. Here Durkheim has his moment, even though the world system also gets its due.

Since independence in 1970, nation-state rituals in Fiji tried to balance democracy and Fijian paramountcy with the uneasy amalgams of balanced Fijian and Fiji Indian customary ceremony. These rituals did not routinize a coherent narrative of political ranks and rights in Fiji. The two messages in the rituals—that Fiji was a plural democracy and that its chiefs had customary prerogatives—failed to clarify how far any nonchiefly political authority could go. Thus, for instance, while the operations of the Native Lands Trust Board regulating Fijian land rights were effectively routinized,[19] the elections were always a crisis. Elections, the constitutive political rituals of many nations, were in Fiji in 1977, 1987, and 1992 contested in form as much as in substance.[20]

Today, even within the chiefs' new political party, established to contest the 1992 elections under the chiefs' new constitution, there are controversies about how candidates should be selected. (Meanwhile Samalia has founded a minor party of his own.[21]) Since independence, Fiji's chartering narrative has been contested, its official rituals have failed to settle the crucial questions, and, as a result, "the nation" is a contested idea, not an experienced reality.

Fiji is hardly the only place in the world where "the nation" is contested at present. I would suggest that the world is full of people and groups of people—such as Samalia, or Col.(now General) Rabuka, leader of the coups, or the colonial British, or the Fiji Labour party—playing—with deadly seriousness—with elements and possibilities concerning order and cosmology, past and future, trying to make up nations and national narratives and routinize them through ritual. The narrative succeeding in Fiji today, unfortunately, is one of violence, division, and inequality.

ACKNOWLEDGMENTS

I thank the late Harigyan Samalia for talking with me in 1984. This essay was written before I learned of Samalia's death in 1992, and therefore I have written of him in the present tense. This is perhaps not inappropriate, given the vigor that characterized his energetic life of prophecy.

I further acknowledge research permission from the Fiji Government for research in 1984–85 and 1986, and from the Republic of Fiji in 1991. For support for the archival research of 1991, I thank the Wenner Gren Foundation for Anthropological Research and Vassar College. I thank S. T. Tuinaceva, archivist, Margaret Patel, and the staff at the Fiji National Archives for their expert assistance. For helpful comments on this chapter, I thank members of the audiences when it was delivered as a paper at departments of anthropology of Vassar College, of Bryn Mawr College, and of the University of Hawaii. And special thanks to Robert Foster and John D. Kelly.

NOTES

1. By *Fijians* I mean the descendants of the Pacific islanders who lived in the islands when Europeans came to Fiji in the late eighteenth century. By *Fiji Indians* I mean the descendants (now third and fourth generation) of South Asian Indians who came to work on the British colony of Fiji's sugar plantations from 1878 to 1919. The two groups are roughly equal in size in Fiji's total population of about 800,000. Their colonial and postcolonial experiences have been very different.

2. From the work of Benedict Anderson in particular comes the emphasis on the nation as one form of "imagined community," particularly one that unites colonized peoples. Another, more ironic, source for thinking about nations imagined are studies inspired by Marx's Eighteenth Brumaire, the revolutionaries envisioning their future in the togas of a past. (And see Chatterjee 1986 on the ways in which "the nation" is derived from colonial discourse and as a colonial category impinges on "nationalist" [anticolonial] movements themselves.) Whether national narratives are conceived, following Durkheim, to be real collective representations that make polities, or whether, following Marx, they are conceived as tales of elites, mystifying underlying power relations, in all, some sort of narrative—historical, cosmological, whatever—is crucial.

3. For a prior use of the term and discussion of the politics of representing tradition, see Linnekin 1983.

4. On British colonial ritual, see Cohn 1983; for the phrase *routines and rituals of rule*, see Corrigan and Sayer 1985 and Cohn and Dirks 1988; on anticolonial and nationalist ritual, see Freitag 1990, Jolly 1991, Kelly 1988b, Lincoln 1987, LiPuma and Meltzoff 1990, Masselos 1990 and n.d., and sections of Foster's (1991) fine review article on nations and nationalism. For a review article on ritual and the making of history, see Kelly and Kaplan 1990.

5. On flag raising as possession, see Dening 1986 on Tahiti, Masselos 1990 on India, and Sahlins 1985 on New Zealand; on flag raising and independence in Vanuatu, see Facey (this volume).

6. Discussing political rhetorical narratives in postcolonial Fiji, Rutz (this volume) notes that chiefly political power tended to construct chiefly legitimacy in terms of the historical relation made between Cakobau and the other signatories and the British queen. Other rhetorical claims replace the queen as source of legitimacy with the Christian God. Rutz's example is Sitiveni Rabuka—who, in his second military coup of 1987, broke Fiji's Commonwealth ties with the queen and proclaimed a Christian republic. It seems to me that this analysis of recent rhetoric has parallels in the competing claims of chiefly colonial officials and prophet leaders in the nineteenth century.

7. Colonial Office, Great Britain (CO 83/139). Correspondence included in despatches between the Governor of Fiji and the Colonial Office, London.

8. For parallels in the Raj, see Cohn 1983 on British Durbars.

9. As noted in note 6, in contest with chiefly colonial officials claiming

colonial legitimacy, prophet-leaders sometimes invoked the Christian God as source of legitimacy. In so doing, they also mobilized the narrative of the power of indigenes as opposed to all "foreign" chiefs, Fijian and British. Thus, in the 1870s and 1880s, Navosavakadua claimed Jehovah to be a Fijian god, an indigenous god.

10. In every village—even those with Tuka temples in the 1880s, or branches of Apolosi's Viti Company in the 1920s—local daily, habitual institutions, rituals, and routines of rule upheld the colonial order. Such institutions were the Methodist church, the colonially designated village headmen, and the local colonially designated "traditional" chief. They included as well the moral calendars of Fijian life, the days of work allotted to church, government, and community, and the fund-raising ceremonies for church, province, and people.

In some places, the local church was the site of Viti Company persuasion, the colonially designated headman himself actually an agent of the company. And, in some very particular locales, Navosavakadua's Tuka or Apolosi's Company have themselves been steadfastly routinized, in text, in oral tradition— indeed, in the very landscape. The continuing power of their local rendering remained in constant contest with, but did not replace, the powerful centralized colonial order (Kaplan 1988a).

11. See Brown 1984 for an account of enactments of these tensions in 1970s and 1980s Indian firewalking rituals.

12. Also interesting in both the text of the newspaper ad and this interview is their self-referentiality, the way that Samalia refers to the dissemination of his words as part of his words. The text of the ad includes the name and date of the paper it appears in; later in the course of the interview, he referred to the number of flyers he had distributed in which he made these prophecies.

13. In my notes I have some versions saying that he spoke of a red cloud, and others saying he spoke of blood on the grass. This may well reflect a confusion of *o* (cloud) and *co* (grass), perhaps my mistake when I wrote up my notes, or perhaps a transformation that took place as villagers passed on to one another and to me accounts of what had been said, or perhaps Samalia prophesied both.

14. This ritual clearly surprised some of the observers, especially when Samalia came out in the white uniform that governors-general wore in colonial days, and identified Lakshmi and Adi Sovanatabua (Hindu deity and Fijian ancestor deity, respectively) as one and the same. But he pulled off this ritual, and made it relatively respectable, because he had prevailed upon Ratu Sir George, the former governor-general, to attend. This came through his connection to the Indian Alliance political organization, a subgroup of the Fijian-dominated Alliance party.

15. While Samalia uses the gendered imagery to represent a complementary interrelationship, it is noteworthy that his gender imagery also replicates British colonial gendered constructions of Fijians and Fiji Indians as masculine and feminine, respectively.

16. Samalia's narrative contradicts the Fijian perspective on the Indian presence in Fiji, which proposes it to be accidental and unnecessary. Scholars' histories, too, have tended to stress the coincidence of colonial Governor Gordon's pro-Fijian paternalism and his experience with indentured Indian labor elsewhere in the British Empire. Scholarly accounts that take "cultures" to be rooted naturally in territories have found the Fijian presence in the islands to be "natural" (taking the Indians—but, curiously, less so the British—to be the odd and excludable members of Fiji's population). Here a world-system perspective makes a contribution—Wolf (1982), for example, would see the Indian presence not as random, but as a typical outcome of world labor processes. For Samalia it is not political-economic forms, but divine imperatives, that have made the presence of Indians in Fiji necessary and inevitable.

17. Here his language echoed two kinds of discourse about respect. The first claimed respect for the sacrifice and contribution of Indian (and all) laborers. Perhaps the most powerful generally known example is a speech by Indian politician and leader of the National Federation Party A. D. Patel to the Fiji Legislative Council in 1946. Second, in the 1980s especially, debates about respect for chiefs were frequent in Fiji's Parliament, often used by Alliance politicians to disparage the opposition by claiming that any disagreement, even by the elected Fiji Indian members of Parliament, and especially any disagreements raised by the opposition, traduced a duty to respect Fijian chiefs. This Fijian political insistence on "respect" for chiefs became increasingly strident, portending the oncoming crisis.

18. As Foster points out in his introduction to this volume, it is especially ironic that the First World now appears to be turning away from the national form while "allowing" or "insisting" on nationness for places like Fiji.

19. The Native Lands Trust Board is the central agency that leases Fijian lands to Indian sugarcane growers.

20. On the "coup from above" in the 1977 elections, see Lal 1986.

21. The party is a transformation of the Girmit Association which, if it were to receive any support, could field Fiji Indian candidates for Fiji Indian voters under the post-coups electoral system. In 1991, Samalia distributed an appeal for people to run as Girmit candidates. The appeal was a calendar, embellished with many of the symbols and slogans of his vision of Fiji, with "Vote Girmit 1992" heading the section of dates. The party had no tangible support in the 1992 election.

REFERENCES

Anderson, Benedict. 1983. *Imagined Communities: Reflections on the Origin and Spread of Nationalism*. London: Verso.
Brown, Carolyn Henning. 1984. Tourism and ethnic competition in a ritual form: The firewalkers of Fiji. *Oceania* 54:223–44.
Bhabha, Homi K., ed. 1990. *Nation and Narration*. London: Routledge.

Burridge, Kenelm. 1969. *New Heaven, New Earth: A Study of Millenarian Activities*. Oxford: Basil Blackwell.

Chatterjee, Partha. 1986. *Nationalist Thought and the Colonial World*. Avon, U.K.: Zed Books.

Cohn, Bernard S. 1983. Representing authority in Victorian India. In E. Hobsbawm and T. Ranger, eds., *The Invention of Tradition*, 165–209. Cambridge: Cambridge University Press.

Cohn, Bernard S., and Nicholas Dirks. 1988. Beyond the fringe: The nation state, colonialism and the technologies of power. *Journal of Historical Sociology* 1:224–29.

Corrigan, Philip, and Derek Sayer. 1985. *The Great Arch: English State Formation as Cultural Revolution*. Oxford: Basil Blackwell.

Darnton, Robert. 1984. *The Great Cat Massacre and Other Episodes in French Cultural History*. New York: Basic Books.

Dening, Greg. 1986. Possessing Tahiti. *Archaeology in Oceania* 21:103–18.

Dower, John. 1986. *War Without Mercy: Race and Power in the Pacific War*. New York: Pantheon Books.

Eagleton, Terry, Frederick Jameson, and Edward Said. 1990. *Nationalism, Colonialism and Literature*. Minneapolis: University of Minnesota Press.

Foster, Robert J. 1991. Making national cultures in the global ecumene. *Annual Review of Anthropology* 20:235–78.

France, Peter. 1969. *The Charter of the Land: Custom and Colonization in Fiji*. Melbourne: Oxford University Press.

Freitag, Sandra B. 1990. *Collective Action and Community: Public Arenas and the Emergence of Communalism in North India*. Delhi: Oxford University Press.

Geertz, Clifford. 1973. Deep play: Notes on the Balinese cock fight. In *The Interpretation of Cultures*, 412–53. New York: Basic Books.

Goldsmith, Michael. 1991. Speech acts, silence and myth: Rhetorical dimensions of the Fiji coup. Paper presented to the Conference of the Pacific Islands Political Studies Association, December, at Monash University, Melbourne, Victoria.

Gordon, Arthur. 1879. On the system of taxation in force in Fiji. Paper read before the Royal Colonial Institute, 18 March. Privately printed by R. and R. Clarke. Newberry Library, Chicago.

Gordon, Leonard A. 1989. *Brothers Against the Raj: A Biography of Sarat and Subhas Chandra Bose*. New Delhi: Viking (Penguin Books [India] Ltd.).

Handler, Richard, and Daniel A. Segal. 1993. Introduction: Nations, colonies and metropoles. In Daniel A. Segal and Richard Handler, eds., *Nations, Colonies and Metropoles*. Special Issue, *Social Analysis* 33:3–8.

Hobsbawm, Eric. 1983. Introduction: Inventing traditions. In E. Hobsbawm and T. Ranger, eds., *The Invention of Tradition*, 1–14. Cambridge: Cambridge University Press.

Hobsbawm, Eric, and Terence Ranger, eds. 1983. *The Invention of Tradition*. Cambridge: Cambridge University Press.

Hocart, A. M. 1969 [1927]. *Kingship*. Oxford: Oxford University Press.

Howard, Michael C. 1991. *Fiji: Race and Politics in an Island State*. Vancouver: University of British Columbia Press.

Jolly, Margaret. 1991. Verbal and visual Creoles: Symbols of nation and secession in Vanuatu. Paper presented at the Annual Meetings of the American Anthropological Association, December, Chicago.

Kapferer, Bruce. 1988. *Legends of People, Myths of State: Violence, Intolerance and Political Culture in Sri Lanka and Australia*. Washington: Smithsonian Press.

Kaplan, Martha. 1988a. Land and sea and the new white men: A reconsideration of the Fijian Tuka movement. Ph.D. diss., Department of Anthropology, University of Chicago.

———. 1988b. The coups in Fiji: Colonial contradictions and the postcolonial crisis. *Critique of Anthropology* 8:93–116.

———. 1990a. Meaning, agency and colonial history: Navosavakadua and the Tuka movement in Fiji. *American Ethnologist* 17:3–22.

———. 1990b. Christianity, people of the land, and chiefs in Fiji. In John Barker, ed., *Christianity in Oceania*, 189–207. Lanham, MD: University Press of America.

Kelly, John D. 1988a. Political discourse in Fiji: From the Pacific romance to the coups. *Journal of Historical Sociology* 1:399–422.

———. 1988b. From *holi* to *diwali* in Fiji: An essay on ritual and history. *Man*, n.s., 23:40–55.

———. 1991. *A Politics of Virtue: Hinduism, Sexuality and Counter-Colonial Discourse in Fiji*. Chicago: University of Chicago Press.

Kelly, John D., and Martha Kaplan. 1990. History, structure, and ritual. *Annual Review of Anthropology* 19:119–50.

Lal, Brij V. 1988. *Power and Prejudice: The Making of the Fiji Crisis*. Wellington: New Zealand Institute of International Affairs.

———., ed. 1986. *Politics in Fiji: Studies in Contemporary History*. Sydney: Allen and Unwin.

Legge, J. D. 1958. *Britain in Fiji 1858–1880*. London: Macmillan.

Lincoln, Bruce. 1987. Ritual, rebellion, resistance: Once more the Swazi *ncwala*. *Man*, n.s., 22:132–56.

Linnekin, Jocelyn. 1983. Defining traditions: Variations on Hawaiian identity. *American Ethnologist* 10:241–52.

LiPuma, Edward, and Sarah Keene Meltzoff. 1990. Ceremonies of independence and public culture in the Solomon Islands. *Public Culture* 3:77–92.

Luke, Harry. 1945. *From a South Seas Diary, 1938–42*. London: Nicholson and Watson.

Macnaught, Timothy J. 1982. *The Fijian Colonial Experience*. Pacific Research Monograph No. 7. Canberra: Australian National University.

Masselos, Jim. 1990. The magic touch of being free: The rituals of independence on August 15. In Jim Masselos, ed., *India: Creating a Modern Nation*, 37–53. New Delhi: Sterling.

————. n.d. India's Republic Day: The Other 26th January. Unpublished manuscript.

Sahlins, Marshall. 1976. *Culture and Practical Reason*. Chicago: University of Chicago Press.

————. 1985. *Islands of History*. Chicago: University of Chicago Press.

————. 1988. Cosmologies of capitalism: The transpacific sector of "The World System." *Proceedings of the British Academy* 73:1–51.

Sanadhya, Totoram. 1991 [1914]. *My Twenty-One Years in the Fiji Islands*. Translated and edited by John D. Kelly and Uttra Kumari Singh. Suva, Fiji: Fiji Museum.

Sukuna, (Ratu Sir) Lala. 1983. *The Three Legged Stool: Writings of Ratu Sir Lala Sukuna*. Edited by Deryck Scarr. London: Macmillan Education.

Tambiah, Stanley J. 1985. *Culture, Thought and Social Action: An Anthropological Perspective*. Cambridge: Harvard University Press.

Thomas, Nicholas. 1990. Sanitation and seeing: The creation of state power in early colonial Fiji. *Comparative Studies in Society and History* 32:149–70.

Toren, Christina. 1988. Making the present, revealing the past: The mutability and continuity of tradition as process. *Man*, n.s., 23:696–717.

Williams, Raymond. 1977. *Marxism and Literature*. London: Oxford University Press.

Wolf, Eric. 1982. *Europe and the People Without History*. Berkeley: University of California Press.

Worsley, Peter. 1968. *The Trumpet Shall Sound: A Study of "Cargo" Cults in Melanesia*. New York: Schocken Books.

Christine Jourdan

Stepping-Stones to National Consciousness: The Solomon Islands Case

Introduction: Three Stepping-Stones

Nationalism is the "in" word in the South Pacific. The sun-drenched island countries with the swaying palm trees of our occidental dream have started to shed the romantic image they had inherited from the colonial era. More pressing images are at stake here, and one of the more important is that of countries sufficiently stable politically and strong economically to attract foreign investment and trust. Political stability would be the proof that decolonization was not only successful, but also worthwhile, for in those newly decolonized countries, the ghosts of the colonial powers are still present, looming over the shaky futures of the tiny islands.[1]

The hope a decade ago was that economic strength would in the end allow these countries to discard foreign aid and be truly independent, a dream that was very much part of the ideology of political independence. Yet rising populations, collapsed commodity prices, dwindling forest and marine resources, and the long-range prospect of rising sea levels are pushing Pacific countries into impoverishment and inescapable dependency. Are these countries nations?

Nations are made; they do not exist naturally. The case of the Solomon Islands I present here illustrates the forces at play in the development of nationhood. The postcolonial state must develop the needed ideological and institutional infrastructure. There are three crucial means by which the ideology of nationhood can be fostered: (1) schooling, inculcating a national consciousness and creating a common frame of reference for the young generations; (2) community of language, providing a medium for the spread of the nationalist ideology; and (3) the development of popular culture, redefining old symbols and creating new ones that cut across ethnic and religious boundaries. I will treat these three means as "stepping-stones to national consciousness."

During the fifteen years that have elapsed since they became independent from Britain in 1978, the Solomon Islands have been busy building and consolidating the state apparatus. However, it has been only over the last five years or so that I have observed the development of emotional associations with the idea that the country may be more than the artificial lumping together of different islands and ethnic and linguistic groups, as well as efforts sustained by the central government to foster in the population the concept of a Solomon Islands nation. Emotional attachment to the idea of "the nation" is more obvious in urban circles than it is in the rural areas, for reasons that will become clearer. This attachment is illustrated and fostered by various public celebrations, such as the celebrations of Independence Day (LiPuma and Meltzoff 1990; Feinberg 1990); by the creation of national sports teams representing the country in international competitions (a Solomon Islands team participated in the 1992 Olympic Games in Barcelona); and by the development of a local body of literature and popular songs focusing on the values, habits, culture, and expectations identified by their authors as being national concerns. All play important roles in nation making. Symbolic displays induce people to watch, enjoy, participate, and, in the end, enlist their identification with a national community. All these symbolic displays are discourses that tell members of the society not only what they are, but more importantly, what they could be: an image of themselves projected into the future. These collective public displays are surface-level representations of a hidden, more secretive, more intimate, and more individual feeling of belonging in the group.

However, it seems to me that additional elements are crucial in conveying to citizens of the Solomon Islands a sense of shared values and expectations, out of which a sense of common purpose in the future is developing. They are the three "stepping-stones" toward a national consciousness: (1) the education system; (2) Pijin as a common language; and (3) popular culture. These focal areas will be essential sites in the emergence of a new discourse, with which people will identify to some degree and which they will help shape. This new discourse will be sufficiently different from earlier discourses predicated on cultural diversity to serve as the binding agent of new identities, yet must be sufficiently reminiscent of them so as not to be too threatening and to be meaningful and symbolically potent. It must therefore seize old symbols and concepts and deploy them for new purposes. Two of these stepping-stones are provided by the state apparatuses and are rooted in the idea that community of language and community of culture (effected through a homogenizing education) will ensure some common ground to a highly diverse population. This is a conception of nationhood very much inherited from the former colonial power. The third stepping-stone, popular culture, develops more or less independent of the influence of the state apparatuses, beyond their control, even though the state may have given the impetus and discreet encouragement that are necessary for its rapid spread.

Nationalism, Otherness, and Independence

Before examining these stepping-stones in detail, and exploring the Solomon Islands case further, I want to pause to reflect on the special character of postcolonial nationalism in the Pacific. There has been an outpouring of writing on nationalism in Europe, its historical development, and its explosive contemporary manifestations. I do not want to add to this flood of words regarding ideologies of roots, blood, land, shared history, and primordial origins, other than to reflect on the role in all this of concepts of Otherness. I will suggest that there lies one of the crucial contrasts between classical ethnically framed Eastern European nationalism and the incipient nationalism of the postcolonial Pacific.

An ethnic minority, whether in an imperial state such as the Austro-Hungarian Empire or in a twentieth-century former conglomerate state such as Yugoslavia, Czechoslovakia, or the Soviet Union, defines its identity oppositionally, vis-à-vis the dominant Other. Nationalist ideology in these classic European forms represents resistance against domination, engulfment, hegemony, and the threat of cultural and linguistic oblivion. Myths of a common past, shared blood, or patrimony are cast oppositionally in relation to the Other that dominates. Whether claims to nationhood succeed or not, identity emerges in relation to the Other, through the dialectic of domination and resistance, incorporation and liberation, denial and realization, in which images held on both sides of the encounter are generated through reciprocal self-definition. The result is an image of Self that makes sense only through the presence of an Other.

For colonized peoples, domination took very different forms. The dominant Other was the colonial master; and nationalist liberation entailed struggle against racially based caste systems, drastic resource extraction, labor exploitation in mines and plantations, land alienation, and imposition of alien institutions and laws. Decolonization was a fight to regain a humanness stripped away by the colonial masters. But in the Pacific, the colonial masters were not the Other fought against in Indochina, or Kenya, or Algeria. Independence was in most places handed on a platter to culturally diverse colonial subjects not at all sure whether they wanted it. Who, then, was the Other in relation to which identity could be defined and nationalism forged?

The first Other is nearby: it is the other ethnic group, on the other side of the river or in the next valley, or on another island, with whom trade and exchange regularly took place, or against whom wars were fought (see as well LiPuma this volume). It is the existence of that Other and the need to assert one's identity vis-à-vis a constructed Other, and not predominantly geographical isolation from one another, that have shaped cultural particularism and the high degree of language diversity in Melanesia, for instance.

The second Other is further removed: it is the world of the colonial or former colonial masters. This colonial world not only brought social chaos, but also required of the groups that came under colonial domination a redefinition of their identity and conception of self, for colonial domination brought a new form of identity, that of colonial subject: a second- or third-class citizen relegated to the newly acquired and pejorative status of "native." It is therefore within the framework of this newly established native citizenship that nationalist movements will emerge. Curiously enough, nationalist movements will seek a redefinition of that citizenship on their own terms, rather than challenging the concept of citizenship itself. The semiotics of the fight will be directly borrowed from the political system that the nationalist movements seek to topple. Interestingly and ironically, most nationalist movements in the Pacific (and in Africa and Southeast Asia as well) have not challenged the artificial creation of new geopolitical entities by colonial powers, beyond the rhetorics that are necessary to create nationalist sentiments. In fact, they may use colonial boundaries as pretexts for imperial expansion, as in the case of Indonesia's seizure of Irian Jaya/West Papua. When independence comes, the one geopolitical entity that will be considered as legitimate, and for which the new ex-colonial state will fight, is the one created by the former colonial power. In subsequent years, internal ethnic tensions may resurface and lead ethnic-based or island-based groups to seek secession from the newly independent country. Bougainville is a case in point (see Ogan 1991).

When we talk of nationalism in the Pacific, and elsewhere for that matter, we have in mind quite often the political format of the nation-state. We thus forget that the nation-state is only one avenue to state-hood, and that successful countries need not be made of one nation.[2] As Rutz (this volume) reminds us, there exist many versions of nationness within the same group of people. Nation making, as we understand it, involves the identification of the majority of citizens with the values of "the nation," and relies essentially on the emotional attachment of the citizens to "the nation." How else could we explain the force of chauvinism, the attachment of many people to the symbols representing their country, and the sacredness attached to such symbols? Witness the hoopla that usually follows flag burnings in times of peace or the scorn that is addressed to conscientious objectors in times of war. This emotional attachment is fostered by the very discourses that people create about themselves as a group and is instilled in the population by the ideologies developed by state institutions. Witness the statement made by John Major, British prime minister, apropos the resistance of various European countries to the Maastricht treaty: "Defenses of national culture are instincts rooted deep in the blood. They are not to be swept away by rhetoric about growth or slogans about unity" (Walsh 1992). As the vast literature on that topic has suggested, nationalism is a narrative of a particular kind, giving to people the sense that they may have something to do together within the political confine of the state.[3]

None of this, however, means that nationalist ideologies need to equate unification of the people with their homogenization: within one geopolitical entity, national consciousness can take many forms and be the result of many versions and interpretations of the same historical events and the same myths. On the other hand, the building of the state implies the establishment of government apparatuses, with or without concomitant legitimacy. The question I am asking is: do processes of state building in the Pacific entail this identification that would go beyond the simple recognition of the legitimacy of the state? Even though symbols of nationhood, such as flags or national anthems, are being used by new Pacific island countries, do we need, in our analyses of these political entities, to associate the process of the building of the state and the process of the building of "the nation"?

It seems to me useful to draw a distinction between the creation of "the nation" and the creation of the state. The two processes rest on different principles and could, in theory, exist quite independently from one another. In practice, the history of the Western world and its capitalist system has shown that in order to survive, the state will seek to legitimize its position by infusing in its citizens the ideology of nationalism (Althusser 1971). What we are witnessing at the moment in most of the recently independent countries of the Pacific are efforts by various states to develop and stabilize themselves, more than blatant nationalism, even though states are definitely using to this end the ideology of nationalism.

Another distinction should be established between countries that have had to fight for their independence (Vanuatu) or are fighting for it (New Caledonia) and countries that have had their independence handed to them on a silver platter (Papua New Guinea, the Solomon Islands, Kiribati, Tuvalu).

In the first case, the nationalist feeling crystallizes around the possibility of independence: the Other is the colonial power, and even though individuals may still identify themselves first and foremost with reference to the ethnic group, a broader frame of identity momentarily overcomes the barriers of ethnicity; new labels appear as people's conception of their identity broadens to encapsulate new symbols that reflect these new levels of identity. These labels may refer to harmonious conceptions of local history and place, to shared expectations, or to a special relationship to the land; and they may be expressed vernacularly. Recall Walter Lini's Vanuaaku Pati (*vanua* being Eastern Oceanic for "place" and *aku* meaning "my"), the name of vanuatu taken by the newly independent country and the name taken by the citizens of that country, ni vanuatu (*ni* meaning "those of"). Or the labels may refer to traumatic elements of colonial history; the term *kanak*, by which Melanesians in New Caledonia call themselves, is a case in point. Borrowed from the sociolinguistic history of the labor trade to Queensland, the word *kanak*, then pronounced *kanaka* (Moore 1986) and borrowed from the Hawaiian *kanaka*, meaning "man" (Clark 1977), was used by Europeans in nineteenth-century Queensland to refer to Melanesians, men and women, who had been indentured to work the sugarcane fields. This term was incorporated into Pacific Pidgin as an extremely derogatory term of reference and address and into Pacific French in the form *canaque*.[4] As Bensa (1990) and Winslow (1991) show, the symbolic and semantic value of the word has been reversed in the current usage by the nationalist movement of New Caledonia and stresses nationalist pride. In the case of nationalist struggle, identity is not only relational, but also oppositional. This opposition catalyzes the crystallization and the binding of nationalist sentiment and conveys legitimation to "the nation."

In the second case, nationalist sentiment is not present at the time of independence. Not having had to think about themselves as a people, citizens of a new country whose independence was handed to them still define their identity very much locally—in terms of their village, their island of origin, or their language group—at the time the country first becomes independent. First and foremost, allegiance will be to one's home place or one's own ethnic group. The former colonial state often will become the oppositional Other, with the result that allegiance to the state will be secondary and often nonexistent. This lack of identification with the state is precisely what undermines the unity and eventual survival of the country. Nationalist sentiments that will spring up in those circumstances will be directed against the former colonial state and will be divisive for the country. Bougainville's struggle for independence from Papua New Guinea illustrates the point. So does the alienation from and opposition toward the independent government by traditionalists such as the Kwaio in the Solomon Islands (Keesing 1992).

We need to stop at this point and reflect on the concept of identity, ethnic or national, because it appears as a leitmotiv of nationalist struggle. The growing literature on the invention of tradition has stressed how much manipulation of history was essential to nationalist claims, in most cases ethnically based. However, focusing on history as shaping the present obscures the fact that history is reshaped because of interests in the present, and not for the sake of the past itself.[5] Often, what is really at stake in the redefinition of history is possible control over the future. In most of the new countries of the Pacific, nationalist sentiments cannot be built on the basis of a common history people have shared: different ethnic groups have been lumped together within the geopolitical boundaries of a country. If anything, ethnic tensions and rivalries surface regularly within the political confine of independent nations and remind us of the arbitrariness of many geopolitical frontiers.[6] Thus, it seems more useful to see nationalist sentiment in such circumstances as being fostered, consciously or not, on the basis of a common future built on a sense of common purpose. Identity is thus defined in terms of a common future, rather than a common history.

I argue that it is a vision of oneself projected in the future that often explains the manipulation of history and the shapes history is given. The strength of history in legitimating the present lies precisely in the fact that it is both objective (a series of facts and events) and subjective (a series of interpretations of the same facts and events). While in their interaction with history, people seem to have a closer relationship with its subjective side, the pseudoscientific nature of its objective side is what gives history its political legitimacy. History thus becomes an essential element of nationalist struggles. However, just as a vision of the past can be constructed, a vision of a common future can be constructed as well. But this imagined community, created not so differently from the ones Anderson (1983) describes, is nevertheless perceived as potentially real. The reality of the imaginary, forcefully argued by Castoriadis (1987), is what gives its force to a projection of identity in the future.

This is what is happening in the Solomon Islands, where an urban-based elite, in government and administrative circles, is trying to promote a nationalist sentiment in the country.[7] This projection of identity creates tensions between the so-called nation builders—those who want to promote the ideology of the nation—and the nation buildees—those who will be caught up in the nation-building process, willingly or not, but whose participation in, acceptance of, and, ideally, identification with the values of the budding nation will be essential to the legitimacy of the national enterprise. This tension should remind us that nation building is not necessarily the result of a consensus (even though some degree of consensus on what the discourse of the nation should be is needed) and is usually the result of the instilling of the national ideology by those institutions and individuals who have the means and the interests to do so. In that light, in the Pacific, just as everywhere else, it may be more useful to think of nationalism as a class-based ideology rather than as an ethnic-based ideology. But we cannot dismiss the role played by ethnic-based ideologies in the legitimation of the national enterprise. We shall keep in mind, however, that towns and cities play a key role in the dissemination of nationalist ideologies: they are cultural market-places, multiethnic and multilingual social worlds, where new ideologies have relatively free rein to develop away from the pervasive control of "custom" (*kastom*), and where the state apparatuses and political elite are well represented.

Back to Stepping-Stones

Schooling

The first stepping-stone to national consciousness is the school, which has proven to be the crucial mechanism for fostering national consciousness in such ethnically complex postcolonial countries as Indonesia and Malaysia. Not surprisingly, we find the same process in the younger countries of the Pacific, such as the Solomons. Through schooling, ideally mandatory so as to reach out to everybody, new ideologies will be instilled in the future generation of citizens; values, expectations, and attitudes will be diffused in standardized forms. Transmitted by such an official vehicle as the school, these values will be endowed with legitimacy. Children learn that systems of knowledge exist that are fundamentally different from the ones their ancestors have relied on, and they are led to believe that control over those systems of knowledge guarantees progression up the socioeconomic ladder. In the mind of the administrators, the school program will perform another function: it will create a common frame of reference for the children, across ethnic and religious boundaries, thus giving some degree of homogeneity to a diverse population.[8]

The school derives its power from two main points. The first is that it transmits social values that are generally upheld by the majority of the adult population and serve the interest of the state: peacefulness, order, discipline, respect of elders, respect for social order—all elements that control both the body and the mind of the child. The second is the transmission of skills through which, it is hoped by parents, an improvement of the social condition of the child (and collectively of the citizenry and the work force) will result. Both points are seductive to parents and explain why schooling is generally popular in the country, even where it is not mandatory; parents will make dire financial sacrifices to send their children to school: school fees represent an important part of the family finances, particularly in areas where absence of cash crops and employment makes money difficult to come by. One often forgets that what is being taught in school, the content of the education program, and the manner in which knowledge is transmitted are the result of a philosophy of education, whether explicitly developed as such or not. This philosophy of education will be applied indiscriminately to all children of the country, thus unifying as one single clientele (it is hoped by the school planners) children with very different sociogeographic backgrounds, different life-styles, and different means.[9]

Those who have looked closely at school systems know that the goal of homogenization planned in ministries of education is not always reached; there is a great discrepancy between what curriculum planners aim at and what the children actually retain from it. Children distort what is being taught to them or simply resist the facts presented to them.[10] Moreover, regional resistance, sheer incompetencies of teachers and staff in some instances, cultural insensitivities, linguistic barriers, and inadequacies or irrelevance of the curriculum in some peripheral areas blur the homogenizing school curriculum. Again it is important to stress that the ideological success of schooling is greater in urban centers than in rural areas. However, beyond the fact that education ensures the reproduction of the servants of the state, and thus the reproduction of the state (Bourdieu and Passeron 1973) as well as the development of a skilled labor force, schooling ensures that children will be exposed to the social values upheld by the state and to a common body of history, literature, and other subjects that will represent a common frame of reference for their future life together. It allows as well for a national sentiment to be fostered in a great majority of children.

The Solomon Islands are no exception. The Solomons inherited from the colonial era an education system that was mostly run by the various religious denominations present in the country. In the earlier years of the protectorate, each congregation had its own curriculum, chose its own language of education, and used its own books. In the later years, the colonial government implemented an education system that was relatively uniform in all the parts of the British Empire. The primers from which children learned to read told the story of Dick and Jane, two young English children growing up in the manicured English countryside and undergoing social experiences that were totally irrelevant to the realities of the local children. The history books taught the history of Britain. Values were those of colonial powers. Those who did well in that system were sent abroad, to England or New Zealand or Australia, to further their education, and they usually came back immersed in the values of the "motherland." It was this first elite generation, well educated, brought up in the British tradition and imbued with British values, who were given the reins of the country upon independence. This process, by then well established in Africa, ensured political continuity of the new country within the confine of the Commonwealth.

As independence was nearing, the content of the school curriculum progressively changed to make more room for local issues. Solomon Islanders started to question the education system. A committee appointed to make a review of educational policy produced a report in 1973 titled "Education for What?"; it analyzed the difficulties of making schooling accessible to all and challenged the relevance and the organization of the education system. It voiced the grievances of parents who found a lack of relevance of education to life in the village: "The present system of education is a foreign one, which does not meet the needs of Solomon Islanders," "Education should aim to make children good men and women in the village," and "The people expect the school leaver to come back and help to improve the village" (British Solomon Islands Protectorate 1973, 31). The recommendations made by the review committee addressed parents' grievances but also went beyond them and reinforced the idea that education should serve the nation. The committee summarized the aims of education in the protectorate as follows (31):

a) To enable each Solomon Islander to understand his environment and the place of the Solomon Islands in the rest of the world.

b) To enable the Solomon Islander to think and develop his reasoning power so that he may face up to and overcome the every day problems with which he is faced.

c) To enable Solomon Islanders to become sound citizens of the Protectorate with an understanding and sympathy of the needs of others.

d) To enable each Solomon Islander to understand his own customs and the customs of others.

e) To promote racial harmony and unity in the country.

f) To improve the quality of life in the Solomons.

g) To offer skills which will enable each Solomon Islander to play his part in the development of his community and country according to his ability and aptitudes.

As a result, not only have Dick and Jane disappeared from the classrooms, but they have been replaced by two little Papua New Guineans living in physical and social environments similar to the ones experienced by young Solomon Islanders. History, this ever important developer of national identification (locally called social studies), brings the heroes closer to home: Maasina Rule, the World War II battle of Guadalcanal,

Sir Jacob Vouza, independence, the first prime minister of the independent Solomons. All these events and people capture the imagination of the children and adolescents. In the evenings, I witnessed the children in my Honiara neighborhood play "war," with the Solomon Islands Labour Corps, temporarily redefined as an army, playing a glorious role alongside the American GIs against the Japanese. Through geography, pupils and students learn about "our Solomon Islands": the name of the various islands and provinces of the archipelago, the beauty of the land, the wealth of the waters, the pride of a people. At the time of homework, in the evening, young children are drilled by their parents into knowing basic facts about their country. Every school day starts with a prayer asking God to protect "our Solomon Islands." Every official occasion at school will be sanctioned with the singing of the national anthem, which the children have learned at school. Localization of the education program has been paralleled by localization of the teaching and administrative responsibilities in the higher circles of education: expatriates' contracts are not renewed.

In education, as in other realms of socioeconomic life, Solomon Islanders assert themselves. Through schooling, many children, and particularly the urban children, grow up and mature with the comforting certitude that they have a country, unified and glorified. They are very attached to this idea, the urban children even more so because they often do not have firsthand knowledge of their parents' culture as rural children usually do. When people develop emotional attachments toward their country, then the seeds of nationalism that have been sown are bearing fruit. I have observed a great discrepancy in that attachment as manifested by urban children and by their rural counterparts. In rural areas, the relevance of the school curriculum to the everyday life of the children is perceived by parents and children alike as remote: parents would like to see their children learn more about their immediate environment and life-style and not so much about wider concerns of the town and the world.[11] This perception causes many children to drop out of school in the early years of schooling, and many simply never attend. But the marketing value of a school education does not escape some parents. I witnessed quite a few bride-price negotiations in some rural areas of the Solomons where fathers were claiming a higher bride-wealth from the kin of their future sons-in-law on the grounds that their daughter had reached year six of primary education.

The impact of the school system on the country as a whole is not immediate, however, and is more obvious in urban areas than in rural areas. Only about fifteen years have elapsed since independence, and it is much too early to assess the unifying role of the school system in the country. At the same time, the precarious economic situation of the country and the saturation of the public service are such that school leavers and graduates find it difficult to obtain the well-paid job that they were told they would get if they went to school and to which they feel they have a right. This employment crisis may very well jeopardize the unifying mandate that curriculum planners and politicians have given the school.

Pijin

The second stepping-stone toward a Solomon Islands nation is Pijin, the lingua franca of the archipelago. It is the communication cement that holds together this rich linguistic conglomerate. As with the other Melanesian countries, the Solomon Islands are characterized by high ethnic and linguistic diversity. Some sixty-four languages are spoken: even though some are closely related, most are not mutually intelligible (Tryon and Hackman 1983). In precolonial times, people overcame the linguistic diversity by being multilingual: they spoke the language of the neighboring ethnic groups or at least had a passive competency. Multilingualism was the rule more than the exception. With the establishment of the British Solomon Islands Protectorate in 1893 came a more widespread usage of the pidgin that indentured laborers from the east of the archipelago had brought back from Queensland. This pidgin, locally called Pijin, and sometimes Pisin, was used primarily to facilitate communication among plantation workers and between British administration officers or plantation overseers and the local population. Progressively, the pidgin became the lingua franca of the plantations, allowing workers from various islands to communicate with one another. By the 1950s, Pijin had become the lingua franca of the male segment of the archipelago. Women, however, because they had no access to the social settings in which the language was used, had no opportunities to learn Pijin. It was used widely as a second language by a male population whose daily social life and main activities were conducted in the much more valorized vernaculars: Pijin was everyone's language, but no one's language.

In the subsequent years, four factors were instrumental in strengthening the status of Pijin as the de facto national language of the country:

(1) the increase in interisland trade and travel, putting people in contact with one another on a much larger scale than had been the case before; (2) schooling, which exposed pupils to Pijin in multiethnic schools; (3) young women learning the language and using it on a regular basis in bigger marketplaces or during their visits to town; and (4) urbanization, through the expansion of Honiara, the capital city of the Solomon Islands. With all sixty-four vernaculars represented in town, Pijin ceased to be a male prerogative and became the "natural" language of the urban world, superseding the vernaculars. In Honiara today, one needs Pijin if one wants to have a social life that goes beyond the limits of the ethnic group. As more and more children from increasingly numerous biethnic marriages are being brought up in Pijin, the command of vernaculars among the young generation in town is diminishing. For an increasing number of children, Pijin is the mother tongue, the only linguistic tool they have at their disposal, apart from the minimal English they acquire at school. Pijin has become the language of the cultural life of the town, with popular songs, cartoons, radio programs, and advertising being produced in this lingua franca.

These developments have contributed to giving Pijin some form of legitimacy (Jourdan 1988) within the urban population and a social prestige that reaches out into the provinces even though some may object to the ever-growing influence of Pijin in the life of the country. This newly acquired social legitimacy puts Pijin in a better position vis-à-vis English, the socially prestigious language inherited from the colonial era and the official language of the country. Pijin had been considered by the British, and by some members of the Solomon Islands elite (who nevertheless used it in most realms of their private and social life), a bastardized language doomed to disappear. It had no place in the education system, no formal and official status, no support system such as standardization and literature. This attitude represents a striking contrast from the way Papua New Guinea and Vanuatu politicians and government treated their local varieties of pidgin, Tok Pisin and Bislama, respectively. In Vanuatu, Bislama became the language of New Hebridean politics as a way to allow the political message of independence to reach out in the provinces (see Facey [this volume]). In Papua New Guinea, Tok Pisin was given the status of a national language and is now used in all realms of social life, even if, in some areas, people resent having to use it.[12]

In the Solomons, the same process has been slower to appear: with the encroachment of Pijin in the social life of the country, the language has begun to be viewed by politicians and administrators as the panacea for the heterogeneity of the country. Its potential as a unifying tool is threefold: (1) it prevents any ethnic rivalry that could stem from one vernacular becoming too visible and important in the country; (2) it is a local alternative to English in a country trying to shake free from its colonial heritage; and (3) being closely mapped onto vernaculars, it is learned quickly by Solomon Islanders, even those (and they are few nowadays) who have not had contact with it from an early age (see Crowley 1990; Jourdan 1985; Keesing 1988). Its usefulness as a language through which political messages can be conveyed to the whole country has not escaped the shrewd eyes of the politicians. As a result, more attention is being paid to Pijin: research relating to its scope, socio-linguistic usages, structure, phonology, and lexicon is now being encouraged by the Ministry of Education and Training. Rumors of a national language policy giving Pijin an official status in the country have been circulating.[13]

Nevertheless, the emergence of Pijin as the de facto national language of the country should not obscure the ever important role played by English in many domains of socioeconomic life: official language of education (even if, in practice, Pijin is very often the de facto language of education [Jourdan 1988]), language of international trade and communication, language of the written media of communication. More and more Solomon Islanders are learning to speak English fluently: to do so opens important economic opportunities, vis-à-vis investors and logging companies and tourists from overseas as well as paid employment. Pijin and English are playing complementary roles in the life of the Solomon Islands, and the ever increasing encroachment of Pijin in the country is not concomitant with the disappearance of English.

Popular Culture

It is in Honiara particularly that one finds the last of the three stepping-stones I have identified: popular culture as generated locally or imported from Western or other Pacific countries. The spread of popular culture is new to the Solomon Islands, but it quickly has caught the imagination of the young urbanites. Soccer matches and rock concerts, T-shirts and videos, marches and banners, dress and hair fashion, new words and new body language, all these contribute to make the cultural world of the town increasingly complex. Gifted musicians have started local string and reggae bands, creating songs that appeal greatly to the public and are being sung in every corner of the archipelago. Interestingly, some of the most successful songs depict the difficulties of making a living in town, an ever recurrent theme in the life of the country. From "Wakabaot long Chinatown," dating from 1969, to "Mama Karae" and "Masta Liu," dating from 1989, these songs express the love for and fear of an urban life-style which many find both exciting and threatening. Not surprisingly, Pijin is the medium of popular culture.

Living in town is new to Solomon Islanders. As people who have no traditional model of an urban life-style, they are continuously creating a culture in which they are immersed. They are both agents and recipients in this process, as marginal participants in a worldwide capitalist consumerism and as cultural creators. In this case, one can confidently argue that this urban culture in the making is being created by urbanites as they live it, although the creative possibilities of urban life-styles are constrained by town structures, the types of socioeconomic activities of urbanites, and the type of social relationships they establish in an urban setting. In that sense, town dwellers are not creating a new cultural world out of a cultural vacuum. For one thing, town life is still connected to life in the villages, through a two-way flow of information that may take the shape of a young thug, sporting sunglasses and a Walkman, going back to the bush, or the shape of a father going to town to collect the bride-price for his daughter. Urban culture in the Solomons is also shaped directly by the influences of the cultural and economic world system. But Solomon Islanders are by no means passive consumers of imported multinational capitalist culture in prepackaged forms; they impose their own creative stamp on the Western phenomena with which they are bombarded.

An interesting example is associated with the movie character Rambo. The film genre in which this character is portrayed as a hero is extremely popular in the Solomon Islands among the male segment of the population.[14] They love the brashness of the character, his strength, his bravado, and his flouting of the authorities if their beliefs and choices go against his own. Christine Ward Gailey (1989) has suggested for Tonga that the admiration manifested for Rambo by the Tongans is best understood as a form of resistance by proxy to neocolonialism. This is possibly the case in the Solomons, but not quite in the same way, as

Rambo resonates more with *ramo*, the traditional warrior of the Melanesian Troika (Keesing 1985) of Big Man, Priest, and Killer than with any form of cultural resistance to imperialism. In traditional lore, a *ramo* is endowed with the qualities and flaws displayed by Rambo in the movies. In town, naughty little boys and brash young men are often called *ramo*, and parents are both afraid and proud of the unruliness of such children. The phonetic analogy of the two words is itself tantalizing: it certainly reinforces the assimilation that Solomon Islanders, and Malaitans in particular, establish between the two heroes.

This set of readings of new and old cultural texts by urbanites in Honiara, individually and collectively, gives its shape to the sociocultural world of the town. People in rural areas are aware that the new urban milieu of the Solomons is extremely different from theirs. Old values—both those of the precolonial era and those of village Christianity—are flouted in town. Villagers object to the changes of behavior they observe, to the laxity in respecting "custom," to the lack of respect for the elders manifested by the young people, to increases in the cost and changes in the content of bride-price, to the escalation of food prices, to sexual laxity and prostitution. Yet they will take in stride most of the facets of popular culture surfacing in town and most of the urban life-styles. This is an interesting paradox. Why object to some aspects of the new cultural world and accept others?

I argue that in Honiara, people will object to social phenomena that threaten them, or impinge directly on and connect directly to valued ways of village life, and will accept, bear with, or ignore those that do not. Popular culture is relatively nonthreatening to Solomon Islands villagers because it is not produced in their social world—a world they know and feel they can control—but in an alien world, already different and out of their control. Not being of the same scale as their own productions, not being ontologically of the same kind, most elements of urban popular culture (its material representations particularly) are perceived by villagers as nonthreatening. They are culturally neutral, not belonging to anyone, but borrowed. It is this seeming neutrality that gives urban popular culture its cultural binding power and allows its innocuous spread in the country. Not being anyone's culture that can be associated with an ethnic group, but being a type of generic culture (Philibert 1990), it overcomes ethnic boundaries: it allows for new shared meanings, symbols, and representations to reach out on a wider scale.[15]

Conclusion: Urban Culture, National Culture

Nation making in the Solomon Islands is not a *chose faite*. People keep on defining themselves locally, with kinship remaining the most important pole of identification. Even in town, kinship still occupies a primary function in the organization of social relationships. However, one increasingly perceives new moods, orientations, perceptions, interpretations, and affinities which, linked to increasing changes in poles of identification, contribute to give national sentiment a stronger base. This gradual transformation is due to the cumulative effect of the three stepping-stones I have analyzed here, and to urbanization.

Towns, as wider cultural marketplaces, allow for new negotiations of meaning to take place while at the same time allowing for wider circulation of new symbols and modes of identification. Nationalism is one of them, negotiated publicly and privately, by urbanites who have to shape a future for themselves away from custom and tradition (*kastom*). It might make sense to think of nationalism as the *kastom* of the urban folk, the ideology that guides definition of Self in the urban setting. Truly, some urbanites are Solomon Islanders before being from Kwara'ae, from Ranongga, or from Makira—particularly among the younger population born and raised in town. Away from the established discourse of "tradition," urbanites create an image of themselves that is reinforced by education and popular culture; it is from this new cultural center and its productions, tolerated with bemusement or admired by rural Solomon Islanders, that the nationalist ideology now emerging in the Solomons is spreading.

Honiara is a cultural center without a past. Barely forty years old, and developed on the remains of the American army base on Guadalcanal, it cannot use its past as a flag of identity; the best it can offer is a new life-style, recognized as the way of the future. It is around this vision of a common future on which they can act that Honiarans develop an original urban culture. It is not surprising that nationalism has more chances to crystallize in that setting. Increasing sharedness of ideas and new poles of identification are possible precisely because of multivocality and multiplexity, those ever more complex, fluid, and situational sets of relationships individuals and social groups create vis-à-vis each other. The cultural creolization that takes place between locally produced and imported foreign elements and ideologies ensures some continuity with ways of contemporary village life, yet it ensures as well the independence of urban life-styles from the control of the village.

In the Solomons, as in many other emergent nations of the Pacific, nationalism is not ethnic based, and it is encouraged by the state apparatuses for a pragmatic reason—to hold the country together—not to situate Solomon Islanders vis-à-vis an external Other or Others. There is too much internal diversity, with Bellonese and Gilbertese and Kwara'ae and Choiseulese, for an ethnically monolithic Solomon Islands Self to be opposed to an external Other. In the absence of a homogenizing *kastom*, the role of the state will be to create one out of

> a compound of cultural traits deemed capable of expressing national identity or unity. As state ideology, the discourse on *kastom* attempts to give credence to a fictive construction: that of an *imaginary mono-ethnism* (Babadzan 1988, 216).

Insofar as it succeeds, this ideology can, in creating an ethnic Self, create an external Other, that will allow the young nation to define itself.

ACKNOWLEDGMENTS

I wish to thank the Social Sciences and Humanities Research Council of Canada for providing a research grant allowing me to spend six months in the Solomon Islands over the summers of 1989 and 1990, researching the relationships between Pijin and the development of an urban culture in Honiara. I am grateful to James Carrier, Ellen Facey, Robert Foster, Michael Jacobsen, Roger Keesing, and John Kelly for the comments they made on the initial version of this chapter.

NOTES

1. I leave aside for the moment the residual French colonial presence in the Pacific.

2. Colonial states and imperial states such as those of Rome, Ottoman Turkey, and Austria-Hungary are good examples. It is a double irony, then, that countries such as Indonesia created as colonial empires must try to reconstitute themselves as nations as well as states.

3. Take, for example, the ideological "war" that is being fought in Canada at the moment between the federal government and the Quebec provincial government. As Quebec prepares itself for yet another referendum on sovereignty, the

federal government is bombarding the population of the country with songs, video clips, and advertising glorifying the country as a whole, celebrating the indispensable participation of all provinces in the nation, and reminding citizens of the historical contribution of their province to the building of the country. This ideological blitz, using emotions to revive nationalism, is aimed at both Quebec and the rest of Canada, trying to convince each party that they do belong together.

4. Interestingly enough, *kanaka* is still being used in the Solomon Islands and in Papua New Guinea to refer to unsophisticated bush people from remote rural areas. In town, the word is used as a derisive term equivalent to *lokol* ("yokel") and stresses the social ineptness or lack of sophistication of new urbanites.

5. Take, for instance, Mexico's recent decision to write a new official history better adapted to the newly established free trade agreement with the United States and Canada, stressing a "libre-echangiste" attitude after one century of protectionism. This new official history, which also transforms former dictator Porfirio Díaz into a hero of the modernization of Mexico, will appear in the free and mandatory textbook distributed to ten- and eleven-year-old children in all primary schools of the country (Sberro 1992).

6. The dismantling of the Soviet empire, the dismemberment of Yugoslavia under nationalist pressures, and the recent vote of autonomy voted by the Slovak government remind us precisely of the arbitrariness of colonial borders.

7. The role of the elite as cultural and political buffer is crucial to the postindependence consciousness. Being urban based, the elite in the Solomon Islands is comfortable with many levels of identities and meaning. For more detail, see Jourdan 1990.

8. To homogenize a population, school is a wonderful tool. The French revolutionaries were quick to perceive its power: within the first years of the Revolution, they had ordered a survey of the state of education in France and had created the basis of a universal system of mandatory education (that was implemented only eighty years later) for all children beyond the age of seven.

9. Equality of access to schooling does not necessarily mean equality of success for the children, but this is not our purpose here.

10. Recall, for instance, that more than fifty years after the introduction of the Russian language in schools by the Soviet government, a comparatively small percentage of the population of the Soviet republics and countries of the former Soviet bloc actually speaks the language, or acknowledges speaking it.

11. Michael Jacobsen (personal communication 24 April 1992) has made the same observation: "In my own study of a community school and its relationship to the surrounding local communities among the Dom people of Simbu Province, Papua New Guinea, I found that communication between school and community is not good . . . This results in an annual student drop-out rate of about 40 percent. Furthermore, the school manages to get into contact with only about 45 percent of the potential mass of students in the area I was working . . . I think this situation has come about because the educational system the school represents, and the skills it installs into the children, do not have anything to do

with the reality the students and their families are living in. The school and the local communities represent two completely different worlds, and there are seemingly no means of bridging them."

12. As is often the case for Motu speakers.

13. In this realm, the Solomon Islands are trailing behind Papua New Guinea and Vanuatu, both of which have given the status of official language to Tok Pisin and Bislama, the local pidgins, along with English (and French as well, in Vanuatu). At a time when the three Melanesian countries are setting the bases of an economic, cultural, and political alliance (the Melanesian Spearhead), the varieties of pidgin spoken in these countries, all mutually intelligible, may prove instrumental in bringing about some linguistic unity in the region. Pidginophony could prove an important tool.

14. Women are not seen in movie theaters and movie arcades in the Solomon Islands, except for a few Chinese or Polynesian women who are escorted there by their kinsmen. These women usually go to see romantic movies but keep away from those that their menfolk relish: Rambo movies, martial arts movies (preferably the old ones with Bruce Lee as the lead), and any other type of film showing war, fights, and other violence. Many of these films are commercial failures in the West and find a second life in the Third World. They come to the country on videocassettes and are usually seen on medium-size screens in small movie arcades where, for an entrance fee of one Solomon Islands dollar, men, young and not so young, pile up in an overcrowded and stuffy room to watch. No harm would come to a woman who ventured alone into these movie houses, but she would be frowned upon by the men and would most likely be driven away.

15. Some resistance appears when the foundations of moral personhood are challenged by urban mores (Jourdan 1991).

REFERENCES

Althusser, Louis. 1971. *Lenin and Philosophy, and Other Essays.* Trans. Ben Brewster. London: New Left Books.

Anderson, Benedict. 1983. *Imagined Communities: Reflections on the Origin and Spread of Nationalism.* London: Verso.

Babadzan, Alain. 1988. *Kastom* and nation building in the South Pacific. In R. Guidieri, F. Pellizzi, and S. J. Tambiah, eds., *Ethnicities and Nations: Processes of Interethnic Relations in Latin America, Southeast Asia, and the Pacific,* 199–228. Austin: University of Texas Press.

Bensa, Alban. 1990. *Nouvelle-Caledonie: Un Paradis dans la Tourmente.* Paris: Gallimard.

Bourdieu, Pierre, and Jean-Claude Passeron. 1973. *La Reproduction.* Paris: Editions de Minuit.

British Solomon Islands Protectorate. 1973. *Education for What?* Education Policy Review Committee Report 1973. Honiara: Government Printer.

Castoriadis, Cornelius. 1987. *The Imaginary Institution of Society*. Cambridge: Polity Press.

Clark, Ross. 1977. *In Search of Beach-La-Mar: Historical Relations among Pacific Pidgins and Creoles*. Working papers in Anthropology, Archaeology, Linguistics, Maori Studies 48. Auckland: University of Auckland.

Crowley, Terry. 1990. *Beach-La-Mar to Bislama: The Emergence of a Natural Language in Vanuatu*. Oxford: Clarendon Press.

Feinberg, Richard. 1990. The Solomon Islands' tenth anniversary of independence: Problems of national symbolism and national integration. *Pacific Studies* 13:19–40.

Gailey, Christine Ward. 1989. "RAMBO" in Tonga: Video films and cultural resistance in the Tongan Islands (South Pacific). *Culture* 9:21–32.

Jourdan, Christine. 1985. *Sapos iumi mitim iumi*: Urbanization and creolization of Solomon Islands pijin. Ph.D. diss., Research School of Pacific Studies, Australian National University, Canberra.

———. 1988. Pidgin's legitimacy. Paper presented at the meeting of the Association for Social Anthropology in Oceania, 19 February, Savannah, Georgia.

———. 1990. No one's culture, everybody's culture: Urbanization in the Solomon Islands. Paper presented at the meeting of the Association for Social Anthropology in Oceania, 24 March, Kauai, Hawaii.

———. 1991. Where have all the cultures gone? Paper presented at the Conference on the New Pacific, 18–19 October, at University of Lund, Sweden.

Kapferer, Bruce. 1988. *Legends of People, Myths of State: Violence, Intolerance and Political Culture in Sri Lanka and Australia*. Washington: Smithsonian Institution Press.

Keesing, Roger M. 1985. Killers, big men and priests on Malaita: Reflections on a Melanesian troika system. *Ethnology* 24:237–52.

———. 1988. *Melanesian Pidgin and the Oceanic Substrate*. Stanford: Stanford University Press.

———. 1992. *Custom and Confrontation: The Kwaio Struggle for Cultural Autonomy*. Chicago: University of Chicago Press.

LiPuma, Edward, and Sarah K. Meltzoff. 1990. Ceremonies of independence and public culture in the Solomon Islands. *Public Culture* 3:77–92.

Moore, Clive. 1986. *Kanaka: A History of Melanesian Mackay*. Port Moresby: Institute of Papua New Guinea Studies and University of Papua New Guinea Press.

Ogan, Eugene. 1991. The cultural background to the Bougainville crisis. *Journal de la Société des Océanistes* 1 & 2:61–67.

Philibert, Jean-Marc. 1990 [1986]. The politics of tradition: Toward a generic culture in Vanuatu. In Frank Manning and Jean-Marc Philibert, eds., *Customs in Conflict: The Anthropology of a Changing World*, 251–73. Peterborough, Ontario: Broadview Press.

Sberro, S. 1992. Le Mexique adapte son histoire à ses nouvelles relations avec les Etats-Unis. *La Presse*, 28 September, p. A20.

Tryon, D., and B. Hackman. 1983. *Solomon Islands Languages: An Inter-*

nal Classification. Pacific Linguistics C-72. Canberra: Australian National University.

Walsh, J. 1992. Europe's puzzling stars. *Time* 140 (no. 12) (September 21):26–30.

Winslow, Donna. 1991. Custom and independence in New Caledonia. Paper presented at the meeting of the Association for Social Anthropology in Oceania, 28 March, Victoria, British Columbia.

Robert J. Foster

Print Advertisements and Nation Making in Metropolitan Papua New Guinea

In May 1985, the National Parliament of Papua New Guinea passed the Commercial Advertising Act, initiated by Ted Diro.[1] According to this act, all commercial advertising in Papua New Guinea must be locally produced by local agencies employing local talent—designers, artists, models, and so forth. Infractions are to be treated as criminal rather than civil offenses.

Letters to the weekly *Times of Papua New Guinea* (hereinafter *TPNG*) by two critics of the act, both expatriate advertising managers, provoked responses from Moale Rivu, then executive officer for Diro.[2] In a *TPNG* article on 12 April 1986, Rivu defended the act as a deliberate effort by the government to promote "nationalism" and "nation building." He asked:

> Is it any wonder that we still find it difficult to be self sufficient in such basic foodstuff as rice and peanut butter? When the Markham factory was in operation it had to compete against imported peanut butter whose agents on numerous occasions used ready-made ads from overseas to promote their products. That, in essence, is the bottom line in this debate on the Advertising Act.

Rivu's nationalism was motivated by mainly economic concerns, the famous "bottom line." It is hardly contentious, however, to maintain that advertising and mass consumption in general are inevitably deeply cultural matters. This is not only a question of cultural imperialism, of resisting "Coca-Colonization"—the flow of images and objects emanating from various dominant regional centers. It is equally a question of the instrumental effects of mass-consumption practices in nation making, that is, a question of the potential for advertisements to present constructs of "the nation" and perforce to define the terms of membership in "the nation."

151

I address this broad question through a consideration of print advertisements taken from several sources: two newspapers, a billboard, and an in-flight magazine. How do these ads construct "Papua New Guinea" and "Papua New Guineaness"? How do these ads and the consumption practices that they publicize enable (if not exhort) the steadily growing population of school-educated, urban-dwelling, wage-earning citizens to imagine themselves as "Papua New Guineans"? To what extent is an emergent urban consumer culture implicated in the processes of nation making in Papua New Guinea (see Jourdan this volume)?

Advertising and "the Nation"

I use two complementary approaches in considering the relationships between advertisements and "the nation"—"the nation" understood here as an imaginative construct (see this volume's introduction). The first approach emphasizes the sociocultural linkages brought about by the spread of mass-consumption practices. Social historians have long observed, for example, that the formation of an imagined national community in the United States during the late nineteenth century was coeval with the birth of modern consumerism (Boorstin 1973; Bronner 1989; Ewen and Ewen 1982; Fox and Lears 1983). Department stores assembled within their palatial confines thousands of big-city dwellers; chain stores replicated these gatherings on a smaller scale in towns across the country; and mail-order catalogs functioned to connect the most remote farmer's family to this expansive network of consumers. The proliferation of images and objects of mass consumption brought the most diverse audiences, including newly arrived immigrants, into not only a developing marketplace, but also an emergent set of shared understandings, memories, tastes, and habits.

The growth of an advertising industry figured largely in this process, inasmuch as advertisements mediated the anonymous encounter between buyers and sellers. Advertisements became important vehicles for the imagination of a community of consumers whose shared consumption practices and ideals put them in experiential unison with each other. Orvar Löfgren (1989a, 373) made this point in reviewing a history of American advertising in the 1920s and 1930s:

> Reading the same ads, listening to the same radio personalities, or watching the same movies created a shared frame of reference for

those growing up during the interwar years, in the same ways as it does for those growing up today.

Circulated through the mass media of newspapers, radio, television, and videos, advertisements continue to expose large numbers of Americans from a cross section of social categories to images of a supralocal world. Put otherwise, shared mass-consumption practices still provide Americans with the means not only for making, remembering, and contesting a common experience, but also for anchoring an imagined national community in ordinary, everyday practice.[3] Benedict Anderson's (1983, 39) arresting description of the "mass ceremony" of newspaper reading comes to mind:

> At the same time, the newspaper reader, observing exact replicas of his own paper being consumed by his subway, barbershop, or residential neighbors, is continually assured that the imagined world is visibly rooted in everyday life.

From this perspective, then, it is possible to regard nations as imagined communities of consumption, "large-scale, non-intimate collectivities unified by the ritualized fantasies of collective expenditure," to borrow Arjun Appadurai's (n.d.) words. Such fantasies circulate at high velocity through the mass media, most familiarly in the form of advertisements.[4]

The second approach, by contrast, does not focus on the specific content of ads—on the "frames of reference" or "ritualized fantasies" that ads exhibit. Instead, it focuses on what might be called the "ad form." I argue that the general *form* of advertisements, however different their specific content, communicates a particular conception of both "the nation" and its constituent "nationals." Accordingly, I approach advertising as "a discourse about and through objects which bonds together images of persons, products and well being" (Leiss, Kline, and Jhally 1990). But I am especially concerned with the general structure of social relations that such a discourse presupposes and naturalizes, a structure of social relations characteristic of commodity consumption in capitalist societies.

More precisely, I am concerned with demonstrating how the ad form at once reflects and constitutes both a definite kind of relationship between subjects and objects (consumers and commodities) and a coordinate relationship between subjects and other subjects (consumers and other consumers) (see Miller 1987). That is, the social relations of commodity consumption implied by ads entail particular definitions of personhood, on the one hand, and of community, on the other. It is my argument that these definitions of personhood and community poten- tially supplement, if not displace, definitions of personhood and commu- nity grounded in social relations of kinship and locality (LiPuma this volume). More importantly, it is my argument that these definitions of personhood and community mesh with a conception of "the nation" as a community of individuals fundamentally similar in their status as "propri- etors" or "owners" of a distinctive reification: "their" national culture (Handler 1985). In this conception, everyone who belongs to a nation is everyone to whom the nation belongs.

My approach, then, follows Anderson (1983) in emphasizing that the generic imaginative construct called "the nation" is specifiably dis- tinctive *in form*. "The nation," whatever its particular characteristics, implies a community that is unambiguously bounded, temporally as well as spatially, and inhabited by people whose manifest diversity belies a latent sameness (Handler 1988, 6). This sort of imaginative construct derives from and gives rise to a variety of processes of objectification in which "the nation" takes on a thinglike form, external to the individual (see Keesing 1989; Linnekin 1990). Such objective forms—flags, cos- tumes, dances, foods, monuments, languages—are "possessed" in com- mon by the individuals constituting the nation as markers of their shared subjective identity as "owners" (Handler 1988, 6). That is, the propri- etors of these forms regard them as elements of a "national culture," as material evidence of an essential national cultural identity. National culture, in other words, emerges as a collection of collectively held things, the discrete, bounded objectivity of which tangibly replicates the conceptual form of the nation itself.

Here I want to consider advertisements as textual vehicles of such objectification. I am not concerned with the intentions of the advertisers themselves—with whether advertisers attempt to enlist nationalist senti- ment in the service of selling toothpaste—nor am I concerned with the putative effects of ads on individual purchasing decisions. My primary concern is not with the particular messages of particular ads, but rather with the rhetorical form common to all ads.[5] By rhetoric, I mean two things: (1) the way in which ads transfer meaning to the commodities that they publicize so as to endow these commodities with a set of "objectively" given qualities (Williamson 1978), and (2) the way in which ads involve consumers as participants in constructing the ad's meaning.

The ads that I examine, I argue, qualify commodities as somehow Papua New Guinean, as embodiments and/or possessions of "the nation." They imply, furthermore, that to consume these commodities is to appropriate the quality of Papua New Guineaness as an attribute of one's person. The consumption of national commodities, then, nationalizes the person. At the same time, each ad implicitly construes the nation as a community of consumption, a collectivity of nonintimate people whose shared consumption practices and fantasies express and constitute their nationality. Membership or citizenship in this community is acquired through acts of consumption so qualified, by participation in the "life-style" represented in the ad.

When taken together, however, these ads leave open the possibility for consumer-citizens to differentiate themselves from each other on the basis of *unshared* consumption practices. Diversity is (re)construed as differential participation within a single universe of consumer activity. Thus, the national community of consumption is neither mechanically solidary nor even organically cohesive; indeed, differentiation of consumer-citizens constantly threatens to expose and create new cleavages (such as class and status divisions) within the community.

I begin the discussion by demonstrating the semiotic logic by which ads impute qualities or attributes to various commodities (Williamson 1978). The particular quality at issue here is nationality, or Papua New Guineaness, a detachable attribute capable of being attached to embodiments as manifestly diverse as sugar and airplanes.[6] This imputation is complemented by a second, namely, the attribution of Papua New Guineaness to the consumer of commodities qualified with nationality. I concentrate in this regard on how ads define the relationship between commodity and consumer as one of "possession" or "having," and I explicate the presuppositions this definition makes about the nature of persons and objects.

The transfer of Papua New Guineaness from commodity to consumer is completed by a third imputation. Consumers are implicitly put into relation with other consumers on the basis of shared *and* unshared consumption practices. Most inclusively, this scheme of social relations defines the nation as a community of fellow consumer-citizens. However, distinctions among consumers are made with reference to a shared understanding of unevenly distributed consumption practices. That is, consumers of specific commodities are constituted as less inclusive totemic groups or "kinds" of people (Williamson 1978; cf. Comaroff 1987). This totemism thereby allows for a diversity of consumer groups within the larger national community of national commodity consumers.

Nationalizing Commodities, Nationalizing Persons

The process of nationalizing commodities in advertising works in more-or-less subtle ways. Ads for state-owned businesses often render the process explicit. Consider this ad (fig. 1) for Air Niugini, the state-owned airline, that appeared a few years ago in a special independence anniversary issue of the *Papua New Guinea Post Courier* (hereinafter *PC*), a nationally distributed newspaper with a circulation of 30,000 in 1985.[7] The top of the page announces: "We're proud to be your airline, PNG." Beneath this caption are four photographs, each of which pictures an Air Niugini employee (two women, two men) holding or touching some piece of airline equipment—a ticket, a cockpit control switch, a tire on the landing gear, a coffee cup. These employees are not only apparently Papua New Guineans, but also "owners" of Air Niugini. The text continues: "As long as PNG has been independent, we have been the wings for the nation. Because we're the airline owned by all the people of Papua New Guinea." Indeed, the airline's claim to be "*Our* National Airline" (emphasis added) effectively blurs all distinctions among owners, employees, and customers. The ad sets up a closed circuit of signification in which the reader is invited to construct the Papua New Guineaness of the employees with reference to the material objectifications of the airline, and to transfer this quality from these objectifications to the "owners" of the airline, the "people of Papua New Guinea" who purchase the services of the airline. In short, "the people of Papua New Guinea" are assimilated to the ambiguously inclusive "Us" implied in the slogan, "Our National Airline."

A similar discourse of collective national ownership is found in ads for Ramu sugar, product of an industry protected by the state against foreign competition. The text of one such ad (fig. 2) proclaims: "From the canefields of Papua New Guinea comes nature's own energy food. . . . The goodness of Papua New Guinea's natural cane sugar can be enjoyed by everyone." Consumption of Ramu sugar thus promises "everyone" (every individual consumer) access to one of Papua New Guinea's natural

We're proud to be your airline, PNG.

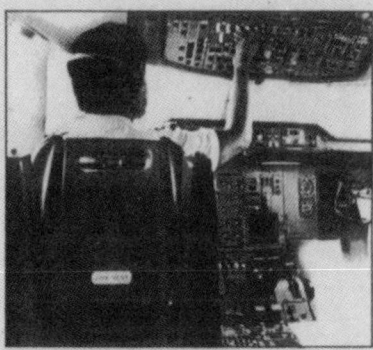

As long as PNG has been independent, we have
been the wings for the nation. Because we're the
airline owned by all the people of
Papua New Guinea.
And together with everyone in
PNG, Air Niugini is proud to celebrate on this 14th
anniversary of Independence.

Air Niugini
Our National Airline

Fig. 1.   Newspaper advertisement for Papua New Guinea's state-owned airline
(*Papua New Guinea Post Courier*, 14 September 1989)

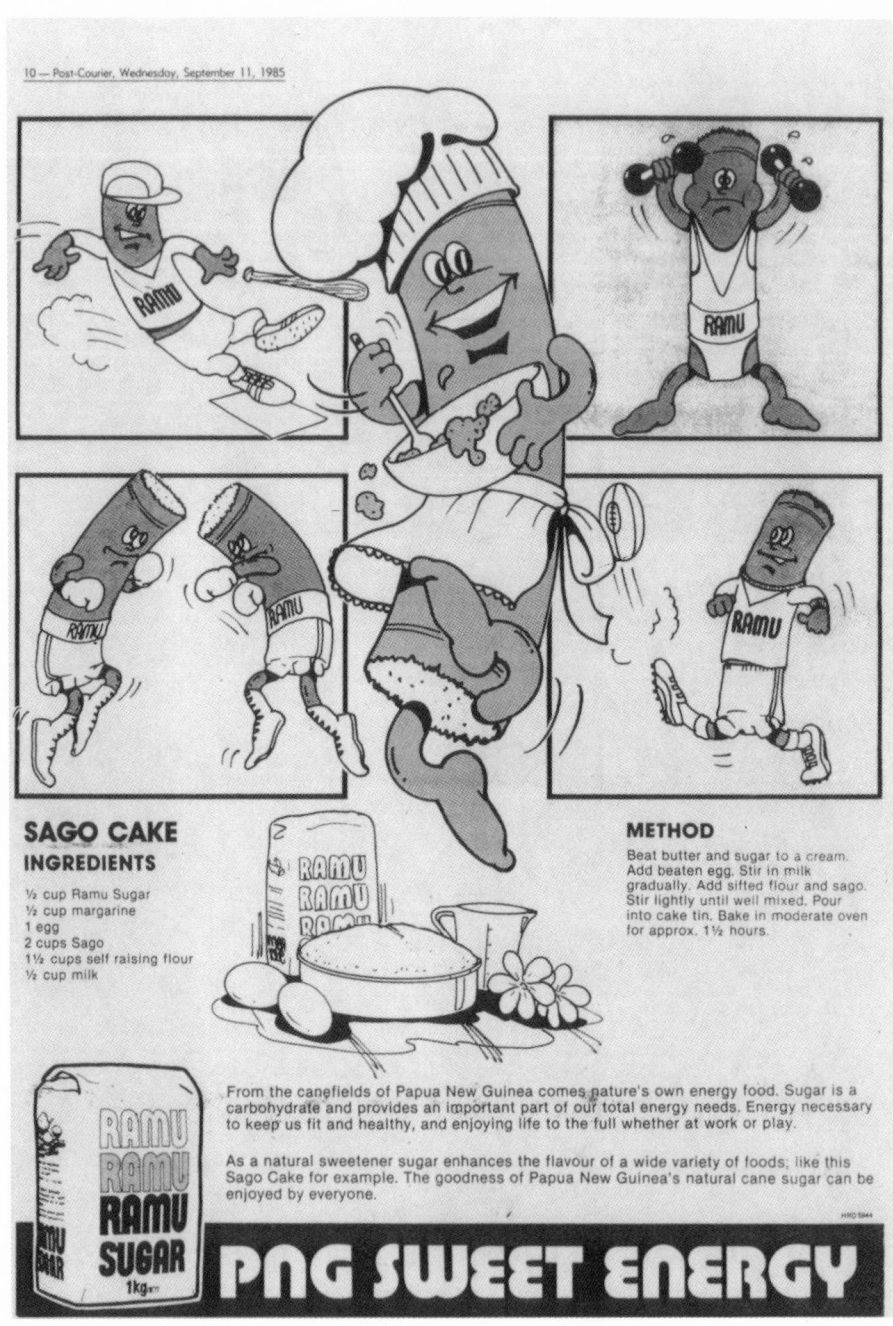

Fig. 2. Newspaper ad for the state-protected sugar industry (*Papua New Guinea Post Courier*, 11 September 1985)

KEEP OUR MONEY IN OUR COUNTRY

CREDIT CORPORATION

Credit Corporation is a 100% Nationally owned company. Invest with us - keep our money in our country and help yourself to interest up to 14.50%. Interest paid quarterly.

FIRST RANKING DEBENTURE STOCK

Write or phone now for Prospectus No. 5

Credit Corporation (PNG) Limited   Phone: 25 5100
P.O. Box 1002, Boroko.

Fig. 3. Newspaper ad for the PNG Credit Corporation (*Papua New Guinea Post Courier*, 27 January 1982)

goods. In a related sense, consumption of Ramu sugar implies consumption of Papua New Guinea itself in the form of one of the land's "natural" products.

Finally, we have two advertisements that apply the argument of national ownership to the one commodity that seems by its abstract nature impossible to nationalize, yet operates as perhaps the most potent and mundane symbol of any national community: money. At the top of an ad for the Papua New Guinea Credit Corporation (fig. 3) runs the heading KEEP OUR MONEY IN OUR COUNTRY. Beneath this advice is a picture of the national flag and a logo of the Credit Corporation. The text reads:

Credit Corporation is a 100% Nationally owned company. Invest with us—keep our money in our country and help yourself to interest up to 14.50%.

Likewise, an ad for the Papua New Guinea Banking Corporation (fig. 4) appeared with the slogan, "Our country, our bank, celebrating together." At the center of the ad is a photograph of a female bank employee, proffering money in a gesture that extends beyond the border of the picture. The reader is implicitly positioned as the recipient of this gift, just as the ad for Air Niugini positions the reader as the recipient of the ticket and the cup of coffee.[8]

Currency, the means of consumption, not only objectifies "the nation," whether in the iconographic forms of pigs and pearlshells or of Michael Somare and the Parliament House—the 50-kina note depicted in the PNG Banking Corporation (PNGBC) ad. Currency also symbolizes the nation-state as one entity in a system of such entities. It is entirely appropriate that the notes proffered by the woman in the PNGBC ad include samples of U.S. and Japanese money, and that the same ad could appear in the in-flight magazine of Air Niugini (*Paradise*, January 1992), captioned "The First Bank You See in PNG," as information for visitors seeking to convert currency. The use of currency, then, practically affirms the existence of a bounded community of consumers, the borders of which are defined by the extent to which the territorial state authorizes the currency as legal tender.

I would suggest that many Papua New Guineans sense these borders despite never having physically crossed them. Their intuition takes the often reported form of stories about the unease people felt at the time of independence when it became necessary to convert Australian dollars into PNG kina. Similarly, I have heard village men in New Ireland recount the history of colonialism and political independence in terms of currency transitions: first we had marks, then pounds, then dollars, now kina. These same villagers would also make sense of inflation in terms of the transition from Australian dollars to PNG kina, accounting for the relatively weak purchasing power of their money to a perceived weakness of the independent government of PNG relative to Australia. Often they would ask me if there were a different kind of money in America, or comment ironically when I informed them that PNG currency and coinage are produced abroad.

It is important to recognize, nonetheless, that the nationalization of commodities is by no means monopolized by the state. The rhetoric of national ownership also appears in an advertisement for Word Publishing Company (fig. 5) that gives an interesting twist to Anderson's observation about the mass ceremony of newspaper reading. The caption asserts:

Fig. 4. Newspaper ad for PNG Banking Corporation (*Papua New Guinea Post Courier*, 14 September 1989)

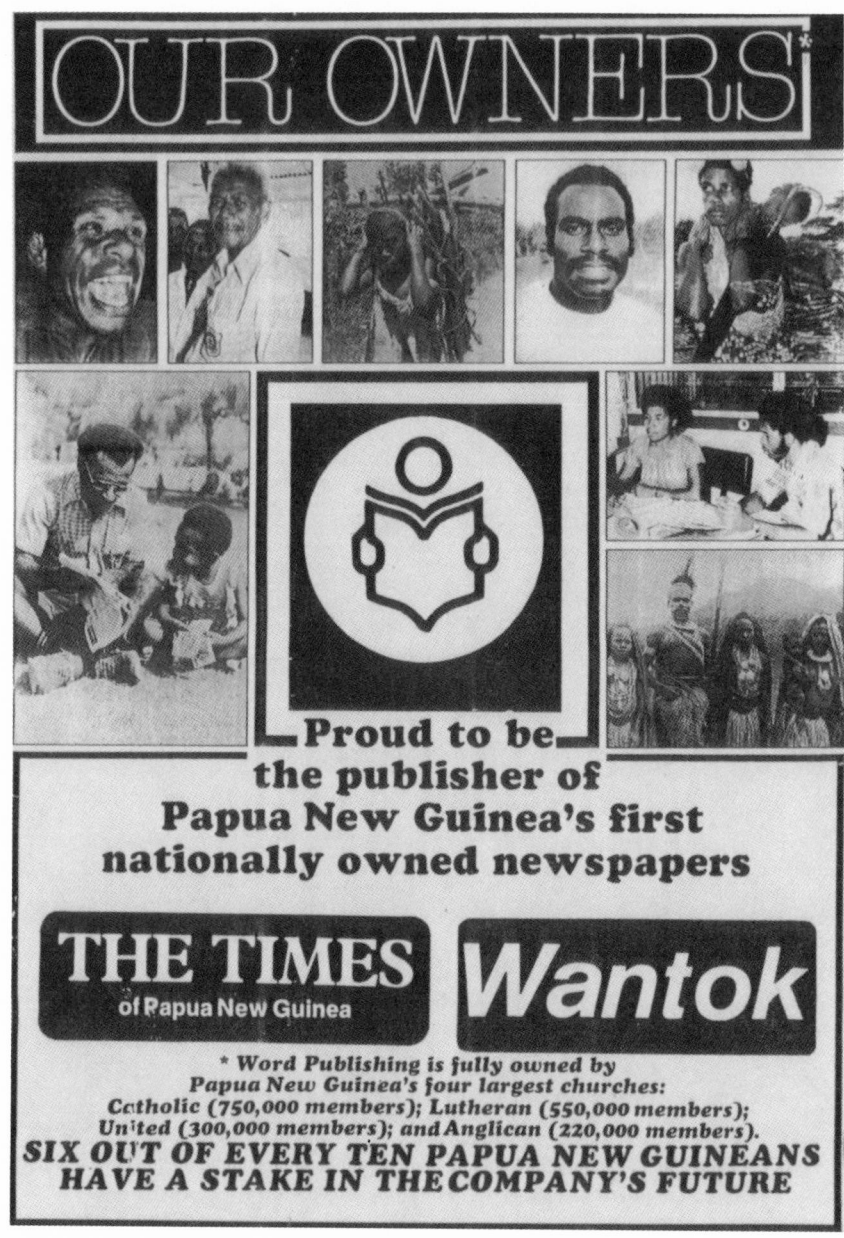

Fig. 5. Newspaper ad for the paper's publisher (*Times of Papua New Guinea*, 11 January 1986)

OUR OWNERS. Underneath are eight snapshots of men and women in urban and rural settings, some dressed in blouses and shorts, others in grass skirts and feathers. The ad claims that Word Publishing is "Proud to be the publisher of Papua New Guinea's first nationally owned newspapers" (the *TPNG* and *Wantok*), and informs the reader that Word Publishing is "fully owned by Papua New Guinea's four largest churches: Catholic (750,000 members); Lutheran (550,000 members); United (300,000 members); and Anglican (220,000 members)." It concludes that "Six out of Every Ten Papua New Guineans Have a Stake in the Company's Future."

What this ad does, semiotically speaking, is to reconcile its own depicted diversity of Christian denominations and of traditional rural and modern urban dwellers through an appeal to joint ownership of the newspapers. That is, at the level of collective ownership, the enumerated members of each church are not Catholics or Lutherans but, rather, Papua New Guineans, all of whom have a stake in the company. Thus, reading these particular newspapers does indeed constitute a mass national ceremony, as Anderson observed, but not merely because it is a shared act of consumption. Here, the newspaper itself is presented as the quintessential national commodity.

Generic Individuals, Specific Consumers

The rhetoric of national ownership makes certain presuppositions about the nature of objects and persons, presuppositions revealed in the following meta-advertisement (fig. 6). Placed by Word Publishing in its *Times of Papua New Guinea*, the ad attempts to persuade other advertisers to buy space in Word's Pidgin-language newspaper, the weekly *Wantok*. At the top in large letters: "He likes to eat RICE and TINFISH." On the left, a large caricature of a man dressed in "traditional" style (grass skirt, feather headdress, and a bone through his nose), carrying a bulging briefcase with several kina notes carelessly sticking out. To the right of this, a text:

> OH! and he . . .
> SHOPS at major department stores, buys different FOODS, likes SOFT DRINKS, enjoys SMOKING CIGARETTES, has a family to feed and CLOTHE, sends his kids to SCHOOL, he owns a CAR, has his own HOME, has money invested in a BANK and in his spare time he likes to play SPORT and listen to MUSIC

Fig. 6. Newspaper ad in English-language paper for PNG's only Pidgin-language paper (*Times of Papua New Guinea*, 8 March 1986)

OH! . . .

and one other thing that advertisers tend to forget—he speaks Pidgin, 90% of the time, as his natural language— unlike English!

Make sure you advertise cost effectively!

There are 2,000,000 Others like him in Papua New Guinea!

Alongside the name *Wantok* at the bottom of the ad are the concluding words, "The only Pidgin newspaper in PNG[.] Ridiculous isn't it?"

Here is a succinct definition of the prototypic consumer-citizen or, somewhat differently, the essential consumer-citizen (apparently male) who underlies the celebrated manifest diversity of PNG's population. At this level of description, the consumer-citizen is generic and virtual, a potential waiting to be realized in the specific forms of specific consumption practices and fantasies. That is, at this level, all consumer-citizens are identical, potential participants in a national marketplace. I would argue that this conception of a generic individual is similar to the conception of a generic human being, endowed with certain inalienable rights, that is promoted by the state in a variety of other contexts, such as state-sponsored campaigns of civil education, trials, and elections (Foster 1992; introduction; LiPuma this volume).

Furthermore, the ad implies that generic individuals distinguish themselves from each other through the work of consuming or appropriating particular objects (Carrier 1990a, 1991; Miller 1988). Such work incorporates these objects into the consumer's definition of his or her social self or personhood. But this implication, in turn, implies a world of anonymous or "neutral" objects, that is, objects "which could be owned by anybody and identified with anybody" (Gell 1986, 113)—in short, a world of personless objects. Of course, this world is no more than the necessary complement of a world of objectless persons, the generic and virtual individuals awaiting specification and realization through acts of consumption that attach objects and persons to each other. "Ownership" or "having" is the means for attaching specific qualities to an otherwise generic persona.

Here I would argue that this view of persons and objects, a view communicated by the rhetorical argument of all ads, directly challenges conventional Melanesian views of objects and persons (Hirsch this volume). On the one hand, the Melanesian person is relational, the precipitate (or node) of numerous and particular social relations (Strathern

1988). This particularity is irreducible, such that the concept of generically identical persons is ordinarily unimaginable.

On the other hand, since the 1925 publication of *The Gift*, anthropologists have been aware of the way in which, for Melanesians, persons and objects generally implicate each other. This is a matter of neither mysticism nor animism. Rather, it is a correlate of social practices—most notably, gift exchange—that embed objects in definite social relations (see Carrier 1990b). That is, there are no unattached or "neutral" objects, objects that could be identified or owned by "anybody."

Nation and Culture as Commodity

One of the effects of the logic of persons and objects operating in ads is to open up the possibility of rendering the nation as a "neutral" object awaiting attachment via consumption to a "neutral" or generic consumer (see Jourdan this volume on the "neutrality" of popular culture). An ad for Nestlé products, also in the special 1989 Independence Day issue of the *Post Courier*, illustrates this possibility (fig. 7). Although part of a transnational corporation, Food Specialities (PNG) Pty Ltd. employs the rhetorical strategy of collective ownership and presents itself as a Papua New Guinea manufacturer. The ad features a drawing of Nescafé Niugini Blend instant coffee, the label of which promises the consumer a beverage made of "100% PNG Coffee." The implication of the ad is that just as the producer and the product are qualified as "100% PNG," likewise will the consumer be qualified.

Perhaps this implication was all the more obvious to an audience already familiar with previously circulated ads that promoted the slogan "PNG Coffee—For PNG People!" Among the ads in this campaign to sell coffee beans grown in the Highlands there appeared one (fig. 8), framed by coffee beans, that illustrated in nine steps "How PNG People Make & Enjoy PNG Coffee." The ad functioned as an instruction manual for making a cup of coffee from scratch, depicting in step-by-step fashion a consumption practice ascribed to PNG people in general. By contrast, another ad in the campaign publicized "PNG's Magnificent 5," five different named brands of PNG coffee (No. 1, Goroka, Namasu, Okka, and Koroma) available for PNG people to consume. Uniformity and similarity are thus portrayed with respect to the generic practice of coffee consumption, while singularity and difference are offered through the consumption of particular brands.

As a sponsor we
are glad to help...

As a Papua New Guinea
manufacturer we are proud
to be involved in...

THE HIRI MOALE FESTIVAL

Food Specialties (PNG) Pty Ltd

Fig. 7.   Newspaper ad for Nestlé products (*Papua New Guinea Post Courier*, 14 September 1989)

Let us return, however, to the Food Specialities ad (fig. 7). It identifies Food Specialties as a sponsor of the Hiri Moale Festival, an independence weekend event in which the Boera villagers of Port Moresby staged songs and dances for themselves and visitors. The *Post Courier* of 14 September 1989 described these songs and dances as "some of the oldest . . . in Boera history," and one old Boera man is quoted as saying, "We do not want to see any exaggerated or made-up dances that do not reflect our culture." The juxtaposition of commodity and "culture" in this context valorizes the advertised products as national commodities by associating them with "authentic" native traditions. This valorization occurs despite the fact that the "authentic" tradition in question is not Papua New Guinean, but Boera, for the definition of the national culture implied in the ad is one of a repertoire of diverse "traditions." That is, each tradition is construed as a variable item in the total inventory of traditions—a brand of tradition. Put otherwise, tradition is itself given the form of the commodity with which it is juxtaposed: discrete, objectified, and valuable on account of its intrinsic properties (see Babadzan 1988; Facey this volume).

There could be no clearer demonstration of the commodification of tradition than an ad campaign for Benson and Hedges cigarettes from the early 1970s, on the eve of formal political independence in 1975. In one set of ads, artsy pictures of various locally made artifacts (such as Sepik carvings) were juxtaposed with a picture of a pack of B&H cigarettes. The

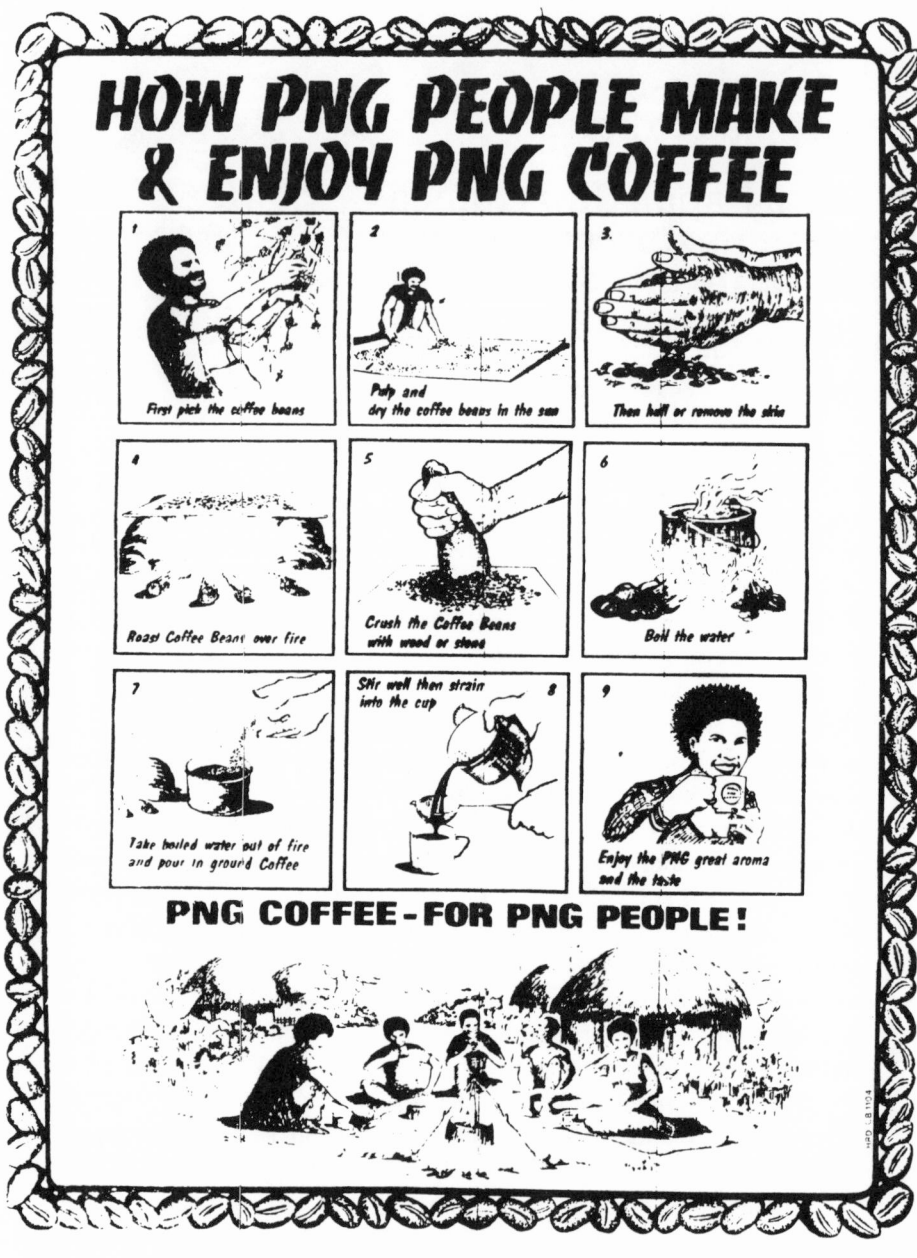

Fig. 8. Newspaper ad promoting consumption of PNG coffee (*Papua New Guinea Post Courier*, 1 October 1980)

caption of the ad announced: "From the Benson and Hedges collection." At the bottom of the ad ran the rhetorical question: "When only the best will do . . . and isn't that all of the time?" The symbolic equation of carving with cigarette pack effects a semantic transfer in which the presumably "traditional" carvings are evaluated as "modern" commodities ("the best") and thereby rendered as a thing to be possessed or collected.[9] Reciprocally, the pack of cigarettes is domesticated and rendered indigenous, an element of local culture.

Precisely this process of metaphorical equation making surfaced in the overdetermined symbolism of a parallel set of ads for a cigarette called Paradise Gold. Two of these ads appeared in December 1974. The first ad is captioned in large block letters: "I AM PAPUA NEW GUINEA." Beneath this is a picture of the Rabaul harbor and, further below to the left, a picture of the product: a pack of cigarettes in a gold box, stamped with a bird of paradise logo. To the right of the product is the following text:

I am the rugged mountain range
I am the field of waving grass
I am the mighty river that flows to the sea
I am the towns and the people of this proud land
And my cigarette is Paradise Gold

Here, the nation, in a soliloquy that equates natural features of the land and human occupants of the same land, discloses its preference for Paradise Gold. That is, the nation itself discloses its preference to smoke, because Paradise Gold is nothing so much as a material embodiment of the nation.

Another ad for Paradise Gold, which appeared in the 11 December 1974 *PC*, sounded these same themes in a slightly different key. The ad "contains" snapshot scenes from a variety of broadly identifiable locales: Rabaul, the Highlands, Port Moresby, Madang, and Lae.[10] Its caption is an invitation, or perhaps a command: "Discover the quality and value of this cigarette made specially for the people of Papua New Guinea." The text continues: "A fine taste of selected high quality tobaccos, presented in a superb personal gold pack. A cigarette to be proud of—a true symbol of Papua New Guinea today." At the bottom of the ad runs the predictable conclusion: "Paradise Gold belongs to Papua New Guinea."

The semiotic form of this particular ad accomplishes what I am arguing that mass-consumption practices have the potential to accomplish more generally: a reconstitution of social geography. A diversity of disjunct locales (communities) are brought into relationship with each other through their shared relationship to some single object of consumption.[11] The "people of Papua New Guinea" emerge as a collectivity—a nation—only in relation to the cigarette made for their consumption. That is, the nation takes the form of a collection of people united by the commodities they jointly possess and consume in common. What are the implications of this definition of collective identity for the definition of personal identity and interpersonal relations? How does a national community of consumption define relations among its citizens?

Totemism: Nationalizing the Commodity

To some extent, the answer to these questions follows inevitably from defining the nation as a community of consumption; for when such consumption occurs within the context of a capitalist mode of production, the nation comprises a collectivity of commodity buyers. To advertise a fish-flavored biscuit—perhaps the paradigmatic Papua New Guinean product—as "Number 1 in PNG" or "New to PNG" is to define PNG as, above all, a delimited marketplace. The citizens of PNG, in turn, are defined as consumers, people who affirm their membership in the nation through commodity consumption.

Commodity consumption, as I have argued, attaches specific qualities to generic individuals. It also predicates relations among such individuals by categorizing them as either fellow consumers, and thus alike, or as consumers with unshared consumption practices, and thus different. These alternatives are not exclusive; consumers who share consumption practices with regard to one commodity (say, coffee) might differ with regard to the brand of coffee they consume (Goroka versus Namasu). Likewise, consumers of a common brand of coffee might differ in their consumption of other commodities (such as tobacco). The possibilities of similarity and difference with other consumers are potentially infinite, and it is this infinite potential that makes it possible for consumers to create for themselves a *specific* individuality. By attaching to one's person, in a continuous act of consumerist bricolage, a unique ensemble of qualities, one can aspire to distinction.

Three ads illustrate how commodity consumption introduces new criteria for differentiating and individualizing persons—how commodity consumption can provide the means for producing simultaneously both a national consumption community *and* subcommunities of consumption.

The first ad (fig. 9) appeared as a billboard on the side of a small shack not far from the government office buildings in Waigani, next to a path that connected these buildings to a Public Motor Vehicle (PMV) stop on Waigani Drive. Various workers from the surrounding offices, as well as people seeking government services, frequented the shack to buy soft drinks, snacks, and cigarettes. The ad is for a coarse cut tobacco called Gold. It pictures two hands, apparently a man's, rolling up some tobacco in a piece of newspaper—perhaps a piece of the classifieds from the *Sydney Morning Herald*, available in many rural tradestores. The caption reads EM NAU, a multivalent Tok Pisin (pidgin) phrase that here expresses an interjection of satisfaction and a recognition of appropriateness on the order of "That's it" or "Perfect."

This cigarette is a popular item of both urban and bush consumption. The ad thus depicts a consumption fantasy with extremely wide geographical distribution. It is accessible primarily to readers of Tok Pisin, but perhaps to nonliterate viewers as well. Moreover, its elliptical form evokes almost entirely through connotation a shared bodily experience, an element of the habitus characteristic of the community of consumption defined by the ad (see Löfgren 1989b). This community is a community of shared tastes and smells. By articulating these otherwise unobjectified sensations, the ad re-presents to people a particular routine—rolling tobacco in a patch of newspaper—as typical of the collective praxis of Tok Pisin speakers. By associating this routine with Gold tobacco, a commodity produced and distributed in Papua New Guinea, the ad makes the boundaries of its implicit community of consumption coterminous with the product's market.

The second ad illustrating our purpose and presented earlier (fig. 2), for Ramu sugar, publicizes a commodity widely, if not universally, available—indeed, the only brand of sugar available in PNG. Ramu Sugar is thus a paradigmatic national commodity ("PNG Sweet Energy"), the consumption of which "can be enjoyed by everyone" and the enjoyment of which constitutes participation in the PNG community of consumption.[12] But notice the recipe for sago cake that appears in the ad. Certain ingredients of the cake—milk and margarine—presume access to a supermarket; it is unlikely that sago cake will be a popular item of bush consumption. To what extent, then, is this recipe an index of an emergent set of urban, middle-class consumption practices? Is this an

Fig. 9. Billboard in Waigani advertising coarse cut tobacco sold
in Papua New Guinea (Nancy F. Foster)

image of the collective expenditures that unite middle-class urban dwellers into a single community of consumption (Jourdan this volume)?
Apparently, the same commodity consumed nationwide provides the
means for defining a less inclusive community of consumption. This
"subcommunity" would be characterized by relatively different habitus,
a differently routinized set of tastes and associations.

That such middle-class consumption practices have taken a discernible enough shape to be parodied is evidenced by a calendar illustration done by Bob Browne, originator of the celebrated Grass Roots comic strip. As shown in figure 10, it depicts "What all the Young Village Kids are Getting Educated to Become: the Yuppies." Note here that these Yuppies synthesize in their consumption practices elements of both a global or transnational marketplace—Walkmans, running shoes, American television programs, instant noodles—and objects with a more local reference—tinned meat and designer-label laplaps. Likewise, the sago cake is identifiably local but at the same time unattributable to any particular local cuisine (say, Baktaman or Iatmul). Is the sago cake one homely item in an evolving national cuisine, that is, an element in a consumer life-style that is neither wholly local nor wholly imported? The question points to one of the tensions inherent in the relationship between mass consumption and national culture: the massive introduction of objects and images produced abroad (Indo-Mie Noodles, Nike jogging shoes, American TV shows) generates a shared experience that transcends local particularity, but which also potentially effaces national particularity. The national community imagined through mass consumption is thus inherently unstable, always threatening either to fragment into subcommunities of consumption or to melt imperceptibly into the transnational flow of commercial images and objects (see Foster 1991).

The third and final ad in our illustration (fig. 11) similarly presents a consumption fantasy with extremely restricted distribution. The ad appeared in *Paradise*, the in-flight magazine of Air Niugini. It is for POSH (Protocol & Overseas Service Hospitality), an agency that provides, among other things, a personalized service for VIPs, executives, overseas visitors and business travelers; hotel and air travel bookings; and air-conditioned, chauffeured cars for city and country trips. Presumably, this ad is intended as much, if not more so, for overseas visitors to PNG as for the small number of local business executives who might purchase the service for their clients. Its caption reads: "When you need to arrive in style . . ." and despite the association with the National Parliament Building (see Rosi 1991) promotes a rather undemocratic, exclusionary sentiment. Style is available to all who have the means to purchase it, but presumably if this were everyone, then style would no longer be style.

Clearly, the advertisement for POSH reiterates that consumption practices and fantasies furnish people with the means for distinguishing

Fig. 10.   Calendar illustration by Bob Browne, circa 1989, parodying middle-class consumption practices in Papua New Guinea (Grass Roots Comic Company)

When you need to arrive in style...

- A *personalised service for VIPs, executives, overseas visitors and businessmen*
- *Programme of meetings and visits arranged*
- *Hotel and air travel bookings made*
- *Met on arrival and assisted through formalities by arrangement*
- *Trips to other parts of the country arranged*
- *Airconditioned chauffeured cars available for city and country trips*

FOR THIS SERVICE WE DO RECOMMEND AN ADVANCE BOOKING

"We are proud to be the leaders in this type of service and we are confident that you will not be disappointed..."

Fig. 11. Magazine ad for travel service agency (*Paradise* 49 [November 1984])

themselves from other people as well as for establishing an imagined similarity or commonality. "The Yuppies" likewise distinguish themselves from village consumer-citizens in their personal dislikes—items stereotypically consumed by villagers: kaukau (sweet potato) and tinned fish. Yet, this sort of differentiation is no more than the complement of the kind of assimilation represented in ads such as the one for Paradise Gold, ads that subsume different locales under the unifying image of a single commodity. If in one case similarity is achieved through shared consumption practices (see note 10), in the other case diversity is achieved through the consumption of different commodities. In both instances—and this is my point—personal identity and interpersonal relations are effectively defined in and through relationship to consumer commodities. Otherwise generic consumer-citizens take on various individualized identities through the various consumer commodities possessed or owned. A new mode for constituting personal identities thus accompanies the establishment of a collective national identity in the form of a community of consumption.

Concluding Questions

Linnekin and Poyer (1990) have made the case that "ethnicity" should be understood to connote a specific ethnotheory of cultural identity rather than some universal feature of social life. This ethnotheory, they explain, rests upon a distinctive ontogeny, or perhaps even ontology—a set of presuppositions about what constitutes a person and what determines collective identities. Its most salient characteristic, in their view, is the privilege given to the "biological inheritance of substance as the determinant of identity" (1990, 7). This presupposition can be broadly contrasted with ethnotheories of identity that privilege environment, behavior, and situational flexibility—ethnotheories that Linnekin and Poyer claim underwrite Pacific conceptions of personhood and community.

For my purposes, the more relevant feature of the ethnotheory of ethnicity is its preoccupation with discrete, bounded individuals (persons or groups), the identity of which derives from putatively innate and essential characteristics. Louis Dumont has long identified this preoccupation as indicative of modern egalitarian individualism, an ideology that renders as "given" the existence of bounded, unitary, categorical individuals. Recently, Richard Handler (1988) has extended Dumont's observations by noting the logical congruence between nationalism and (possessive) individualism; both define integrated, autonomous units as primordial entities.

My questions, then, are these: Are such ontological presuppositions being communicated as an aspect of nation making in the new Melanesian states? If so, how?

I leave aside here the question of whether presuppositions about bounded, categorical personal and collective identities are a necessary feature of all versions of "the nation" (Kapferer 1988; Kelly this volume). Instead, I want to suggest that such presuppositions are indeed being communicated in Papua New Guinea, at least, and communicated in a number of ways. Perhaps the most visible of these ways is the undertaking of the state to expose people through formal schooling and periodic public campaigns to a moral ideal of citizenship based on the inalienable human rights of all individuals (Foster 1992). But perhaps the most effective of these communications is one that is more subtle.

I refer here to the way in which the ontological presuppositions of capitalism and nationalism interpenetrate and reinforce each other. As LiPuma (this volume) points out, "the association of the nation with commodities"—explicitly rendered in some advertisements—"objectifies the nation in such a way as to imbue it with the properties of capitalist commodities": discrete, bounded, intrinsically valuable—a reality apart from and independent of its creators. He continues:

> When linked and likened to a commodity, the nation appears to be "objective" rather than socially constituted; it appears as primordial rather than historical; it appears as "necessary" rather than contingent; and it appears as a unified, autonomous reality.

In this sense, then, participation in mass commodity consumption potentially functions as a practical training ground for the development of a national style of consciousness (as defined in note 6), for such participation conditions one to the presuppositions of categorical identity that define what a nation is and what a national citizen is. Not only is the world of commodities a world of bounded, external objects, but it also is a world in which subjects are related to such objects only externally, by "having" them. One "belongs to" a nation or "possesses" a national culture much as one has or possesses commodities. When such "having" (or "not having") becomes the dominant, taken-for-granted mode in which one relates to the object world, the idea of being a national citizen who "has" and/or "needs" a national culture follows unproblematically.

ACKNOWLEDGMENTS

I thank the following institutions for supporting my research on nationalism and national culture in Papua New Guinea: the Center for International Studies, University of Chicago; the National Endowment for the Humanities; the American Council of Learned Societies; and the Australian-American Educational Foundation. This essay has benefited from the comments of James Carrier and of audiences at seminar presentations at the University of Sydney, the University of Adelaide, Australian National University, and Curtin University.

NOTES

1. Diro, then a backbench-member of Parliament (MP) from Central Province, was both deputy prime minister and head of the People's Action party until a scandal over corruption forced his resignation in 1991.

2. Government delayed enforcement of the Commercial Advertising Act as the result of requests presented by local business executives to Karl Stack, then minister for industrial development, at a public meeting organized by the Chamber of Commerce in July 1985 (*Papua New Guinea Post Courier*, 29 July 1985). A grace period of 540 days, into 1987, was subsequently approved by Parliament (*Post Courier*, 19 November 1985). In 1990, then Communications Minister Brown Sinamoi announced that he would use the provisions of the act to stop the overseas production of company and annual reports (*Pacific Islands Monthly*, February 1990).

3. Thus, for example, the inclusion of a picture of a jar of Vegemite in the video that introduces visitors to the mission of the National Museum of Australia in Canberra, and the postcard reproduction of a Sunlight soap advertisement from the 1920s on sale at the souvenir stand.

4. This approach converges at points with that taken by Karl Deutsch in his *Nationalism and Social Communication* (1966 [1953]). Deutsch argues that the ability to communicate effectively defines membership in a *people* or *nation* (terms that are not synonymous for Deutsch). He stresses, moreover, that such communicative efficiency does *not* require a shared language. Alternative "facilities," including, I suggest, primarily visual advertisements and shared consumption practices, equally enable social communication—mutual understanding of memories, associations, habits, and preferences. I emphasize, however, that

shared "language" for communication does not imply social solidarity; shared languages facilitate arguments and disagreements as well as consensus.

5. If consumers do not recognize this by no means self-evident rhetoric, then they will not be able to decode the message of an ad, that is, to recognize the ad *as an ad*. While this might seem a moot point in, say, the contemporary United States, it is particularly germane in contemporary Papua New Guinea, especially rural Papua New Guinea. However, note that consumers who contest, reject, or obviate the message of an ad nonetheless respond to the ad's rhetorical devices.

6. Consider in this regard Deutsch's (1966 [1953], 172) definition of national consciousness: "National consciousness . . . is the attachment of secondary symbols of nationality to primary items of information moving through channels of social communication. Not wit, but 'French wit'; not thoroughness, but 'German thoroughness'; not ingenuity, but 'American ingenuity . . .'"

7. See Filer (1985) for some informed speculation on the identity of the readership of the *PC*. I would emphasize that although the newspaper reaches only 3 to 4 percent of the total population, its main constituency includes the urban-dwelling politicians, bureaucrats, and business people with most access to the financial and technical means for nation making in Papua New Guinea (see, for example, fig. 6; cf. Anderson's remarks about the "reading classes" of nineteenth-century Europe [1983, 73 ff.]). Put differently, its main constituency is the emerging middle class of urban Papua New Guinea—the population of main concern in this chapter.

8. Both ads seem to have been produced by the same firm, Samuelson Talbot.

9. The tradition-versus-modernity contrast appeared more explicitly in other cigarette ads from the same period that juxtaposed pictures of Highlands-style round houses with the Port Moresby skyline.

10. This motif was used more recently in Toyota's "Wheels for the Nation" campaign, in which ads picture different types of Toyota trucks in various locales.

11. In this regard, it is possible to compare the pilgrimages of colonial administrators (from province X to capital to province Y) that Anderson (1983) interprets as a potent force in first making a national community imaginable to the journey of Jumbo, the elephant sponsored by South Pacific beer. Jumbo traveled from Lae to the Mount Hagen show, stopping at various towns along the way, in a procession that linked communities through reference to the beer. Jumbo's movements were regularly reported in the *Post Courier*, thus linking newspaper readers throughout the country to the elephant's progress (*PC*, 31 July 1973, 1 August 1973).

12. The anthropologist James Carrier, in his reader's report on this volume, reminded me that the introduction of Ramu raw mill sugar and the disappearance of CSR (Australian made) refined sugar were not greeted happily by many Papua New Guineans, who thought the more expensive domestic product compared unfavorably with its foreign predecessor. These consumers might well reject the message about enjoyment communicated in the ad. But—and this is

my point more generally—to reject the message about enjoyment is not necessarily to reject the implicit message about Ramu sugar being a commodity owned by the nation; indeed, it could be because a consumer has accepted the implicit message that the person is aggravated by the claims of the explicit message— that is, Ramu sugar might be perceived as an inferior national commodity and hence a poor reflection on "the nation." This perception of Ramu as a national commodity was in any case evinced in some of the letters to the *Post Courier* that expressed support for the product.

REFERENCES

Anderson, Benedict. 1983. *Imagined Communities: Reflections on the Origin and Spread of Nationalism*. London: Verso.
Appadurai, Arjun. n.d. Communities of consumption: Public life in contemporary India. Typescript.
Babadzan, Alain. 1988. *Kastom* and nation building in the South Pacific. In R. Guidieri, F. Pellizi, and S. J. Tambiah, eds., *Ethnicities and Nations: Processes of Interethnic Relations in Latin America, Southeast Asia, and the Pacific*, 199–228. Austin: University of Texas Press.
Boorstin, Daniel. 1973. *The Americans: The Democratic Experience*. New York: Random House.
Bronner, Simon J., ed. 1989. *Consuming Visions: Accumulation and Display of Goods in America, 1880–1920*. New York: W. W. Norton.
Carrier, James. 1990a. The symbolism of possession in commodity advertising. *Man*, n.s., 25:693–706.
———. 1990b. Reconciling commodities and personal relations in industrial society. *Theory and Society* 19:579–98.
———. 1991. Gifts, commodities, and social relations: A Maussian view of exchange. *Sociological Forum* 6:119–36.
Comaroff, John. 1987. Of totemism and ethnicity: Consciousness, practice, and the signs of inequality. *Ethnos* 52:301–23.
Deutsch, Karl. 1966 [1953]. *Nationalism and Social Communication: An Enquiry into the Foundations of Nationality*. Cambridge: MIT Press.
Ewen, Stuart, and Elizabeth Ewen. 1982. *Channels of Desire: Mass Images and the Shaping of American Consciousness*. New York: McGraw-Hill.
Filer, Colin. 1985. What is this thing called "brideprice"? In D. Gardner and N. Modjeska, eds., *Recent Studies in the Political Economy of Papua New Guinea*. Special Issue, *Mankind* 15:163–83.
Foster, Robert J. 1991. Making national cultures in the global ecumene. *Annual Review of Anthropology* 20:235–60.
———. 1992. Take care of public telephones: Moral education and nation-state formation in Papua New Guinea. *Public Culture* 4:31–45.
Fox, Richard Wightman, and T. J. Jackson Lears, eds. 1983. *The Culture of Consumption: Critical Essays in American History, 1880–1980*. New York: Pantheon Books.

Gell, Alfred. 1986. Newcomers to the world of goods: Consumption among the Muria Gonds. In Arjun Appadurai, ed., *The Social Life of Things*, 110–38. Cambridge: Cambridge University Press.

Handler, Richard. 1985. On having a culture: Nationalism and the preservation of Quebec's *patrimoine*. In G. W. Stocking Jr., ed., *Objects and Others: Essays on Museums and Material Culture*, 192–217. Madison: University of Wisconsin Press.

———. 1988. *Nationalism and the Politics of Culture in Quebec*. Madison: University of Wisconsin Press.

Kapferer, Bruce. 1988. *Legends of People, Myths of State: Violence, Intolerance, and Political Culture in Sri Lanka and Australia*. Washington: Smithsonian Institution Press.

Keesing, Roger M. 1989. Creating the past: Custom and identity in the contemporary Pacific. *Contemporary Pacific* 1:19–42.

Leiss, William, Stephen Kline, and Sut Jhally. 1990. *Social Communication in Advertising: Persons, Products, and Images of Well Being*. New York: Routledge.

Linnekin, Jocelyn. 1990. The politics of culture in the Pacific. In Jocelyn Linnekin and Lin Poyer, eds., *Cultural Identity and Ethnicity in the Pacific*, 149–73. Honolulu: University of Hawaii Press.

Linnekin, Jocelyn, and Lin Poyer. 1990. Introduction. In Jocelyn Linnekin and Lin Poyer, eds., *Cultural Identity and Ethnicity in the Pacific*, 1–16. Honolulu: University of Hawaii Press.

Löfgren, Orvar. 1989a. Anthropologizing America (review essay). *American Ethnologist* 16:366–74.

———. 1989b. The nationalization of culture. *Ethnologia Europaea* 19:5–24.

Miller, Daniel. 1987. *Material Culture and Mass Consumption*. Oxford: Basil Blackwell.

———. 1988. Appropriating the state on the council estate. *Man*, n.s., 23:353–72.

Rosi, Pamela. 1991. Papua New Guinea's new Parliament House: A contested national symbol. *Contemporary Pacific* 3:289–324.

Strathern, Marilyn. 1988. *The Gender of the Gift: Problems with Women and Problems with Society in Melanesia*. Berkeley: University of California Press.

Williamson, Judith. 1978. *Decoding Advertisements: Ideology and Meaning in Advertisements*. New York: Marion Boyars.

Part 3
Unmaking Nations?
Local Appropriations of "the Nation"

Eric Hirsch

Local Persons, Metropolitan Names: Contending Forms of Simultaneity among the Fuyuge, Papua New Guinea

Introduction

The making of a national culture in Papua New Guinea (as in other nation-states) is, in part, a conscious project formulated and enacted by agents and agencies of the state. One of the uppermost goals of this project is to create a particular "style" of imagined community by inculcating in each citizen a notion of temporal and spatial simultaneity particular to that "national culture." A focus on this cultural project alone, however, provides too limited a perspective on the process of making a national culture, especially in Papua New Guinea, because the national culture project coexists with local cultural projects[1] that also attempt to sustain particular styles of temporal and spatial simultaneity (imagined communities). But these projects are imagined differently from that formulated in national terms. In particular, the goal of the national culture project is to reconfigure local cultural projects so that they are seen to conform to the imagined ideal—a goal often described as movement from "tradition" to "modernity" or as "development." This goal of reconfiguration exists in an uneasy relationship with the perspective and cultural logic of the local project. In most cases, it would seem, the making of a national culture is the *unintended consequence* of local cultural projects being pursued within the wider context created by the nation-state and its project of culture.

I have made such an argument in an earlier article that focused on the adoption of betel nut consumption among the Fuyuge, and in Papua New Guinea more generally (Hirsch 1990). This chapter develops the theme of unintended consequences. In particular, it will be argued that it is only by considering the *interaction* between national and local cultural projects that the making of a national culture can be understood in its

185

full complexity. In this chapter, I will suggest that a crucial site where this interaction can be studied is the contending forms of temporal and spatial simultaneity engendered in the national (metropolitan) context and in the local (village) context, particularly around the enactment of collective ritual.

Spatial Simultaneity: Taurama

In the revised edition of *Imagined Communities*, Anderson (1991) provides a series of insightful commentaries on the changing apprehensions of space associated with a nationalist consciousness. One of these is the European practice, first started in the sixteenth century, of naming places in colonized lands as "'new' versions of . . . 'old' toponyms in their lands of origin" (187). We thus find New York, New London, and New Orleans in the New World coexisting with their "older" counterparts in the Old World.

One consequence of this practice was that it provided the capacity for the "residents" (creoles) of these colonized lands to "imagine themselves as communities *parallel and comparable* to those in Europe" (Anderson 1991, 192, emphasis added). The subsequent revolutionary and nationalistic struggles in the New and then Old World were predicated on the idea of preserving this parallelism and simultaneity; as Anderson stresses, the intention was to rearrange the distribution of power within the former empire, not to keep the empire intact. The novelty of this trend was that in empires from former times, the dream was often of replacing the old center with a new one (191).[2] Anderson's discussion highlights some of the "spatial" preconditions for the emergence of a trend toward nation making and national consciousness.

What is suggestive about Anderson's discussion of spatial simultaneity is the way it shares similarities with the ethnographic situation described in this chapter. Among the Fuyuge, the similarity arises because place-names, as derived, for example, from the PNG capital of Port Moresby, exist parallel and coterminous with their place-name counterparts in the village—not as new versions, but as what we might call "namesakes" (*yasi*). The parallelism is also meant to imply comparability, as in the European example. The example of an urban place-name in the village context does suggest that a desired redistribution of power is implicit in this practice, but it is a redistribution that is predicated on a different starting point from that of the Euro-American example.

Among the Fuyuge, who live in the mountains northwest of Port Moresby, there was a small garden called Taurama. The garden was looked after by a widower named Yavi who was about sixty years old. Yavi was considered of "chiefly" status. On many days he would go off in the morning to the garden, often accompanied by his son's wife, and return in the late afternoon with sweet potatoes for himself, his other relations, and his pigs. I asked him on a number of occasions about the name he had chosen for the garden. His remarks were to the point and not expansive. The name did derive from the place-name in Port Moresby. He had visited this place on a number of occasions and was impressed with its material and financial abundance. Other than this, he did not feel there was any more to say. He even seemed amused that I should take an interest in the name of his small garden. After all, there were a number of places throughout the valley that had names found in and around Port Moresby and other coastal locations—Elevala, Samaria, Bautam, and so on. In naming his garden Taurama, Yavi was drawing an analogy between this produce-filled metropolitan context and his own garden. We will return later to the use of such analogies in other Fuyuge contexts. A theme pursued in this chapter is that Fuyuge men and women draw on experiences, images, and names associated with the metropolitan context of Port Moresby, in particular, to recontextualize local cultural processes of spatial and temporal simultaneity.

For those not familiar with the place-names of Port Moresby, a brief word about the name Taurama is in order. Taurama is the name associated with one of the major shopping districts in the capital. Taurama Road is now one of Port Moresby's important thoroughfares, and takes its name from the conical hill at its terminus on the coast. The name Taurama conjures up, for me, an image of metropolitan life in Port Moresby—busy shops, large department and food stores, banks and the central post office, streets full of cars and people (Papua New Guinean and European), and so on. It is a place with an abundance of goods and the hustle and bustle of people engaging in money transactions. It feels very "modern."

For Papua New Guineans, depending on their own circumstances and perspective, the place may conjure up some of this image, but also one very different. From the perspective of Fuyuge men and women, to be a part of the Port Moresby Taurama is to participate in a world of market relations, commodities, and money which are greatly valued but to which access is limited in the Fuyuge context. At the same time, it is to be a part of a world where one is generally an outsider, with little means to engage in such relations, and where one does not have a place. There is thus a tension intrinsic to a place like Taurama that was repeatedly emphasized by the Fuyuge; of it being both highly desirable but also a place where one can live only according to money.

Two Models of Personhood and Agency

It is of note that the original edition of *Imagined Communities* concentrated on, among other key topics, changing apprehensions of time. In revising the book, Anderson came to realize that the original thesis "lacked its necessary coordinate" (1991, xiv). I previously drew on Anderson's discussion of temporal simultaneity as a way of discerning, from the vantage point of the Fuyuge, the emergence of a "national culture" in Papua New Guinea (Hirsch 1990). Anderson's earlier argument linked the origins of a national consciousness to the development of print capitalism and its widespread dissemination. It was this historical process that engendered both new notions of temporal simultaneity and new notions of "imagined community." He stated (with reference to the ordinary, newspaper-reading citizen of the contemporary United States):

> He has no idea what they [the other 240 million citizens] are up to at any one time. But he has complete confidence in their steady, anonymous, simultaneous activity. (1991, 26)

While Anderson's discussion focused on the consumption of print commodities and the discursive practices thus fostered, I focused on the use of marketable commodities (such as betel nut). The argument suggested that two forms of simultaneity were engendered through these practices, but they were of a nondiscursive character (Miller 1987). One form was "in time" with a metropolitan life-style, associated with the consumption of betel nut and other commodities; the other was "out of time" given the ideas of cosmological centrality construed in Fuyuge ritual and the use of betel made in this context.

In what follows, the differences of spatial and temporal simultaneity between these contexts should be seen in relation to two models of personhood and agency with which they are associated: one "modern" (Western), as primarily engendered in the metropolitan, consumer context of Port Moresby, and more generally by the institutions of the nation-state;[3] the other "Melanesian" and primarily engendered in the village-based context of Fuyuge. The Melanesian person has been described as follows:

> The [Melanesian] person is construed from the vantage points of the relations that constitute him or her; she or he objectifies and is thus revealed in those relations. The agent is construed as the one who acts because of those relationships and is revealed in his or her actions. (Strathern 1988, 273).

By contrast, the "modern" (Western) person is imagined to exist prior to her or his relationships, as a unitary self, with (universal) rights and obligations. As a consequence, the agent is someone who is responsible for her or his own actions (Strathern 1988, 141–42).

This contrast also has implications for the way we understand the person from the perspective of particular and collective relations. Strathern (1988, 278) cites the example of a Kewa (Southern Highlands) pig-kill which closely resembles similar events enacted among the Fuyuge. The focus in this example is on the presence of a visitor, observing the event from the sidelines, who has come to receive a shell or some pork:

> He scrutinises the pig killers as they make their ceremonial gifts of shells and pork. His glance unifies them, and in his view they constitute a whole. This is his value; each pig killer can, by putting himself in the spectator's place, see himself as a member of a unified group. Long before the visitor arrives on the scene, therefore, local pig killers anticipate his reactions. What will he think if he sees them make a bad job of it?

By contrast, Jameson (1991) has provided us with an interesting insight into the general character of such relationships in the metropolitan context. His formulation is predicated on the assumption that the person, as an individual, is connected to other persons or collectivities of which she or he has no immediate knowledge or experience. It is in this context that Jameson introduces the idea of a "gap" or rift to characterize this "connection." He draws on the notion of "cognitive mapping" to elucidate this idea (415–16):

> [a] gap between phenomenological perception [the local positioning
> of the individual subject] and a reality [totality of class structures in
> which she or he is situated] that transcends all individual thinking or
> experience, but which ideology . . . attempts to span or coordinate,
> to map, by means of conscious and unconscious representations.

According to Jameson, one of the dilemmas of the modern (the postmodern) individual is the extent to which this gap becomes unbridgeable with ever increasing processes of globalization and urban alienation.

In the "Melanesian" context, we can also speak of a gap between the "here and now" of phenomenological experience and an imaginary sense of absence to which the person is connected. But this gap is not spanned or coordinated, as in the modern (Western) context, by the force of ideology intent on regulating the "rights" or "obligations" of the individual through moral-legal dictates. Rather, the gap is spanned by relationships that "anticipate" the absent image(s) revealed in contexts such as collective ritual: it is in these contexts that the diverse perspectives of persons—as composed of multiple relationships—achieve a singular perspective of unity (Strathern 1988, 274–88).

This contrast between the "Melanesian" and the "Western" is not meant to indicate the existence of two pure "cultural" types. It is also not intended to suggest that "Melanesian" and "Western" denote two unrelated contexts. Rather, it is suggested that these are two contexts that have emerged as seemingly opposed (e.g., village versus city) through the advent and development of the colonial and postcolonial national state, where previously such a contrast did not exist. Through the processes associated with missionization, colonialism, and postcolonialism these two models of personhood and agency have increasingly come to contend with one another in Papua New Guinea. This essay suggests that they have come to contend around two forms of spatial and temporal simultaneity: one made increasingly visible in ritual contexts, the second through forms of metropolitan life-style and consumerism (as subsets of an emerging "national culture"). The first context is one in which a man like Yavi is very much at the center; the second context increasingly holds the attention for Fuyuge of a younger generation.

In rituals (*gab*) performed by the Fuyuge, the creation of this simultaneity is conceptualized as an "achievement" of holding things together: of men, women, and objects from diverse locales coming into a single village for the period of the ritual's enactment (see Hirsch 1994).

Men, women, and objects are thus simultaneously in the same space and at the same time for the enactment of the stages that form the images of the ritual. Upon completion of the ritual, this simultaneous spatial and temporal presence is abandoned, only to anticipate a similar ritual in a different locale in the future where such a simultaneity is again striven for. The ritual village thus creates a center which persons and objects on the periphery move toward and then again move away from; the task is to try to hold things together in order to realize this image. This is a demonstration of power (*kagava*). The process of creating an analogy between Yavi's garden and the metropolitan Taurama is, as I will indicate, implicated in this process.

In the metropolitan context, I want to suggest, another sort of simultaneity is achieved. This simultaneity has less to do with the movement of persons and objects to specific locales, one space at one time; rather, it is based on the movement of objects to different spaces, for example, domestic spaces for use (consumption) at potentially the same time. Simultaneity in this context is achieved from the perspective of the individual—from his or her distinct spatial location. The person acquires (or does not acquire) and appropriates objects via the market through money earned by wage labor. Moreover, the objects themselves are supposed to continually change—the ever-presence of newness is one of the defining features of modern consumerism (Campbell 1987). This concept of simultaneity presupposes the capacity of the person to anticipate—and, in a sense, desire—the tempo of constant change. At one level, this capacity is engendered by the work process itself, in which it is only through money that one is able to procure objects through the market. At another level, it is the market itself that displays this need for money through the ever changing range of consumables available. This sense of motion is particularly expressed through fashion, music, and the visual images of advertising. My general argument is that analogies are increasingly drawn between the first simultaneity and aspects of the second as one generation "takes the place" of the next in the Fuyuge context.

The Fuyuge

The Fuyuge are swidden horticulturalists who live in the Wharton ranges about 100 kilometers northwest of Port Moresby. The Fuyuge number around 14,000, and their population is divided among five river valleys. Each of these populations has distinct origins and migration histories.

Prior to European intervention, the Fuyuge did not conceptualize themselves as a linguistic and cultural unit. Even today, the name Fuyuge is
rarely used. Rather, the largest unit generally recognized is that of the
river valley. Men and women will speak instead of "living inside" a river
valley (for example, the Udabe, which has the largest population and
where the present research was conducted). Within each river valley, the
population is divided into a number of named units based on shared
ideas of territory and dialect. These are referred to as "places" (*bu*) or
more commonly "homes" (*em*).[4] I lived in the *em* of Visi, which has a
population of roughly 450.

The river valleys in which the Fuyuge reside are imagined through
the bodily symbolism of head and base. The imagery of head and base,
which is used to conceptualize the positioning of territorial units in the
river valley, is replicated in the way internal groupings are conceptualized. In this context, the imagery is transposed to the symbolism of a
tree or body and is given visible expression in the *gab* ritual (the word
gab can be translated as describing a notion of wholeness). The ritual is
enacted by an *em* or section of an *em* and consists of pig-killing events
and exchanges that are linked to periods of dancing and life-crisis rites.
There is an established protocol to these enactments in each *em*.

Men and women say that they come together to organize and perform a *gab* around a person known as *amede*. I translate the word amede
as "chief" (Hallpike 1977; McArthur 1971; see Wagner 1986 and his
discussion of the *orong*). A chief in turn only manifests his capacities in
the collective context of the *gab*. The Fuyuge say that without a chief,
they cannot perform the *gab,* and without the performance of a *gab*,
they cannot sustain themselves as unshameful men and women.[5] To
appear shameful is to appear inefficacious and thus without purpose.

The Fuyuge person is conceptualized as brought into being and
brought out of being through the social actions of others. Each person is
composed of skin (*hode*), which they acquire from both their father and
mother. The cultural significance of *hode* is an image. Men and women
imagine themselves as sharing a similar skin in the manner analogous to
that of a tree sharing a number of branches from a single origin or base
(see Hirsch 1994 for a more extensive discussion of this and other elements composing the person).

The Fuyuge have valorized a number of life-crisis rites associated
with personal growth and maturity and also with personal decay and
death (Hirsch 1987). These life-crisis rites in turn are associated with the

experience of ever-increasing social centeredness from growth into maturity, and then with ever-increasing peripherality from decay into death. This can also be correlated with ever-increasing and then ever-decreasing degrees of visibility and efficaciousness. The performance of these rites is never self-fulfilling, and the rites are structured around the concentrating together of persons and wealth objects from both close at hand and distant into a *gab* space. The task of such concentration is always fraught with uncertainty—depending on the will or desire of others.[6] It is in relation to such uncertainty, and particularly in the context of the *gab*, that the person of the chief is conceptualized as pivotal to achieving one talk (*av*), one work (*soso*), one mind (*sisibe*). The person, as analogous to the home, then, moves into and out of periods of uncertainly sustained spatial and temporal simultaneity.

Connecting the Local and the Metropolitan

Younger and older Fuyuge have diverse experiences of the colonial and postcolonial world. These experiences impinge on the sense they have of what the *gab* ritual should "look like" and how it should be replicated from the ancestral and mythological past. In this respect, men of a younger generation are said to "take the place" of their fathers—that is, to take their place in demonstrating the capacity to "hold things together" when the latter no longer want to make visible their efficacy through talk and action.

I did not conduct research among the Fuyuge who live outside their mountain region. At the same time, though, I talked in depth with my Fuyuge hosts about their varied urban experiences. Discussions about Port Moresby figured often in the Fuyuge village context. During periodic visits to Port Moresby, I also came across villagers who had gone to the city for stays of varying lengths, but who expressed no desire to live in the city for an extended period of time.

On one occasion, I was buying some vegetables from the market near Waigani (in Port Moresby) and noticed out of the corner of my eye someone I recognized. It turned out to be a young Visi man named Kog who was standing on the side of the market. He slowly came over and greeted me. We talked for some time about my brief stay in the city, and I asked him when he was planning to return to the village. He told me soon, in a vague sort of way. As it turned out, it was to be many more weeks before he did return. He was newly married and had left his wife in the village during his visit to the city. They had no children. He had come to Port Moresby some months earlier. The reasons he gave for leaving the village were themselves rather vague. At one level, it was about going to Port Moresby to look for money; at another level, it was about going to Port Moresby simply because it was there (see Strathern 1977 for similar observations about Hageners in Port Moresby).

With the exception of this young man, I did not recognize anyone else at the market that day. It was clear, though, that the people buying and selling produce came from a number of different regions. Many knew each other, but many did not. This is a typical place in the urban setting of Port Moresby, where goods can be exchanged for money and where people like my village friend can come and watch from the sidelines, while others engage in the transactions. This place creates a context of simultaneity that holds together the perspectives of agents from diverse locales and experiences: many who are connected by nothing else than being in this space at this particular time. Unlike the contexts in the Fuyuge, this place, as it has come into existence through European urban planning, does not "anticipate" relationships. It is where agents come for many different reasons (buying, selling, looking), but it is not implicated in their person in the way a garden leads to the feeding of guests at a ritual where exchange relationships are constituted; the garden anticipates the exchange, which anticipates further relations with persons and places (see Strathern 1988, 281).

Some months after this encounter, I was inside my village house after returning from a stay in a nearby village. The nearby village had just completed a small *gab* as a lead-up to a large *gab* that was to take place in Visi some months later. I was one of the first to return to the village, tired from many days of observing the events of the ritual. I had a cassette tape of the Pretenders and began to play it on my cassette recorder. The rock music momentarily transported me to a world outside that of the Fuyuge. A short time afterwards, a young man, Elleli, appeared at my door. He was from the neighboring *em* of Kase and was making his way back to his village from the same ritual. I turned off the music and joined him outside.

He told me how he heard the music as he came close to my house. Upon hearing the music, it made him feel a certain way inside. He described how listening to such music immediately made him think about being in Port Moresby, walking around the streets. As he said, hearing this Western music made him long to be in Port Moresby at that very moment. The music also evoked a sadness in him in relation to this longing.[7]

The sentiments about Port Moresby expressed by Elleli can be seen in relation to the small *gab* he had just left. As a young married man, with a young son, Elelli is expected to do much of the work requiring visible strength in the ritual context. But at the same time he must wait for the efficacious men (*aked*) to decide when events of the ritual will take place (pig killings, dances, distributions, and so forth). In other words, although Elleli has a clear place in the ritual, the timing and pace of the ritual are achieved by men who seem to move "too slowly." The pace and feel of Port Moresby, as exemplified by the Western music, evoke a different sense of motion.

This contrast was further highlighted by another Visi man. Dube was someone with whom I developed a very close relationship during my period of fieldwork. He explicitly expressed thoughts that someone like Elleli only seemed to be able to feel. Dube was ten to fifteen years older than Elleli and had four young children. He had worked for a period on a coastal plantation and also had experience as an unskilled laborer in Port Moresby. Since marrying, however, he only traveled to Port Moresby for short, periodic visits. Unlike the two younger men described previously, Dube no longer traveled to Port Moresby for a "walkabout" or related activities.

On a number of separate occasions, Dube expressed to me his frustration with the amount of time he thought it took to complete specific events of the *gab*. He was particularly vocal about the amount of time that dancers took to prepare their headdresses before performing. The preparations were a stage in the process of the ritual that could last anywhere from several weeks to several months. Alternatives to such lengthy preparations were known and increasingly being used in the Fuyuge context. One such alternative involved the substitution for decorated dancers performing from dusk to dawn of guitar-playing youths and an all-night "disco." Although this form of performance was not used for "major" *gab* events, Dube expressed the view that such a substitution would be a good thing. He was critical of the *aked* for allowing so much time to be "wasted" on the dances, for example, when there was other work to be done (such as growing coffee and engaging in "development").

At the same time, when Dube was asked to perform in such events, he was always "in place." His feelings of frustration originated partly, I suspect, from the more "disciplined" work regime that he had experienced on the coast and in Port Moresby. He was also frustrated, as other men and women were more generally, about the lack of a road among the Fuyuge; this lack epitomized the lack of opportunities for production of cash crops and development. As it turned out, discussions about a road to the coast figured highly during my stay among the Fuyuge. At one stage, I learned from officials in Port Moresby that there were no plans for such a road and none had been announced. In addition, the likelihood was slim of a road being planned in the future, given the relatively small population of the area and the high cost involved. Nevertheless, the hope persisted, as did the discussion around this topic.

I remember on several occasions in the village the experience of sudden and intense excitement that seemed to grip the place when word began to circulate that a road to the coast was to be started. Dube was often the first to inform me of this prospective event. Many of the men would begin to plan among themselves how they would organize the work and who would go to meet the bulldozers making their way from the coast. This sort of excitement would usually last for one to two days and gradually recede into the background to be rekindled at a future time. I was never able to discover where these rumors originated from. I suspect that men and women arriving back from Port Moresby at the small, mission airstrip (about a four-hour walk away) often brought news back from the coast which made its way down the valley. In the process of traveling over such a distance, the communication became transformed to meet certain local expectations and hopes. This particular preoccupation with a road is expressive of a more general concern among the Fuyuge. The desire for a road is related to the need the Fuyuge create for centers, for spatial and temporal simultaneity as realized in the *gab* ritual. They create the need for a center by the concept of branches of which the person is composed: the branches create the need for a base, just as a base provides the support for the branches. This is the image of *hode*, skin, the display of the capacity to hold things together where the chief is seen as pivotal (see Hirsch 1994).

The views expressed by Dube echo in a peculiar way those of others made from an outside perspective. One of the most frequent complaints found in patrol reports and as expressed by present-day officials and missionaries is the amount of time the Fuyuge are said to devote to the enactment of their rituals. This preparation for and performance of rituals is said to inhibit their involvement in producing cash crops or engaging in more "rational" pursuits with their time. In fact, specific local legislation exists restricting the amount of time that can be devoted to the killing and distribution of pigs.

The Fuyuge have over the years devised numerous techniques to circumvent these constraints and are often perplexed by the complaints of the government officials who remonstrate against their ways of raising pigs and conducting ritual. The widower Yavi exemplifies a view typical of the *aked* and of a generation that has not experienced wage labor outside of the Fuyuge context. As he expressed it to me on one occasion, "This is our way. We feed the pigs and then kill them in the *gab*. We do not know any different way."

The garden of Yavi at Taurama, we will remember, is used to cultivate sweet potatoes to feed himself, his relations, and his pigs. Each one of these pigs will find its way into a particular *gab* setting. They will be known as pigs originating from Yavi and have been fed from food grown at Taurama. This place-name is thus implicated in the relationships that constitute Yavi as a person and become visible in the various transactions in which he is involved. However, not every person is able to transform the name of a place in this way. Yavi is recognized as an *amede* who is able to speak in the center of the *gab* village plaza at key moments of the ritual. He is one of a handful of men from Visi who are widely known in other *em* throughout the valley. He is one of the men who is conceptualized as facilitating the achievement of "one talk," "one mind," and "one work" in ritual contexts where otherwise uncertainty is seen to prevail. He is able to make visible and explicit these sorts of analogies. Yavi is seen as a person who can unify the perspectives of agents originating from diverse places or contexts into the common purpose of the *gab*: he is thus able to make the diversity of places from which persons originate "cohere" in spatial-temporal simultaneity for the duration of the ritual (see next section).

By changing the name of his garden to that of Taurama, Yavi is also effecting a change in how this place is known and perceived in the minds of others. For such a change to be accomplished it must be associated with a person seen as able to effect changes in the minds of others: somebody seen as "worthy," to borrow the Usen Barok notion (Wagner 1986) that captures well a similar Fuyuge perception. Such a change would be ignored and derided if (unthinkingly) attempted by some of the younger men I have described.

Changed Contexts, Quicker Tempo

There is a historical depth to these processes which was captured by Williamson (1912) earlier this century. Williamson visited the Fuyuge (whom he refers to as Mafulu, the most southwest Fuyuge population) during 1909 for three months. He particularly noted the prominence of the *gab* ritual in Fuyuge social life. His visit was three years after the first Catholic mission station was founded in this region. In fact, the book he based on this visit, the first "ethnological" research among the Fuyuge, devotes an entire chapter to the description of a typical ritual and the events and stages involved in its performance. What is clear from his account is that a *gab* was the focal point of social life in any given locality. What is also evident is that other seemingly nonritual activities, such as pig raising, gardening, trade, and so on, anticipate the enactment and performance of the *gab*, either within the home locality or those more distant. Williamson's account is scattered with descriptions and pictures of *gab* villages in various states of use and decay. What is explicit in his account is the extent to which the Fuyuge surroundings are shaped by both the anticipation of the *gab* and the remnants of the *gab* that have been performed.

When I came to live among the Fuyuge during the mid-1980s, I was struck by the extent to which the *gab* still had a prominence in Fuyuge social life similar to that described by Williamson some seventy years earlier. I have elsewhere described a number of "changes" that have occurred in the sequencing of the ritual over this period (Hirsch 1987, 1988). At the same time, the changes that have been brought about have occurred as a way of sustaining an image of personhood and agency achieved in the *gab* context.

Prior to the 1950s, very few Fuyuge men or women had extended experience of the areas outside of their region, especially Port Moresby and the coast (the exception would be male carriers who made periodic visits to the coast to bring back goods with the missionaries). After this period, young adult men were sent to the coast on short-term contracts to work in and around Port Moresby. Since this time, movement to and from Port Moresby and other coastal areas (for example, to work on plantations for wage labor) has become a regular feature of Fuyuge social life. In this way, the continuing centrality of the *gab* ritual in the Fuyuge context has been ever increasingly framed by experiences generated outside the Fuyuge context. This was often expressed to me in polarized terms as follows: between the ways of the "whites" as exemplified in Port Moresby and the way of the "true" people (*an a tae*) as exemplified by the Fuyuge; between a life based on money and a life in which food, housing, and water are free.

A contemporary *gab* will have its origins in the life-crisis rites associated with aspects of youth and increased maturity and/or that of old age and death. What I want to touch on here is the spatio-temporal dimension implied by these processes. When men and women of an *em* or *em* section decide that they will "kill pigs" for their "sons" and "daughters" and/or "mothers" and "fathers," a place is chosen at which to construct a *gab* plaza (*endant*) and enclosing village for this purpose. This becomes the first visible sign to surrounding *em* that local social life will soon intensify around that place. The site chosen is usually a small hamlet, which is enlarged to form a plaza and to accommodate numerous houses and special men's houses, where *aked* sleep and gather to talk with *amede*, around its perimeter.

The men and women who come together to build individual houses around the plaza will at other times reside in small hamlets located in close proximity to gardens used to feed themselves and their pigs. During the time period in which the village is being constructed and for the duration of the later *gab* events, the men and women will move between this village and their more disparately located hamlets. As indicated when describing the widower Yavi, the uniting of persons for this purpose is not a self-evident fact. Men and women from their diverse vantage points (hamlets) experience a sense of collective purpose of "one mind" and "one work" (*gab*). The same holds true for the other categories of participants in the ritual: invited dancers, supporters in the pig-kill, exchange partners, and so on. Each one of these participants must be "pulled" from his or her respective place and assembled in the space of the *gab* at the appropriate time.

The manner in which this joining and concentrating is conceptualized is analogous to that of places on a common path that are brought increasingly together. In speeches by *aked* in one place, other local men and women are told how they need to join with their counterparts in an adjoining place to make their way to the *gab*: men and women need to "hurry up" in their gardens and get ready to move. The following is a speech by one of the hosts of a small ritual enacted before he and his group set off to the main *gab* as dancers, in their role as supporters of the hosts:

The people on that side, all of you gather and go inside the men's house. The people on that side, gather and go inside that men's house. Everyone go inside the house. Dancers, you sit on the verandah, divide the food and give it to those on the inside of the house. Io [an *aked* from the *gab*], now I am going to send your dancers to you . . . [He then begins naming the roads along which groups of supporters traveled to reach this village. After each set of connected roads, he says, "This is your betel nut."]

Hosts [lit.: fathers of the *gab*] this is your betel nut. Bring it up, chew it and if you want to get any guests go now or you will be too late. I am going to cut the rope from your pig [i.e., the dancers] and it is going up.

This is followed in turn by a speech from another one of the hosts:

Hosts you know there is no food at the *gab* and you can see there is no food here. People with guests in Moresby, take this pig, eat it and if you have any guests in Moresby you had better get them up here quick. Moresby and guests from anywhere else don't wait, don't take a break. You just go. Hosts if you go to get guests don't spend 2–3 weeks, or else you will be late. Dancers when you get up to the place for making headdresses and when Easter approaches, then we will stop. Dancers, you listen, you know this is Easter time. Dancers you eat this food and then tomorrow go up to the headdress house. Don't wait for the hosts, you have work to do. What you have come here for, you go and do it. When you get up there everybody look after themselves. Walk around properly. You people know the law. Don't go and spoil the place. I see that you don't get the law properly. Councillors, police officers, and committee, you must enforce the law. If you break any law look out.

Each such connection is achieved by replicating in miniature the *gab* to which they will become attached. For example, in the *em* of Visi where these processes were observed in detail, supporters of a *gab* prepared and entered the villages of their neighbors by staging a small-scale *gab*. This was performed several times as the increasingly large group moved geographically closer to the main *gab* village before entering it and replicating the process again. A similar process would occur among the invited dancers from another *em* and those supporters they "pull" to increase their dancing numbers.

Over the period of many months in any particular *em*, ever increasing degrees of centeredness are achieved, which in turn create the experience of increasing degrees of spatial and temporal simultaneity. This simultaneity is precariously held "in place" within the confines of the *gab*, during which the most anticipated events of the ritual (dances, life-crisis rites, and pig-kills) are completed. Upon completion of the distribution of the pig, the men and women participating in the *gab* leave the village and return to their more disparate, hamlet-based social life. The *gab* village itself is left to revert to a hamletlike place. In the coming years, before it is completely abandoned, it may occasionally be used as a place for connecting up to a *gab* in a neighboring *em*.

These ethnographic observations can also be compared to the earlier account of Williamson (1912), who highlights many of these same processes. In addition, the popular accounts of the Fuyuge provided by the missionary Dupeyrat (based on the writings of Fastre, which were completed during the 1930s) also focus on these "joining" and "concentrating" dimensions of place intrinsic to the performance of the ritual (Dupeyrat 1955; Fastre n.d.)

In my account, unlike these earlier accounts, Port Moresby and the coast generally appear as the widest context of places that are connected into any locally based *gab*. Nowadays, with greater movement among the Fuyuge, Port Moresby, and the coast, men and women staging a *gab* need to consider "pulling in" persons from these distant contexts (as made evident in the speeches described earlier). A specific category of "road" is now frequently invoked, that of "Mosbi," when discussing the persons resident and/or visiting there. Men are now "sent off" to Port Moresby (taking a plane from the mission airstrip) in order to notify specific men and women of the timing of an upcoming *gab*. The "simultaneity" that men and women attempt to achieve in the ritual now has to contend increasingly with the actions of men and women who are located in different spatial and temporal settings.[8] The places, and movements between them, in the "Mosbi" context do not "anticipate" the *gab* in the manner of the *em*; they are ordered according to a different cultural logic. But, paradoxically, the achievement of personhood (that of men in particular) is nowadays caught up with acquiring "experience" of Port Moresby or the coast in various ways (wage labor, "walkabout," card playing, and so forth).

Local Persons, Metropolitan Names

When I first came to live among the Visi, men and women would delight in pointing out to me places where a *gab* from the past had been staged. They would indicate where the men's houses were located, who slept where around the plaza, and what dancers and other guests were invited. Often, to my then untrained eye, there was little evidence of what could be inferred as a village. Different men and women would emphasize different places, sometimes coinciding with the stories of others. What became clear after a brief period of time was that these were discourses as much about "themselves" (their name) as features of the local topography.

But this was not a discourse about "fixed identities" in relation to "changing" places. Rather, the continual emergence and/or disappearance of a *gab* and the places that anticipate it (gardens, hamlets, and the like) are a manner of thinking about and making explicit the relationships that constitute the person and his or her name; and it is this "name" as analogous to the places that is seen as continually anticipating forms of joining and concentration. Men strive to make ever more visible their name. This was evident, for example, when I visited *em* distant from that of Visi. Men such as Yavi were names that were immediately recognized. But this visibility is achieved as a consequence of enabling multiple others to attain simultaneity in the collective contexts of the *gab*: by focusing particular and diverse perspectives and relationships to a common purpose. As a consequence, the "names" of local others (men and women) become more visible (Hirsch 1994, 700–702.).

Men and women at once delight in the thought of the *gab* but also emphasize how hard one must work. This is not simply the work of physical labor (carrying wood and food, moving pigs) but also what we might call "coordination"; of getting persons and objects into the appropriate spaces at the appropriate times. It is only in this way that the momentary simultaneity of the ritual can be achieved—of coordinating the multiple relationships that constitute the diversity of persons involved. Once it has been assembled and the dances, rites, and exchanges performed, it has served its purpose and thus anticipates the next such event in a different place.

This achievement of name is increasingly framed by need to bring relationships contained in Port Moresby into the Fuyuge construed order of simultaneity. However, since the 1950s, when money first entered the *gab* as an exchange object, this sense of achieved personhood has become increasingly associated with the experience of a different order of spatial and temporal simultaneity, the order of the Port Moresby–coastal context. This in turn implies a different conception of personhood and agency. In the Port Moresby context, there is not for young men the "hard work" of the *gab* and what this implies for the achievement of name. Instead, there is the "walkabout" and the sense of standing at the side of a market and watching money transacted and profit made. There is also the excitement of a place like Taurama with music blasting out of the shops, numerous commodities for sale, and betel nut vendors on every street corner. In such a place, it is not possible to feel the sense of "coordination" that efficacious men like Yavi enact in the *em* context. The experience of simultaneity engendered in these contexts is completed through consumption. To participate fully in this process, a person requires money to buy the commodities. This enables the person, as an individual, to constantly recreate spatial and temporal simultaneity in personal experience. The "coordination" or "mapping" of this collective process is from an individual vantage point (Jameson 1991).

But at the same time, to be in such a place, is in a manner of speaking, to be "out of place." Men and women repeatedly asserted how life in Port Moresby was a life lived after money: without money one could not eat, drink, or sleep. Unlike other cultural groups, particularly coastal groups like the Mekeo, the Fuyuge have virtually no stake in the urban context (see Hau'ofa 1981). This sense of "peripherality" is not lost on the Fuyuge and is directly related to their intense desire for a road to the coast. A man like Yavi has visited Port Moresby on a number of occasions. He has direct experience of Taurama and so his use of this name is not derived from a view afar. In transforming the place-name of his garden to that of a name currently recognized far and wide in Papua New Guinea, Yavi is engaging is a cultural act that would be well recognized by his ancestors. It is through the analogies of naming that he is attempting to "pull" that which is potentially "out of time" and "out of place" into a context where it anticipates the simultaneity achieved in the *gab* ritual. In so doing, the name Taurama becomes part of the process of making the name of Yavi and those with whom he is connected more visible.

The reason I focused on this name and became preoccupied with it was because it seemed "out of place" to me. But this was because I was operating with a different conception of "place" than that of my Melanesian host. Following Strathern, it could be said that in the English (Euro-American) view: "[P]ersons acquire identity from the places they are at, modified by where they have come from and where they are going. Places stay, persons move" (1991, 117). By contrast, "Melanesians . . . are, culturally speaking, already there. They make the places travel" (117). Taurama among the Fuyuge is less a fixed locale than a context from which analogies can be drawn. It is about bringing something into view; about creating a particular intentional space—a particular relation between foreground (Yavi's plot of land) and horizon (Port Moresby). More generally, it is about displaying the capacity to hold things together in a particular sort of way (analogous to the Fuyuge notion of *hode*, skin).

It is an open question, though, whether the form of simultaneity achieved in the *gab* will prevail in the future, or whether that associated with a place like Port Moresby or Taurama, based on individual consumerism, will be ascendant. What seems clear is that it is a tension that will continue to preoccupy the generation that follows people such as Yavi, just as it preoccupied his generation in its own way. Port Moresby–Taurama will undoubtedly endure in the future, but whether it will be primarily viewed from the perspective of the ritual village or that of the shopping consumer is, in essence, the question at the core of interactions which form Papua New Guinea's emergent "national culture."

ACKNOWLEDGMENTS

The research on which this chapter is based was conducted during 1983–85. The research was made possible by financial support from the Wenner-Gren Foundation, Central Research Fund, University of London, and the London School of Economics and Political Science. For their helpful comments on various drafts of this chapter I want to thank Gerd Baumann, Robert Foster, John Kelly, Harvey Whitehouse, and the seminar participants in the Department of Anthropology at the University of Manchester. Any errors in either fact or form are solely my own. I also want to thank the Papua New Guinea national and provincial (Central Province) governments for allowing me to conduct my research. Finally, my greatest debt is to the Fuyuge, and especially the people of Visi, for allowing me to live among them.

NOTES

1. I am using the notion of "local cultural project" as a shorthand for practices pursued in particular contexts, which locals see as central to the way their social lives are structured. This includes such "classic" cases as the *moka*, *kula*, and *tee* as well as the present case, the *gab*. The fact that such practices may or may not have come to take on this centrality in the context of colonialism is beyond the scope of this chapter (cf. Thomas 1992).

2. For this sense of parallelism to have important political consequences, Anderson (1991, 188) suggests that "it was necessary that the distance between the parallel groups be large, and that the newer of them be substantial in size and permanently settled, as well as firmly subordinated to the older." Unlike the populations of Scotland, for example, which was gradually absorbed into the larger political-cultural unit of the United Kingdom, the Americas met these conditions.

3. Foster (1992) has drawn attention to examples of "moral education" initiated by the PNG state which attempt to reconcile "traditional" practices in the urban context—such as betel nut chewing and spitting—with Western models of proper individual behavior and conduct in relation to such practices.

4. In previous publications, these have been referred to as parishes (Hirsch 1987; 1990). I now find the label of *home* more appropriate.

5. A man or woman will commit suicide out of shame (*fafi*) if their close relations refuse to kill pigs in their name when they have reached the "white hairs" life-crisis rite. During my stay among the Visi, a woman at the "white hairs" stage of her life threw herself off a cliff when her husband refused to kill pigs for her.

6. Speeches in such settings refer rhetorically to whether an action will be "true": for example, whether enough pigs or food will be collected to properly perform the exchanges and distributions; or whether the dancers will appear strong and beautiful (see Strathern 1988, 181).

7. Listening to Elleli's desire for the streets of Port Moresby, made explicit by this music, conjured up the image of the *flaneur* described by Baudelaire and Benjamin. As they observed, "the *flaneur* [is] the spectator of the market" (Frisby 1985, 252).

8. In a related discussion that focused on the incorporation of betel nut (mountain and coastal) into Fuyuge ritual, I indicated how "[t]oday whether Fuyuge ritual is set in motion or comes to a halt depends on the movements of men who venture from the ritual village to bring back the betelnut bunches" (Hirsch 1990, 27).

REFERENCES

Anderson, Benedict. 1991. *Imagined Communities: Reflections on the Origin and Spread of Nationalism*, 2d ed. London: Verso.

Campbell, Colin. 1987. *The Romantic Ethic and the Spirit of Modern Consumerism*. Oxford: Basil Blackwell.

Dupeyrat, André. 1955. *Festive Papua*. Translated by Erik de Mauny. London: Staples Press.

Fastre, P. n.d. *Manners and customs of the Fuyuges*. Typescript. Translation of *Moeurs et coutumes Foujoughes*. 1937–39. Translated by M. Flower and E. Chariot. De Boismenu College, Boroko, Papua New Guinea.

Foster, Robert J. 1992. Take care of public telephones: Moral education and nation-state formation in Papua New Guinea. *Public Culture* 4:31–45.

Frisby, David. 1985. *Fragments of Modernity: Theories of Modernity in the Work of Simmel, Kracauer and Benjamin*. Cambridge: Polity Press.

Hallpike, Christopher R. 1977. *Bloodshed and Vengeance in the Papuan Mountains*. Oxford: Clarendon Press.

Hau'ofa, Epeli. 1981. *Mekeo: Inequality and Ambivalence in a Village Society*. Canberra: Australian National University Press.

Hirsch, Eric. 1987. Dialectics of the bowerbird: An interpretative account of ritual and symbolism in the Ubade Valley, Papua New Guinea. *Mankind* 17:1–14.

———. 1988. Landscapes of exchange. Ph.D. diss., Department of Anthropology, London School of Economics.

———. 1990. From bones to betelnuts: Processes of ritual transformation and the development of a "national culture" in Papua New Guinea. *Man*, n.s., 25:18–34.

———. 1994. Between mission and market: Events and images in a Melanesian society. *Man*, n.s., 29:689–711.

Jameson, Frederic. 1991. *Postmodernism, or, The Cultural Logic of Late Capitalism*. London: Verso.

McArthur, M. 1971. Men and spirits in the Kunimaipa Valley. In L. Hiatt and C. Jayawardena, eds., *Anthropology in Oceania*, 155–89. Sydney: Angus and Robertson.

Miller, Daniel. 1987. *Material Culture and Mass Consumption*. Oxford: Basil Blackwell.

Strathern, Marilyn. 1977. The disconcerting tie: Attitudes of Hagen migrants towards home. In R. J. May, ed., *Change and Movement: Readings on Internal Migration in Papua New Guinea*, 247–66. Port Moresby and Canberra: Papua New Guinea Institute of Applied Social and Economic Research, in association with Australian National University Press.

———. 1988. *The Gender of the Gift: Problems with Women and Problems with Society in Melanesia*. Berkeley: University of California Press.

———. 1991. *Partial Connections*. Savage, MD: Rowman and Littlefield.

Thomas, Nicholas. 1992. Substantivization and anthropological discourse: The transformation of practices into institutions in neotraditional Pacific societies. In James G. Carrier, ed., *History and Tradition in Melanesian Anthropology*, 64–85. Berkeley: University of California Press.

Wagner, Roy. 1986. *Asiwinarong: Ethos, Image, and Social Power among the Usen Barok of New Ireland*. Princeton: Princeton University Press.

Williamson, Robert Wood. 1912. *The Mafulu Mountain People of British New Guinea*. London: Macmillan.

Ellen E. Facey

Kastom *and Nation Making:* *The Politicization of Tradition* *on Nguna, Vanuatu*

Introduction

In this volume, Foster (introduction) and LiPuma outline what areas must be investigated if we are to be able to achieve some understanding of the structure and process of nation making in the contemporary Pacific. To take LiPuma's (this volume) phrasing of these matters,

> an adequate understanding of those structures and strategies used to objectify "the nation" and create national identity must consist of three aspects. The first defines the conditions and consequences of encompassment by capitalism . . . ; the second aspect maps out the social mediations . . . by which nations construct themselves . . . ; and the third grasps the ways in which these mediations are imbued with meaning, appropriated, and used by local communities.

In this chapter, my primary purpose is to consider this third aspect of nation making—the use made by local communities of the social mediations through which various agents construct nations. I will elucidate this process with reference to events that transpired on the island of Nguna in the central region of Vanuatu during the two years immediately prior to Vanuatu's 1980 declaration of independence as a republic.

To avoid losing sight of the other aspects of nation making pointed to by LiPuma, one must link the local level of political process to the national level of political process. In general, then, this chapter is concerned with how the images and narratives of nationhood that are generated through nationwide political processes are interpreted and used by local communities. More specifically, and in terms of the case of Nguna, it offers an answer to this question: why did the Ngunese embrace the

Vanuaaku Pati ("the VP"), the archipelago's first indigenous party, and the party that ultimately became the first to rule the new nation? What social mediation(s) made sufficiently compelling sense on the local level that the vast majority of Ngunese would so strongly attach themselves to the national values espoused by the VP?

To foreshadow the argument presented below, the phenomenon of *kastom* ("custom" or "tradition")—its origin, use, and effect—will provide the major clue in solving this puzzle. I will document the politicization of *kastom* that took place at the national level in the late 1970s. It will then be argued that this particular construction of tradition was the preeminent influence on Ngunese perceptions of and response to the Vanuaaku Pati, and that this preeminence was a direct result of specific elements of that construction and of the way in which they were presented and delivered to the Ngunese population.

Vanuatu and the Vanuaaku Pati: A Brief History

It would be more correct here to refer to the country as the New Hebrides or Les Nouvelles Hébrides, as it was until 30 July 1980. It was then the world's only remaining "condominium," meaning that it had a double colonial presence and heritage, being jointly administered by Britain and France, each of which maintained its own health, education, trade, and other systems. To certain pro-independence expatriates as well as to the incipient, indigenous, intellectual elite of the 1970s, this only spelled double trouble. To them, the condominium government was more accurately known as the "pandemonium government" and the condominium of the New Hebrides itself as the "conundrum of the New Hebrides."

In 1971, the New Hebrides Cultural Association was formed. Within a few months it was renamed the New Hebrides National Party and, finally, in 1977 became the Vanuaaku Pati (Plant 1978, 195). As such, it became the first and only indigenous political party in the New Hebrides, in contrast to the preexistent, almost entirely European parties. In classic condominium style, of the two largest parties, one was made up largely of English-speaking British expatriates, the other of French-speaking French expatriates.

Alienation of land quickly became the central concern of the Pati's platform. As Jolly (1992, 332) observes, "a rapacious policy of European land alienation was established" in Vanuatu. The result: as of 1968, Europeans, who constituted only 3 percent of the population, held a full

36 percent of the land. New Hebrideans, who made up 95 percent of the population, held formal title to only 64 percent of the land. The statistics were even more lopsided in terms of land actually in use: approximately 50 percent of all land in use was owned by Europeans (Sope 1975, 19). Consequently, this issue was paramount throughout the archipelago.

At the same time, however, there were major obstacles to be overcome by the VP in terms of its appeal from one area to another. Although the New Hebrides then had a total population of only roughly 100,000,[1] internal divisions within the New Hebrides were many, based on such contrasts as rural–urban, educated—uneducated, British-educated (and therefore speaking English as a second language) versus French-educated (and therefore speaking French as a second language), and Christian (of various sorts) versus non-Christian (often glossed as "pagan") (Sope 1975, 35).

Faced with the problems generated by such division and diversity, the Vanuaaku Pati leadership made several critical decisions in order to put forward the Pati as a national political party. They established Bislama, the pidgin lingua franca, as the language of New Hebridean politics, and used it via the medium of the radio, taking their message to the general populace with great effect (cf. Jourdan this volume on the role of Pijin in the Solomon Islands). They then employed Christianity as a central bulwark. Their leader, Walter Lini, was himself an Anglican priest, and most of the leaders and supporters were active Christians. Indeed, in May 1973, the Presbyterian Church of the New Hebrides declared its support for "responsible self-government," which was the Vanuaaku Pati's overarching goal. In tandem with this association with Christian beliefs and values, official VP policy stressed preservation of traditional values and life-styles—*kastom*. Conversely, the VP was trying to create itself in the image of "government," as it knew it. My own introduction to the politics of the day illustrates clearly these processes at work.

As a postgraduate student at the University of Sydney, I initially made plans to fly to the capital, Port Vila ("Vila"), in December 1977. As a Canadian, I was only required to "pass" through the British "side" of the condominium government. My permission came deceptively quickly, with no questions or problems. On 1 December, however, a scant few weeks before my departure, I received a terse cable from the British Residency's Research Office informing me that the residency had reversed its decision to allow me entry to the Central District, CD 1.

Several violent incidents and an air of unrest and of hostility toward Europeans led residency officials to feel that they "could no longer assure [my] security," because I was a 23-year-old, female, individual researcher.

Phone calls to contacts in Vila soon yielded the information that the leaders of the Vanuaaku Pati had boycotted the national election of 29 November and, instead, had declared a People's Provisional Government (PPG) that same day. There had been a large, armed demonstration in Vila and scuffles in some of the small towns on other islands, and the officials of the existing governments feared that these isolated acts of violence might spread and worsen.[2] Therefore, all outsiders were being denied entry in order to avert potential conflicts with international implications. In the weeks that followed, however, these concerns abated. Through news reports and more phone calls, I learned that the acts of violence had not escalated and the situation was seen as having stabilized. I applied for reconsideration of my application, and the British Residency's permission was reinstated.

I arrived in Vila late in January 1978 and within a few days was granted an interview with the British Residency officer in charge of foreign researchers. He made two things crystal clear: first, that, in view of the present situation, my position was to be a neutral one. My behavior was to be strictly apolitical, no matter what pressures might be exerted on me locally to act otherwise, and no matter how my own political views might predispose me to act. (He cited the example of a researcher who had recently been on one of the northerly islands and had taken to wearing T-shirts that advocated that island's secession from the [yet to be] nation. I was assured that the residency would not tolerate a second such embarrassment.) Second, under no circumstances was I to begin making any anthropological inquiries of any sort, or to travel beyond Vila's boundaries until I had chosen a precise location for my work and had the location approved by his office. Violating any of these restrictions on my activities and comportment would result in immediate cancellation of my research visa.

The area in which I had proposed working was considered by all and sundry to be a Vanuaaku Pati stronghold. If this were indeed true, I wondered what the chances were of my being able to maintain the completely neutral stance required by the residency; would it be possible without undermining my position in the local context? I had been advised entirely unofficially, but equally firmly and baldly, that official permissions were not enough, given the continuing claim of the Vanuaaku Pati to being the People's Provisional Government. So I would have to "pass" the VP's inspection as well. I had become a participant—if naive—and a resource—if unwilling—in its efforts both to establish its competence as the People's Provisional Government and to assert the legitimacy of its claim to formal, official standing.

Approaching the VP's Vila headquarters with some trepidation, I applied for leave to go to Nguna, a site chosen for theoretical reasons and approved by the British Residency's Research Office for more practical ones, especially its proximity to Vila in case of a recurrence of political unrest. The Vanuaaku Pati leadership then in turn put the question into the hands of representatives of the Nguna-P̃ele Cultural Association (P̃ele being the island immediately adjacent to Nguna), which was a self-help group for urbanites originally from those islands. Only much later did I realize that, while the association ostensibly served as a social and financial support network for those Vila residents, it also functioned as a local branch of the Vanuaaku Pati.

After a long, hot wait over the next month, numerous visits to their office, and, finally, a stern lecture from Father Lini himself, I was eventually given the go-ahead. This consisted of a small blue piece of paper with my name, occupation, destination, and permitted length of stay typed on it: an illegal PPG "passport."

The Local Context: Nguna

Nguna, covering an area roughly 5 by 10 kilometers, was home to just under one thousand people in 1980, all of whom had had at least a few years of schooling and virtually all of whom spoke at least three languages (Ngunese, Bislama, and English or French, or both). They made their primary living from subsistence horticulture (manioc, taro, yams, and such) and from cutting copra.

Since the nineteenth century, this population has survived some terrible experiences and massive alterations of various sorts—tragic losses due to diseases, the advent of cultivating cash crops (first arrowroot, then copra, and, finally, with little success, coffee and cocoa), adoption of Presbyterian Christianity, and a shift from matrilineal to patrilineal transmission of chiefly titles in the hierarchical chiefly system (see Facey 1981, 1983, 1988).

Under these circumstances, it is remarkable that today bearers of these traditional, chiefly titles not only exist, but also continue to inherit lands that are tied to their titles as well as to dominate in the other two power structures that govern island life: the local Presbyterian church body (the pastor and approximately a dozen elders) and village councils. Not surprisingly, then, the people of Nguna are intensely interested in their own past; unity and continuity are recurrent themes of the discourse in which they engage regarding their own culture. As they put it, however, life is precarious. And, as they often say, to the bedevilment of the ethnographer, things are "good, but not good, too."

Take language as just one example. It is a source of pride, yet also a source of concern. The entire Bible and many of the standard Presbyterian hymns have been translated into Ngunese, which, relative to the other major languages of Vanuatu, is fairly easy to learn. In fact, it is already spoken by a comparatively large number of nonnative speakers (especially among Efate residents). Aware of this, a few Ngunese in 1980 anticipated that, in the context of independence, Ngunese might be chosen to replace Bislama as the country's third official—and only indigenous—language, alongside English and French. (So far, it has not.)

Consequently, there is annoyance over the insistence by past administrators of the French school on Nguna that their students should speak French at all times, even in the playground. Likewise, the Ngunese dislike the fact that their children who live in Vila and attend school with speakers of many different native languages communicate with their playmates in Bislama and therefore seem to have lost competence in the Ngunese language. Nonetheless, outsiders who settle permanently on Nguna—the majority being women who marry in from other islands—are not long in learning the language, and they are expected to stop using Bislama as soon as possible. Europeans who do likewise, be they missionaries, anthropologists, or doctors on clinic inspections, are considered to be demonstrating respect for their hosts if they make even a minimal effort to speak Ngunese.

At the same time, there has been and will continue to be what conservative Ngunese perceive to be a deterioration of Ngunese, due both to the loss of vocabulary rendered irrelevant by sociocultural change and to the intrusion of English, French, and Bislama words and expressions. So there is cause for concern for those who are interested in the language as part of traditional culture or *kastom*.

Finally, it is also true that language is a primary means of measuring social as well as geographical distance, and this is as true on Nguna as it is elsewhere. Groups on neighboring islands who speak very similar dialects of the same language are said by the Ngunese to "turn" or "skew the language" slightly. This gives them cultural common ground with the people of Nguna, while simultaneously defining them as different. The farther one goes geographically, the wider the linguistic gap, and the greater the perceived cultural difference. Therefore language, while primarily viewed as a basis of unity and its use and present social relevance as evidence of continuity with the past, is subject to opposing forces and can be used for opposing purposes as well.

Similar comments might be made of the opposing movements—centrifugal and centripetal forces, if you like—that are in evidence in Vanuatu's educational system as found on Nguna (see Facey 1983). But when it comes to religion and politics, a different movement is apparent.

Throughout the colonial period, Nguna demonstrated a high degree of stability. Since conversion was completed at the turn of the century, there have been no major reversions to "pagan" beliefs, nor have competing religious factions emerged as has been the case elsewhere in the archipelago, such as in Southeast Ambrym (Tonkinson 1981) and in Tanna (Brunton 1981; Lindstrom 1982, 1990).

It isn't that other denominations haven't tried. The Seventh-Day Adventist Church, for example, has gained some converts among the Ngunese residents in Vila, plus a few on Nguna and the neighboring offshore islands. In 1978, they applied to the local Presbyterian District Session for permission to construct a Seventh-Day Adventist church on P̂ele. Permission was denied, the session members wanting to retard what they saw as potential competition. Their decision was predicated on the conviction that, since this area was "brought into the Light" by a Presbyterian missionary, only the Presbyterian church has historical validity. To its adherents, any person who abandons it for another church and faith is betraying, even denying, the faith of his or her forebears.

Ngunese political life shows a similar trend. Traditional politics on Nguna were never characterized by ostentatious public competition between individuals, actual or aspiring "big men" in the classic sense, nor are they today. There are a few men whose words carry more weight than those of others, and this fact is not satisfactorily accounted for by comparing their relative positions in the chiefly hierarchy. Personal attributes and skills—a good command of local "history," verbal eloquence, and sheer presence—certainly single out some chiefs over others.

There are also interpersonal conflicts between chiefs, but their supporters do not operate publicly as followings in open opposition to each
other. Political differences are not thrashed out on Nguna by rival factions as they often are on Tanna, Ambae, and elsewhere in Melanesia.
This does not mean that there are no differences, no long-standing
animosities and scores to settle; but, in order to realize the ideal of
unity—or, at the least, to give the impression of striving toward it—such
conflicts are suppressed as people attempt to conceptualize, and to portray, their community as a cohesive, coherent whole.

With these facets of the local context in mind, we can now examine
the local view of national politics and, more specifically, Ngunese perceptions of the Vanuaaku Pati and its goals.

Ngunese Perceptions of the Vanuaaku Pati

Modern party politics, in the abstract, are condemned by many Ngunese.
Indicative of this is the Bislama term, *politik*, which literally translates as
"politics" but, as the Ngunese use it, has a thoroughly pejorative connotation. Its oppositional structure makes modern politics for many Ngunese
a largely useless, often destructive, enterprise characterized by heated
argument, efforts to deceive, and even incitement to violence of members
of one party against those of another. Consequently, the general Ngunese
opinion is that a one-party government is far better than one with two
parties or more. The latter is seen as only counterproductive, as different
policies merely generate argument and lead ultimately to inaction.

Having had parties thrust upon them by the condominium powers,
however, the Ngunese have responded characteristically. Since the incep-
tion of the indigenous Vanuaaku Pati, the people of Nguna have come to
support it virtually universally. What little opposition there appears to
be to the Pati is expressed only privately. Dissenting individuals are
loathe to controvert the image of their community as a single-minded,
unified collectivity. Were they to do so, they would leave themselves
open to being accused of being antisocial, disruptive of the peace that is
thought to derive from such unity. Under pressure to conceal their difference of opinion, such individuals feel powerless and resentful. Their
public silence is evidence of the constraints that the shared value of unity
places on individuals in this society.

The reasons behind the strong support of the Ngunese for the VP must be sought in the grass roots image of the Pati, which diverges in a few major respects from the public image projected by the Pati's leaders. On Nguna, support took on many of the characteristics of a cargo movement, some of which are quite similar to those apparent in Jimmy Stephens's Nagriamel movement on the northern island of Espiritu Santo.

Two historic eras came into play in the development of the conception Ngunese held of the nature and potential role of the Pati: the period during which Melanesians were expelled from the cane fields of Queensland; and World War II, when many Ngunese were exposed to, and very much impressed by, American soldiers stationed at nearby Havannah Harbor. These soldiers, Jolly aptly points out, were "foreigners who seemed both more powerful and more generous than the British and the French" (1992, 336; see also White and Lindstrom 1990).

Following the passing of Queensland's Repatriation Act of 1906, the New Hebrideans returned home. At some point thereafter, a tale emerged on Nguna, perhaps elsewhere as well, of New Hebrideans having handed over money to an American, "Mr. Nichol" [Nickle?]. He was to hold the money in trust for New Hebrideans, and make it grow—Americans being renowned for this facility—until such time as he would return the entire sum. Release of these funds, now estimated at anywhere from 5,000 to 50,000 British pounds, had one string attached, however: the New Hebrideans must be flying their own, and no one else's, flag.

These ideas were alive and well in the years immediately preceding independence, and the VP fitted in neatly with them. Informants used a lock-and-key metaphor, the VP being the key in relation to the lock that holds secure an endless flow of wealth deriving from the original "investment" of New Hebridean workers abroad via the mediating and financially creative American, "Mr. Nichol."

As a result, the VP's ceremonial raising of the flag of the People's Provisional Government on 29 November 1977 was a heavily symbolic event at more than one level. It marked the VP's declaration of their authority; but it carried with it, as well, the promise of independence which to some was both sign of and prerequisite for a new era, an era of unparalleled material prosperity in a Western mode.

Alongside this rather messianic dream, the VP represented other hopes to many of the Ngunese. Two virtues of the Pati often explicitly

stated by Ngunese were that it was "all black" and that it would therefore rid the country of Europeans. What the VP announced in its press
release of 4 December 1977 was that one of the People's Provisional
Government's aims was to achieve "a democratic way of running the
country, socially, economically, and politically . . . [and] to drive out the
British and French colonial governments from Vanuaaku" (in Plant
1978, 201). This is not the same, however, as saying that one's aim is to
drive out all Europeans.

In addition, the Pati's expressly stated aim of repatriating native
ownership of the land and preventing future acquisition of land by foreign speculators was widely hailed. Likewise, the Pati emphasized the
importance of preexistent local authority structures as a major component of *kastom* to be retained in the future. Finally, the Pati's philosophy
and organization were basically democratic, based on local "political
commissars" and a committee system for disseminating information and
carrying local wishes to the Pati leaders. The consensual base of the Pati
was highly approved of, according to the people I interviewed on
Nguna.

The Ngunese of the 1970s and 1980s have found themselves in a situation rather like that which faced their great-grandparents at the end of
the last century. The major influences of that era were the labor trade,
initiation of wage labor and cultivation of cash crops, and severe depopu-
lation. The experience of the last few decades on Nguna is similar: large
numbers of people, particularly young men, are absent for extended
periods. Moreover, those who return bring different values and habits
which are in conflict with local values and therefore sometimes socially
disruptive.

In both periods, socioeconomic and cultural changes have resulted
in what could be called a state of ideological crisis, by which I mean that
contradictory notions abounded, and proponents of different social constructions of reality were vying for ideological control. At the turn of the
century, the new Christians emerged victorious from this ideological
confusion; more recently, the supporters of the Vanuaaku Pati have.

Certainly other ni-Vanuatu societies have gone through similar
crises. What distinguishes Nguna is the fact that in both instances, not
only have the preexistent leaders managed to maintain their dominance,
but the society has also maintained the appearance of unity. The

Ngunese eventually all became Christians; there were neither resistant pockets of paganism nor eventual reversions to paganism, nor did any significant degree of support emerge for alternative ideologies such as cargo. Just so have virtually all Ngunese become Vanuaaku Pati people.

Kastom: Local and National

In the 1982 special issue of *Mankind*, Roger Keesing drew our attention to various types of "neo-traditionalisms" proliferating in Melanesia. In each case, "custom" or *kastom* (the Bislama term meaning "traditional cultural elements") has become and been enthusiastically taken up as a political symbol for various purposes. In Keesing's research with mountain dwellers of Malaita in the Solomon Islands, he found the Kwaio to be a group still relatively quite isolated, resistant to religious proselytization, and still following an essentially "traditional" life-style. Yet there, too, custom is a political rallying cry by even this group who "have never accepted the terms of colonial subjugation" (Keesing 1982b, 357).

In the same volume, Robert Tonkinson reported a similar process at work in the southeastern part of the island of Ambrym in Vanuatu (see also Tonkinson 1981). Ambrym's is a vastly different situation from that of the Kwaio, the Ambrymese having long since become deeply involved in Christianity, cash crop production, and migratory wage labor. Yet, in this context, too, *kastom* has played a tremendously prominent role in recent years, being the occasion of enormous amounts of discussion and activity. These examples show, as does my own research on Nguna, that the concept of "traditional culture" or "custom" has arisen in cultures whose histories and contemporary situations contrast greatly. Why should Nguna be included among them?

It is clear that the Vanuaaku Pati won Nguna with its "*kastom* within Christianity" stance. Nothing else would have supported the local status quo, grounded as it is in the tandem structure of the chiefly system and the Presbyterian church leadership. There are certainly many other historical, social, and ideological factors that came into play in Nguna's enthusiastic reception of the Pati, but local cultural ideals of unity and continuity and their relation to the Pati's rhetoric of "*kastom* within Christianity" were undoubtedly the most powerful factors in Nguna's wholesale support of the Vanuaaku Pati.

Kastom has come to form the basis of the Ngunese conception of their society, embodying the essential distinctiveness of Ngunese society as an integral entity vis-à-vis all others. It invokes both the unity and the continuity through time of the social whole. The Ngunese-language equivalent of *kastom* is a phrase that translates literally as "the way of doing (things) of the Land."

It is clear that the Ngunese feel that contemporary activities and behavior should approximate these standards; there is considerable difference of opinion, however, as to the actual substance of the standards. The core of *kastom* for the Ngunese is still the traditional chiefly system. Yet, to contemporary generations, Christianity is also regarded as traditional even though its European origin is fully acknowledged (cf. Rutz this volume). The essence of Ngunese culture for the Ngunese, then, is the duality that Tonkinson's (1981) phrase "*kastom* within Christianity" captures very neatly.

These realities are clearly illustrated in the following "psalm" (original in Ngunese, my English translation here), a poem which was circulated, without specific authorship, during a VP rally on Nguna in August 1979:

First Psalm

Chiefs and leaders of religion in the land
Your names should be kept sacred
Your dominion should be clear
So that you might be respected
Your dominion should be as [it was] when
The ancestors first walked there
In accordance with the desires of the whole people
You should give us true and honest help
You should forgive us
And direct the life of the people
As we do with our children
You should not lead us into temptation
But deliver us out of the
Hands of Whites, [our] attackers
And those who would take our land for nothing.
We trust completely that the dominion is
Yours, the Strength and the Truth
Which calls forth respect from all the people.

Several elements in this "psalm" are worth noting: the close mirroring of the Lord's Prayer; the juxtaposition and equation of political leaders with religious leaders (line 1); the idea of a return to the "proper," *kastom* way of doing things, from time immemorial ("when/The ancestors first walked there"); and the reference to struggle against aggressive, usurping foreign powers ("Whites, [our] attackers/And those who would take our land for nothing"). Most especially, note the concept of the "dominion" (*namarakiana*, meaning a Ngunese chief's jurisdiction as well as the literal area over which he holds sway) and the trust and social contract that is presumed between "You" (chiefs and religious leaders) and "We" ("all the people").[3] What is the mediating element in this relationship? Not surprisingly, land. And with that are fused in this "psalm" the very same set of elements offered as the VP political package in the pre-independence years: a fusion of Christianity, traditional authority, repatriation of land, and the European in the image of thief and villain.

Conclusion: National Unity and Its Discontents

Around 1975, the *preexisting* process of conceptualizing a whole larger than the local community or region took a sudden turn—not for the better or the worse, but for the political. Given a name, "cultural identity," this process became the focus of political action, just as it had in other new and emergent Pacific nation-states. That is, for the first time in history, Vanuatu, as a concept of a hoped-for entity distinct from the condominium of the New Hebrides, became an object of indigenous political activity. But, if said to be a goal, cultural identity is also a tool, a notion manipulable for political purposes.

In the 1970s educated ni-Vanuatu achieved the perspective that Alan Howard observed among educated Rotumans, wherein a growing segment of the population, "recognize[s] the value of . . . custom for its own sake, from a moral-ethical point of view" (Howard 1970, 150). Howard goes on to say that the educated elite "can also recognize [custom's] significance as a source of common identity and make efforts to endow custom with dignity" (150).

This describes equally well what happened in 1980 in Vanuatu. Having become the new nation's prime minister, Walter Lini (1980, 290) proposed a restructuring of the nation's self-concept in a volume commemorating its independence:

We believe that small is beautiful, peace is powerful, respect is honourable, and that our traditional sense of community is both wise and practical for the people of Vanuatu.

While traditional values and life-style are encapsulated in the notion of *kastom*, founding a national cultural identity on such a concept is not an easy task. As others (especially Lindstrom 1982 and 1990) have pointed out, *kastom* is an extremely variable entity and therefore the source of much dispute within even very limited geographical areas. Indeed, in many parts of Vanuatu it is actually the major idiom in terms of which cultural differences are expressed, compared, and evaluated relative to one another. Paradoxically, this is also *kastom*'s great strength as a political idiom for unity and historical, cultural continuity. When used abstractly by the Vanuaaku Pati leaders, it can sometimes transcend local variation and avert conflict.

But in many places *kastom* has been the cause of much division. A concrete example of this is presented by Larcom (1982, 1990) with regard to the Mewun of South West Bay, Malakula (Vanuatu).[4] First, "[t]heir older perception of *kastom* as commodity—knowledge, rituals, objects, etc. to be bought, sold or exchanged at will—has been supplemented by the more wide-spread notion of *kastom* as a stable body of traditions, unshared as well as shared" (1982, 330). More recently, the Mewun have been using the concept of *kastom* legalistically in local courts set up by the national government to arbitrate disputes of various kinds.

LiPuma (this volume) suggests that as local cultures, based on principles unlike those upon which the modern nation-state is based, are "enfolded" within such nation-states, "the entire set of relations that define collective self-definition" as well as the very notion of the social person are reconfigured. According to Larcom (1990), this is exactly what is happening in South West Bay as the Mewun (1) make judgments that run counter to and are altering their concept of "person"; and (2) invent a kind of Mewun culture based on objectified icons of identity rather than on shared values. As she puts it,

Mewun kastom, which once referred to a repertoire of transferable performances, techniques, and artifacts, is now used to denote a unique culture identified with the Mewun as a group. This new notion of Mewun kastom is defined by inalienable material items and practices as well as by the exchange relationships they signify. (Larcom 1990, 177)

Similarly, the enshrining of *kastom* can disenfranchise as easily as it enfranchises. Just as privileging a particular line of descent in an ideology of substance and belonging functions to exclude some as well as to include others, so does privileging *kastom*. In an ironic footnote, Philibert (1986, 270) nicely summarizes a case of what LiPuma terms internalizing the cultural Other, wherein the foreigner comes from within rather than from outside of one's cultural frame of reference:

> Those coming from the islands made fun of peri-urban villagers for their lack of rituals. A villager from the peri-urban village of Erakor sent a recorded message to Radio-Vanuatu explaining that the reason they had so few traditions left was because they sacrificed them in order to bring about the new social order. Other islanders, he went on to say, now benefit from this new social order by coming in droves to Port Vila to seek employment. He then suggested to those who mocked them that, if it was really the way they felt about *kastom*, then they ought to go back home to their island to practice their beloved *kastom*.

Apparent and asserted public consensus notwithstanding, *kastom* is also problematic on Nguna. Two specific cases will serve to illustrate the sort of contestation that it has created (or, perhaps, simply tapped).

During my second field trip to Nguna, I had a very unpleasant if enlightening encounter. In the company of a senior man whom I knew very well, I was walking to a rendezvous with several of his peers, some of whom were chiefs of high title. We were going to discuss some details of traditional ceremonies and other "*kastom* matters" which I had agreed to record and prepare in booklet form at their request and instruction. As we approached the village, a tall man in his mid-thirties appeared, barring our path. Referring to me in the third person, and punctuating his remarks by stabbing the earth with his iron digging-stick, he began to berate my companion for telling this white woman things about local practices. According to him, I was no doubt in the employ of someone (European and male) in Vila or elsewhere to whom I would relay this sensitive information. The eventual result, he warned my friend, was that, having gotten what he wanted from these gullible old men, my "boss" would come to Nguna and turn this knowledge against the local people. Armed with this understanding of *kastom* rules of land ownership, he would prove that many of the locals are not, in fact, native to the areas in which they live and garden. Therefore (by some logic which neither my companion nor I could comprehend), he would be able to take those lands away from those people and throw them out.

When the fellow finally had begun to cool off, my friend was able to reason with and reassure him of the innocent nature of our discussions. But the experience served to confirm my feeling that there was a lot of suspicion abroad about me in a larger context of fear of and hostility toward Europeans in general. And rights are a hot topic on a small island with a growing population and too much land taken up by aging stands of coconuts. Talk of *kastom* inflames suspicions by raising matters of the legitimacy of specific land claims and even of the legitimacy of privileging or prioritizing rival types of claims to land-use rights. Insiders fear being labeled outsiders for concrete purposes, and they fear outsiders' powers to force such alienating redefinitions upon them.

The second example of contestation engendered by *kastom* bears directly on this point. It relates to the observation that Foster, LiPuma, and Larcom all make about material items often becoming commoditized in the nation-making process, thereby creating a sort of artifactual trafficking in culture. Objects are equated with national identities as they are exhibited in decontextualized ways, especially in multicultural exhibitions, world fairs, and the like.

Something of this sort was transpiring on Nguna in the weeks immediately preceding the country's first National Arts Festival, held 1–8 December 1979 (before there was even an independent "nation" as such). The following exchange took place in the village I was then living in as people were discussing what customary clothing should be made to be worn at the dance exhibition:

> PERSON 1: "Well, how was it we used to make [a certain item of apparel]?"
> PERSON 2: "Uh, I think the *kastom* way was like this [explanation]."
> PERSON 3: "Well, we'd better get it right; because, if we don't, if it isn't the real *kastom* way, those Whites in Vila are going to look at it and just laugh at us."

It is apparent from this exchange that these Ngunese villagers felt compelled to create something that would be seen to be authentic and that they feared judgment from outsiders, both white and native. This is the insidious side of *kastom*, as it becomes the measure by which different local groups feel they are to be judged. Their own local cultures are turned into material icons on this new, higher stage—the national level for inventing, comparing, and competing for acceptable identities. As these examples from various parts of Vanuatu indicate, nation making has diverse local effects, and many of these are alienating and provocative of division. The enshrining of *kastom* is a more complex and volatile process than its proponents in the Vanuaaku Pati may have anticipated. Its effects are to reinvigorate old arguments as well as to generate new ones over old issues—in this case, land, legitimacy, and authority, among others.

NOTES

1. Vanuatu's population as of 1990 was estimated at 160,000, having been growing rapidly throughout the 1980s (*World Fact File* 1990).

2. Plant (1978, 201) describes the events of 29 November 1977 as follows: "[On November 29] . . . the Vanuaaku flag was pulled down by opposition party members in Santo town, and in Vila the British police used tear gas to disperse a crowd of 300–400 VP opponents, armed with 'sharpened sticks and lumps of wood,' who were massed in front of the Pati's headquarters in Rue Higginson. Six people were injured and threats were made against the lives of two British officials (the Commandant of Police and the British District Agent) who subsequently left the country."

3. A second "psalm," circulated along with this one, bespoke of the betrayal of one particular local leader, in much the same vein as the first. Because its referent is both more specific and less thinly veiled, however, I prefer not to reproduce it here.

4. Prior to independence in 1980, Malakula was spelled Malekula.

REFERENCES

Brunton, Ron. 1981. The origins of the John Frum movement: A sociological explanation. In Michael Allen, ed., *Vanuatu: Politics, Economics and Ritual in Island Melanesia*, 357–77. Sydney: Academic Press.

Facey, Ellen E. 1981. Hereditary chiefship in Nguna. In Michael Allen, ed.,

Vanuatu: Politics, Economics and Ritual in Island Melanesia, 295–313. Sydney: Academic Press.

———. 1983. Ideology and identity: Social construction of reality on Nguna, Vanuatu. Ph.D. diss., Department of Anthropology, University of Sydney.

———. 1988. *Nguna Voices: Text and Culture from Central Vanuatu.* Calgary, Alberta: University of Calgary Press.

Howard, Alan. 1970. *Learning to be Rotuman: Enculturation in the South Pacific.* New York: Teachers College Press.

Jolly, Margaret. 1992. Custom and the way of the land: Past and present in Vanuatu and Fiji. *Oceania* 62:330–54.

Keesing, Roger M. 1982a. *Kastom* in Melanesia: An overview. In R. Keesing and R. Tonkinson, eds., *Reinventing Traditional Culture: The Politics of Kastom in Island Melanesia.* Special Issue, *Mankind* 13:297–301.

———. 1982b. *Kastom* and anticolonialism on Malaita: "Culture" as political symbol. In R. Keesing and R. Tonkinson, eds., *Reinventing Traditional Culture: The Politics of Kastom in Island Melanesia.* Special Issue, *Mankind* 13:357–73.

Keesing, Roger M., and Robert Tonkinson, eds. 1982. *Reinventing Traditional Culture: The Politics of Kastom in Island Melanesia.* Special Issue, *Mankind* 13:297–399.

Larcom, Joan. 1982. The invention of convention. In R. Keesing and R. Tonkinson, eds., *Reinventing Traditional Culture: The Politics of Kastom in Island Melanesia.* Special Issue, *Mankind* 13:330–37.

———. 1990. Custom by decree: Legitimation crisis in Vanuatu. In Jocelyn Linnekin and Lin Poyer, eds., *Cultural Identity and Ethnicity in the Pacific,* 175–90. Honolulu: University of Hawaii Press.

Lindstrom, Lamont. 1982. *Leftamap kastom*: The political history of tradition on Tanna (Vanuatu). In R. Keesing and R. Tonkinson, eds., *Reinventing Traditional Culture: The Politics of Kastom in Island Melanesia.* Special Issue, *Mankind* 13:316–29.

———. 1990. *Knowledge and Power in a South Pacific Society.* Washington: Smithsonian Institution Press.

Lini, Walter H. 1980. The future. In Walter H. Lini et al., *Vanuatu: Twenti Wan Tingting Long Taem Blong Independens,* 282–91. Suva, Fiji: Institute of Pacific Studies, University of the South Pacific and South Pacific Social Sciences Association.

Philibert, Jean-Marc. 1990 [1986]. The politics of tradition: Toward a generic culture in Vanuatu. In Frank Manning and Jean-Marc Philibert, eds., *Customs in Conflict: The Anthropology of a Changing World,* 251–73. Peterborough, Ontario: Broadview Press.

Plant, Christopher. 1978. Current developments in the Pacific, New Hebrides 1977: Year of crisis. *Journal of Pacific History* 13:194–204.

Sope, Barak. 1975. *Land and Politics in the New Hebrides.* Suva, Fiji: South Pacific Social Sciences Association.

Tonkinson, Robert. 1981. Church and *kastom* in southeast Ambrym. In Michael

Allen, ed., *Vanuatu: Politics, Economics and Ritual in Island Melanesia*, 237–67. Sydney: Academic Press.

———. 1982a. *Kastom* in Melanesia: Introduction. In R. Keesing and R. Tonkinson, eds., *Reinventing Traditional Culture: The Politics of Kastom in Island Melanesia*. Special Issue, *Mankind* 13:302–5.

———. 1982b. National identity and the problem of *kastom* in Vanuatu. In R. Keesing and R. Tonkinson, eds., *Reinventing Traditional Culture: The Politics of Kastom in Island Melanesia*. Special Issue, *Mankind* 13:306–15.

White, Geoffrey, and Lamont Lindstrom, eds. 1990. *The Pacific Theater: Island Representations of World War Two*. Honolulu: University of Hawaii Press.

World Fact File. 1990. Edited by Roger East et al. New York: Facts on File.

Michael Jacobsen

Vanishing Nations and the Infiltration of Nationalism: The Case of Papua New Guinea

Introduction

Political ideologies are normally perceived by both politicians and social scientists as one of the most important vehicles for the creation of nationhood. National ideologies, shaped in a nationalistic framework, have especially taken up great space in the discussions of the processes behind nation making (Anderson 1983; Gellner 1983). However, national ideologies alone do not create a nation-state. The actual implementation and entrenchment of governmental institutions, both political and administrative, also have to be taken into account. They must be the primary bearers of the national framework, if the nation is to have any continuity.

One of the important things when discussing nationalist ideologies and the creation of a national culture is to define the targets—the audience—for this aspect of nation making. I am not thinking of the individual actors as such but, rather, the different social domains in which these individuals act.

This consideration of social domains is especially important in the case of Papua New Guinea, where nationalism and a national culture are still in the making. To be able to measure the overall impact these constructs have on the Papua New Guinean society per se, one has to define the social domains of this nation. There are basically two domains of interest in this connection, the urban and the rural. The latter comprises by population about 85 percent of Papua New Guinea, the former about 10 percent. The remaining 5 percent covers the gray areas, or perhaps better, the overlapping areas between the urban and rural domains.[1] These domains are not to be conceived of as closed and isolated in relation to each other. On the contrary, there is a massive movement of people between them, thereby making them interrelated parts within an overall social whole.

There is not a general sense of nationhood or oneness among Papua New Guineans, a coherent and distinct set of commonly accepted characteristics that define Papua New Guineanness. Fragments of such characteristics can be found in the major political and economic centers in the urban areas such as Port Moresby, Lae, Madang, Mt. Hagen, and maybe Goroka. If one tries to define a public or national culture in, say, the provincial capital of Simbu Province, Kundiawa, one has to look for it in the government offices and at Radio Simbu.[2] Outside these institutional representatives of the nation-state, the only other loyalties to be found are those that revolve around kin-based relationships. If one furthermore deducts the more indirect mechanisms behind the creation of a national culture—for instance, commodity consumption, education, legal action, and Christianity, which also in themselves have to be assessed critically due to local recontextualizations—then the town as such does not constitute a manifest focal point for a dominant national culture, neither for the people using the town nor for the few tourists who dare to visit it. Rather, Kundiawa is virtually a small town, a service center for business and shopping.

After now having confined the exponents of nationness to the major urban enclaves, one might speculate about the viability of the project: the creation of the nation, Papua New Guinea. It is of vital importance that the message of nationalism and the development of a national culture penetrate the different societal domains to create a coherent national entity. However, because the various political and ideological attempts and the somewhat subtle mechanisms of nationhood have failed to penetrate the vast rural areas, some kind of resistance to this penetration must persist. I am not necessarily talking about organized sociopolitical resistance toward this penetration in the form of *kastom* ("custom" or "tradition") groups and/or sociopolitical movements. Rather, I would like to point to a systemic resistance, one that no ideology in itself can break down or transform, as ideology itself is only part of what it takes to create a nation.

In taking a systemic approach to the analysis of the creation of a nation, it is not enough to analyze the ideological constructs. One also has to analyze the implementation and entrenchment of the economic relations of production, because they are the ones that, among other things, are to reproduce both the political and institutional foundations of the new nation.

The low level of national awareness among the different cultural groups in the hinterlands of Papua New Guinea is remarkable. All the modern sociopolitical institutions are implemented—Parliament and provincial governments together with their respective administrative supporting institutions—but the effectiveness of these different institutions is minimal. Even capitalist relations of production have for the most part only managed to penetrate the subsistence economy in the sphere of circulation. By this I mean that capitalist social relations of production[3] have not replaced or fundamentally transformed existing forms of production praxis in the rural areas, thereby subsuming these other forms under capitalist production in the form of, say, commodity production. Instead, an adjustment of those other forms of production has developed such as to accommodate both a market economy and the necessity of subsistence production. We thus have a production form that has its own specific characteristics, and is therefore not just a disguised form of capitalist commodity production, as some theorists would have it (for example, Bernstein 1979, 431). This situation has had a damaging effect for the nation-state in its inwardly oriented development. The prevalence of subsistence production in the rural areas means political and economic autonomy for the local communities, and thus less ability for the nation-state to control them. The capitalist economy in its most advanced form—that is, where the social relations of production are the dominant form of economic relations—is confined to a few economic enclaves, spread throughout the nation.

This development, or rather lack thereof, tells us something about the integrity of the local communities, the so-called traditional cultures. What I would like to emphasize in this chapter is that the process of nation making is slowly coming to a halt precisely because of the integrity of the local communities. I will go even further than that and postulate that the local communities are subverting the nation-state itself, thus rendering it self-contradictory in its very constitution.

In this chapter I address the following questions: what will happen when the contradiction between the foreign-designed Papua New Guinean nation-state and the indigenous culture groups that make up the national hinterland becomes too great to suppress, both politically and ideologically? And what will happen when the indigenous culture groups realize the ideological nature of their incorporation into this national framework, thereby leaving them, in effect, without any possibility of directly influencing the further development of the nation-state (see LiPuma this volume)? Will such a realization upset the processes of harmonization within the nation, processes that are of vital importance for the entrenchment of the idea of nationhood, thereby questioning the legitimacy of the nation-state itself? Or will it produce different degrees of displacement among the various social strata within "the nation," thus endangering the whole process of national integration?

The answers to these questions have to be found beyond ideological or political explanations because they mostly pertain to a social domain that, again, only constitutes a minute part of "the nation." As previously suggested, one also has to turn to the institutional framework that constitutes or activates the nation and incorporate analysis of how the factual political and administrative setup articulates with the indigenous culture groups if one wishes to address the total process of nation making.

Such an approach leads to the ultimate question: what would happen if the overall conceptual and institutional framework of the Papua New Guinean nation-state changes; if the notions of nation and nationalism are no longer accepted as "natural"; and if new societal structures are demanded, or suggested, by the indigenous local cultures and/or international capitalism? Following these lines of inquiry, I shall try to show how the nation-state of Papua New Guinea might be, in a not too distant future, sandwiched between local demands and international pressure. Consequently, the nation-state of Papua New Guinea might be forced to reorganize its basic societal structures and institutions to meet these new demands, thereby transforming itself in the process into other, perhaps more appropriate, societal constructs (see LiPuma this volume).

The discussion begins by describing the establishment of Papua New Guinea as a nation-state, emphasizing the political and intellectual milieu in which the national framework was created. It then goes on to describe the encounter between this national structure and the local communities, stressing the interaction and possible incompatibilities between the two. Leaving the Papua New Guinean scene for a moment, a discussion of Western Europe is provided on the latest developments in relation to nationhood and nationalism. After taking up some recent trends there, the focus is again turned toward Papua New Guinea and the Melanesian scene to see if the trends depicted in Western Europe can be found there and what consequences this might have for the future of nation making in Melanesia.

The Introduction of the Modern Political System

On 16 September 1975, Papua New Guinea became independent. As a new member in an exclusive club of third world nations, this new nation presented itself to the world community as a decentralized representative democracy, confined within a unitary state form: a notable achievement in the Third World, where the order of the day for new nations was and is more-or-less well-camouflaged dictatorships.

This type of political system does not originate in Papua New Guinea but, rather, is the result of a long historically conditioned political development in Western Europe. How did this type of political system turn up in Papua New Guinea, and what has become of the original types of political systems in Papua New Guinea? Have the latter disappeared as a consequence of the hardships of colonialism and the establishment of the modern nation-state, since no trace of them can be found as contributing elements to the making of this new nation? The logical answer to these questions is that there is no historical continuity between past and present in contemporary Papua New Guinea, or to put it in another way, there is no room for the real past in the real present, as this part of the past is obviously considered unsuitable in the making of both the present and future.

These assumptions can be verified by looking at the way in which the Papua New Guinean nation-state came into existence. Leaving aside the pre- and postcolonial economic integration of Papua New Guinea into the world economy, and concentrating on the development of the modern political system, one finds that despite what some nationalists see as a further development of the traditional political systems, representative democracy is a foreign import and as such has nothing to do with the original political traditions anywhere in Papua New Guinea.

In the first place, the coalition government led by Chief Minister Michael Somare in 1972 was kept together not by a common political-ideological platform based on a comprehensive alternative strategy of development, but by opposition to Australian colonization. In other words, the spirit of nationalism in a neotraditionalistic disguise was *not* the main inspiration behind the political forces leading to independence. Neither did the relatively peaceful transition from colonial to postcolonial status leave any room for aggressive political mobilization: extra-parliamentary activity was extremely weak. There were no "congress" parties as in India, no revolutionary fronts, and no mass movements of protest to constitute a foundation for producing nationalist ideology (Loveday and Wolfers 1976, 103).

In this vacuum of public discourse, the Somare government hired an advisory team. It was recruited through the Overseas Development Group from the University of East Anglia, then the most radical center for development studies in the United Kingdom, and headed by Michael Faber. This advisory team was cosponsored by the United Nations Development Programme (UNDP) and the Australian Government.

This was an auspicious conjuncture: an advisory team offering an alternative charter for development and a new reformist government looking for one. It resulted in the Report on Development Strategies for Papua New Guinea (the Faber Report), which contained the basis for the Eight Point Improvement Plan adopted by the Somare government in 1972 (Fitzpatrick 1985, 22–24).

Here it is interesting to note the terms of reference within which the Faber team worked: after the 1968 "revolutions" in the Western nations but before the major economic recessions in the early 1980s, which ushered in postmodernism with its antisystemic ideology. Instead, the intellectual mainstream adhered to the various socialist strategies carried out, for example, in some African countries such as Tanzania. Even though these theoretical approaches were not explicitly spelled out in the final Eight Point Improvement Plan, one easily can find the underlying themes of Maoism, the Tanzanian experiment, and the "cult of appropriate technology," to use a phrase from Fitzpatrick (1985). After all, the Faber team could not have openly used these references. They would not have gone down well in Australia, one of the team's main sponsors.

It was only in the beginning of 1975 that the first Papua New Guinean nationalistic fingerprints on the new political guidelines appeared. They were mainly those of the deputy chair of the Constitutional Planning Committee (CPC), Father John Momis, and the philosopher and lawyer Bernard Narokobi. Together they drafted the preamble of the constitution, and a list entitled National Goals and Directive Principles, which were incorporated into the constitution of Papua New Guinea.

However, even though these nationalistic fingerprints did "naturalize" (or culturalize) the imported political ideological guidelines, the coalition government still had to rely on foreign advisers to further develop the political system according to the Eight Point Improvement Plan.[4] Therefore, on 28 February 1974, two consultants, Professor R. Watts from the Queen's University in Kingston, Canada, and Professor W. Tordoff from the Department of Government at the University of Manchester in the United Kingdom, were appointed by the CPC to "advise the committee on relation between the central government and other levels of government" (Tordoff 1985, 197).

The CPC, chaired ex officio by Somare, wanted a decentralized form of government within the framework of a unitary state system. This was actually an old debate, dating back to 1965, about which political system to choose. The major choice then stood between a federal system and a unitary system of government. Eventually, the CPC advocated a unitary government structure, but with a substantial degree of political and administrative decentralization.[5] Papua New Guinea as we know it today became a reality.

Beside the heavy European influence in the creation of the Papua New Guinean nation-state, an important question must be raised. Where are the traditional societies in this new national construct? As already mentioned, they are not incorporated into the basic structures of this new society. Why? It is tempting to assume that they are not incorporated because there is no structural room for them. They are, in other words, structurally incompatible with the newly implemented societal structures. The only room left for this incompatible majority, then, is in the ideological realm, expressed in a nationalist construct such as "Papua New Guinean Ways," in which the more spectacular features of the different local cultures are turned into a generalized cultural theater where "traditional" dances, costumes, artifacts, and so forth are displayed.

The Creation of the State and the Development of Nationalism in the Third World

Why this state of affairs? Is it really necessary to have a nation and a nationalism to have a Papua New Guinea? Is it conceptual conventionalism on the part of the Westernized Papua New Guinean elites that, together with the Western European intellectual elites, created these societal constructs? Given intellectual links, one must pose the questions in another way. Since the different intelligentsias share the same perception of how to create, or rather shape, a modern society—overlooking, or maybe even suppressing, alternative and perhaps more viable societal possibilities—then one must take a closer look at the origin of their common conceptual constructs.

The concepts of nation and nationalism have their origin in the development of the capitalist mode of production in Europe. Capitalism, however, is not confined to the Old World. Because of its dynamic and expanding nature, it spread throughout the Third World through colonialism and imperialism, thus creating the foundations for the present world order. What is of interest here is that when capitalism or, more precisely, capitalist relations of production became entrenched in different parts of the Third World, nationalist ideologies and the development of nations simultaneously began to appear, initiated by emergent national elites. The expansion of capitalism from the Old World to the New World was thus not restricted to a specific economic system, but also included specific societal frameworks that made the economy operate more smoothly. The irony of this state of affairs is that it was the colonialized people themselves—in the case of Papua New Guinea, a small, Westernized elite—who "created" this "new" societal framework, perpetuated their own political and economical inferiority, and thereby allowed a further entrenchment of the capitalist relations of production.

As in many other parts of the Third World, the different Melanesian nations express themselves officially in a specific form of nationalism which can be termed *neotraditionalism*. This form of nationalism usually consists of a combination of "Essentialism," or the reification of an indigenous way of life, and "Epochalism," or the spirit of the age, to use concepts developed by Geertz (1973). He describes the relationship, or rather, the tension between the two (243): "to move with the tide of the present and to hold on to an inherited course," which "gives new state nationalism its peculiar air of being at once hell-bent towards modernity and morally outraged by its manifestations." Geertz is here referring to the schism that develops when the ideological manifestations of capitalism fall short of the actual socioeconomic developments, exposing a reality that contradicts the ideological expositions. In relation to Papua New Guinea, I only have to mention the nonincorporation of the local cultures into the national framework and the devastating force of regionalism and separatism in relation to nationhood to make my point.

The main task for this neotraditionalistic nationalism is to create a collective "we," a national identity, the aim of which is to coordinate an otherwise culturally heterogeneous national hinterland. The purpose of this exercise is to avoid or prevent the development of alternative forms of "internal" nationalisms, which in the last instance might have a destabilizing or even disintegrative effect on national cohesion (Geertz 1973, 238–49).

In the Melanesian context, one finds these pseudocultural national ideologies in the pan-Melanesian construction of the "Melanesian Way" (Narokobi 1980, 1983). As constitutive parts of this pan-Melanesianism, one finds more "local" forms of nationalism, say, the concept of ni-Vanuatu and Papua New Guinean Ways. These political-ideological constructions, usually developed by national elites, are substantiated by their incorporation into their respective national constitutions. In the process, the ideological constructions are formalized and thus made part of the rest of the national state and power apparatus.

A further effect of this substantiation and formalization of the national ideologies is that other ideological and political forms of leadership, such as the precolonial ones, are excluded and subordinated to the national one. In this way the national ideology consolidates its position vis-à-vis other rival forms of leadership in the same overall societal context. The different constitutions are thus the very charter by which the new nations legitimate themselves, both internally and externally (Ghai 1983, 55).

In the case of Papua New Guinea, it is explicitly stated in the national constitution, both in the preamble and throughout the main text, that Epochalism and Essentialism— that is, introduced social and political ideas and indigenous forms of social, political, and economic organizations—are to coexist under the common designation of Papua New Guinean Ways.[6] There are, however, two major problems with this coexistence. The first is that the apparent symmetry between the two is in reality an asymmetry, because the indigenous customs and traditions are for all practical purposes subordinate to national laws. The second and most important problem is the way in which this subordination is defined. The basic premises here are the fundamental rights of the individual as defined in the constitution.[7] These rights are based on Western philosophy and values and can seriously undermine the bases of the traditional authority, for example, the right to exercise jurisdiction, to impose sanctions, to exile, and to restrict mobility (Ghai 1983, 55–58; see also LiPuma this volume).

In short, it is the state that defines the nation of Papua New Guinea through the national ideology of Papua New Guinean Ways, and not vice versa. In this way, it is the encompassing and ordering power of the state that maintains the nation as a coherent entity. The failure of the power of the state to maintain coherence in the whole order it circumscribes therefore threatens the integrity of the nation. It follows that the fragmentation of the state is also the fragmentation of the nation.[8]

Contextualizing the Nation-State

It is thus easy to understand the importance that the national leadership attributes to the development of an appropriate national ideology, based on a concept of individuality and citizenship, in creating a coherent nation-state. According to their convictions, those who control and implement a dominant national ideology are also those who are able to control the culturally heterogeneous national hinterland. This means upholding and further developing a sense of national identity and nationhood at the expense of local communalism and kinship ties.

There is, however, one major problem. As previously noted, there are intimate connections among capitalism, nationalism, and the creation of "the nation." Consider a nation where capitalist social relations of production are for the most part confined to economic enclaves and otherwise weakly represented throughout the rest of the nation—that is, mainly confined to the sphere of commodity production—thereby allowing the "primordial" societies a high degree of reproductive autonomy, which makes them somewhat independent of the national society. What consequences does this have for national legitimacy and the further entrenchment of the national institutions with respect to these "primordial" societies? Who, then, does such a nation represent?

As I have argued, the creation of the nation Papua New Guinea was an elitist exercise, heavily aided by Western experts. Furthermore, the indigenous cultures have not been incorporated into the official nation-making process; they have been perceived as constituting archaic and thus useless remnants of times past. The only use these remnants of the past have is to legitimate the present. This is quite evident in the nationalist ideology of Papua New Guinean Ways.

It is thus clear that there are two major types of societies in Papua New Guinea that coexist but apparently do not interact. To take a closer look at this apparent lack of intersocietal interaction or articulation, I leave the national domain and concentrate on provincial and local domains in order to ascertain the degree of entrenchment of the nation.

On the basis of my fieldwork in Eastern Highlands Province in 1986–87, which concentrated on the establishment of introduced political and administrative institutions, the filtering down of nationalist ideologies, and the local response to these developments, it appeared almost immediately that it was very difficult to compare national and provincial politics. For one thing, national ideologies were nonexistent in the provincial domain, and political parties, which can be perceived as the spearhead of new political ideas and as the link between national and provincial politics, were met with widespread skepticism by provincial politicians (cf. Facey this volume). Most politicians declared themselves independent of party politics because they, according to themselves, represented the people directly. National politics and politicians were generally regarded with great suspicion and often associated with nepotism.

Further down the political system at the local government level, hostile relations existed between councilors and provincial politicians because both felt they competed for the same resources handed down from the national government. Furthermore, the councilors accused the provincial politicians of slowly killing the local government councils by taking over ever more of the councils' functions. The working relationship between the two levels of government, the local government councils and the provincial government, was generally not effective.

The provincial administration, which in 1987 was divided into the Department of Eastern Highlands (the local branch of the national bureaucracy) and a Provincial Secretariat (a special secretariat for aiding the provincial government), worked rather well. However, both parts of the administration were hampered by underqualified personnel and a constant turnover of staff, a state of affairs that for the most part was conditioned by a nationally dictated localization process which, according to provincial understanding, aimed at transforming Eastern Highlands Province for Eastern Highlanders exclusively.

The relationship between the provincial politicians and the administration can best be described as asymmetrical to the advantage of the administrators. This description was especially true for the relationship between politicians and the Provincial Secretariat. As the personnel of the latter generally had university degrees in administration and thus were capable of managing and manipulating the complicated bureaucracy, the politicians had great difficulties in working with the secretariat and understanding how to manipulate it to their advantage. And because they had to rely heavily on the secretariat for help, the politicians de facto had less power than the personnel employed to assist them.[9]

The politicians were not only hampered in their work by a powerful secretariat and administration, but also the conditions under which they became politicians had an important influence on their political maneuverability. By comparing how one becomes a local leader, or "big man," if you like, with how one becomes a provincial politician, it was possible to disclose a close relationship between local demands for development and the performance of the politicians. The latter were perceived by the local communities as a magnified local leader who only handled provincial politics, which consisted mainly of getting development projects back to each leader's constituencies. Local politics were taken care of by local leaders, clan leaders, and "big men." In the event that politicians did not fulfill the expectations of their constituencies, they were replaced at the next election with new representatives. A detailed investigation of how the different local communities chose their representatives to the provincial government showed that it was clans or sections of clans in alliance that promoted their candidate and that accordingly exerted a degree of control over the politicians.

These close ties between a politician and his constituency largely explained why the politicians did not embrace the political parties. Political parties were and still are not popular among the village people. According to informants, villagers feel that political parties do not serve their interests because they act according to their party platform and not individual (i.e., clan) interests. As a result, village people prefer independent politicians.

Local interests are also registered within the administration, especially through people employed there as public servants. As mentioned earlier, there is a great turnover of staff, mostly due to the localization process. This process of earmarking positions within the administration has created a possibility for the local communities to influence decision making within the administration. As in the case of the provincial politicians, employees take their clan affiliations with them into the administration and are as such vulnerable to pressure and demands from their clans. On the other hand, many employees use their position within the administration as a stepping-stone for a political career, which is why most are not positively interested in their job as administrators. They are just waiting for the right moment to resign and try their luck as politicians, a position that carries much greater prestige in their local communities than does being a government employee.

It is clear that there does not exist a sharp division between the introduced and indigenous sectors in the nation-state. In fact, they interact in a highly complex way. The interesting point here is that modern society does not act as a juggernaut with respect to the indigenous societies, eradicating them on its way to supremacy. On the contrary, it seems as if the indigenous cultures have the ability to infiltrate the modern political and administrative institutions, thus slowly transforming and domesticating them to suit the interests of the local communities. This being the case, the entrenchment of modern society in the national hinterland—here, the Highlands region—has come to a standstill; over time, modern society must change its basic institutions to conform to the indigenous setting. This change has consequences for the modern society as its founding institutions slowly evolve into somewhat uncontrollable hybrids that generate unpredictable feedback for the encompassing nation-state. Modern society as a tight and well-structured entity is thus slowly cracking up at its constitutional foundation.

One of the important ingredients behind this process is the integrity of the indigenous cultures. During a second period of fieldwork among the Dom people in Simbu Province in 1990, this integrity was the object of intensive study. The main topics of research were how the local communities perceive modern society in all its complexity, with special emphasis on how modernity is incorporated into the local universe (Jacobsen 1992).

The Dom people, who live about ten kilometers southwest of the provincial capital Kundiawa, are mainly subsistence farmers and coffee growers. Now and then they sell different produce for the market, but it is not a requirement for economic survival. They are in the luxurious position of being able to withdraw or (re)enter the market economy at will when the need for using money arises. This flexibility is possible because all Dom residing in the Dom territory have access to a piece of land on which to subsist, either from their agnatic or affinal kinsmen.[10] Accordingly, no young men are forced to migrate because of lack of land. Another circumstance that similarly discourages young men from taking up wage labor is that there is no head tax to pay. The provincial government abolished it in 1985 and replaced it with a retail sales tax system.

In general, the Dom people are closely connected to their clans and kin groupings, and accordingly to their ancestral land. People do migrate, especially young men, but this is mostly for a shorter period of time, usually when a specific need for money arises, typically in connection with marriage and compensation payments. Some people also migrate in search for wage labor for longer periods of time, but only a few have no intention of returning to the home community. The pattern of migration can thus be characterized as circular.

This situation gives these communities great leeway in minding their own business. They only engage directly in the "outer" society when specific occasions arise, say, at local government, provincial, and national elections, and the few occasions an agriculture specialist visits them to tell them how to improve the output of their coffee production. People do visit the provincial capital regularly to buy rice, beer, tinned fish, and other foodstuffs when they have money. Otherwise, they just visit the town for a spin, meeting friends, drinking beer, and hoping for something to happen. As such, the town as a materialized expression of modernity does not have great importance in people's lives.

In discussing the national and provincial government as the political representatives of the modern society, local leaders and people in general distinguish rather sharply between these institutions and their own local community. This distinction is based on a principle of priority: the local community occupies the all-important place in the lives of every individual. Here one's identity is formed through different processes of socialization into one's respective subclan, and here people are born, marry, and die. This, then, is the center of their life cycles. "The nation" and all it stands for are something "out there" which only become reality on specific occasions, for instance, at national election time. In this regard, as in the case of the provincial politicians, national politicians are perceived as an extension of their local communities, and as such are expected to deliver "development" back home—a difficult task, it seems, when one looks at the turnover of politicians at national elections. Yet people are proud of Papua New Guinea as an independent nation; and "by the way, there is an important compensation payment coming up at Damamene tomorrow!"

The provincial government is often perceived as an extended forum for local politics. It is not a question of what the local community can do for the provincial government but, rather, what the provincial government can be pressed to do for the local community. The means for obtaining specific services from the government are politicians and the public servants. The general attitude toward the provincial government is pragmatic: what can it do for you? If nothing, then *"maski"* ("forget it" in Tok Pisin). It is thus not seen as a political forum but, rather, as a source of wealth which can be tapped if only the right means are employed. Otherwise, the provincial government is something that can be found in the provincial capital; it is not really important for the day-to-day life in the individual local community.

The administrative institutions of both the national and provincial governments are remote and considered foreign institutions. They normally come into one's mind when one is related to a government employee who might get one a job some time in the future. Again, these official institutions only come into existence when something special happens: landslides ("now the landowners can get compensation for the gardens destroyed; the government did not pay that much for the land when they bought it for the road in the first place!") or campaigns for new agricultural products ("a very good chance of getting free seedlings!"). In between these kinds of events, the official institutions, which make up a key part of the modern sector, exist only remotely in the minds of the people.

I nearly forgot the ideological dimension. Melanesian Way, Papua New Guinean Ways, or other political ideological constructions—what is that? Never heard of it! After giving some information about these ideological constructs, most of the leaders say: "Bullshit. *Em i tok win, tasol* ['It's only useless talk']. We Dom people are special. We are different from the Sinasina, Gumine, Era, and Yure people. We are proud of that."

On the basis of such statements, it can be seen that the indigenous cultures not only have their integrity intact, but also are slowly infiltrating the modern society in its most important institutions, thereby alienating these institutions from their own structural settings. The process of nation making is thus arrested by the very hinterland it was supposed to integrate and homogenize.

This situation poses some important questions. What happens when the national hinterland remains heterogeneous, that is, sustains its overwhelming cultural pluralism? Does this mean national disintegration in the long run? If the politicization of traditional cultures has not yet occurred, then perhaps another process—one even more dangerous for the nation—has been set in motion. Have we been witnessing the emergence of an intersystemic process of articulation? As pointed out earlier, the indigenous cultures were not incorporated into the foundation of the modern nation-state Papua New Guinea for two major reasons. First, in the early phases of nationhood, the enthusiasm for the ideology of representative democracy within the boundaries of a unitary state overshadowed the existing societies and their potential contributions to the making of the new nation. Second, the incorporation of the indigenous cultures into the introduced society became increasingly impossible as the complexity of the national society increased. This lack of incorporation has had the apparent effect that the indigenous societies became even more elusive, inward looking and disaffected, thereby making them difficult for the nation-state to "domesticate" and incorporate.

As this chapter has shown, however, the introduced and indigenous societies do not exist as two separate noninteracting entities. On the contrary, they interact in a complex way despite the fact that the local communities are still not incorporated into the basic structures of the nation-state (except in the ideological realm). Even though the indigenous culture units have been forced to conform to changing sociopolitical circumstances during the colonial and postcolonial period, this does not mean they have lost their specificity during the process. Their communal integrity is intact, and furthermore, they more-or-less consciously articulate themselves with the different introduced political and administrative institutions, thereby subverting the functional capacity of the latter. For the present, the outcome of this process has been that the different national institutions slowly become institutional hybrids, thereby endangering the whole process of nation making.

Nations, Nationalism, and the Encompassing World Economy

One can well question whether the whole concept of nations and nationalism is an appropriate construct for a postcolonial Papua New Guinea. Is the application of nationhood, with all its specific institutional and ideological entailments, merely the result of conceptional conventionalism on behalf of the national elites? This seems to be the case.

Here it is important to remember the historical specificity of nationhood. Like any other phenomena created in the course of history, nations and nationalism have a limited life span, whereafter new forms of societal organization develop. Here I make a brief reference to contemporary Europe to stress my point.

It is an established fact that during the last two decades, the international capitalist world economy has gone through rapid change that has taken the form of moving from nation-specific processes of production toward international processes of production. One of the driving forces behind this development is industrial specialization in the fields of high technology and mass communication.[11] This means that the international economy achieves a higher degree of mobility, so that the economic centers of the world are no longer fixed or concentrated in a single region as in former times. Now there are several economic centers located throughout the world, the most powerful of which are situated in East and Southeast Asia, for instance, Japan, South Korea, Hong Kong, and Singapore. The old centers, the United States and especially Western Europe, are now in a state of recession, or reconstruction, if you like. This does not mean that this part of the world economy is in decline but, rather, that it is restructuring its productive forces to meet the new demands of the international economy.

The growing fluidity of the world economy also means that the old forms of imperialism, normally delineated in center-periphery models, no longer are the sole form of large-scale relations of exploitation. Now, every form of economic relations has to be filtered through this world economy, which as a result has become an entity in its own right. Consequently, all nations, both the so-called industrial nations and the developing ones, have to relate to this world economy, thereby subordinating themselves to this entity.

A good example of this national subordination to a changing world economy is Western Europe. For example, Friedman (1989) has called attention to a process of European deindustrialization put into motion by the relocation of world economic accumulation to new centers. This deindustrialization has curtailed each individual European nation's abilities to accumulate capital, which, as a further consequence, has led to an undermining of the national ethos in each nation (1989, 62). The safety net of nation making and nationalism that early capitalism created to safeguard its future development has now been transformed into a kind of straitjacket for further expansion (see Gellner 1983).

To break this deadlock, recent developments have taken two directions. The first is regional economic cooperation, comprising almost all the Western European nations, the European Economic Community (EEC). The long-term plan of this organization is to create the framework for a new world economic power center to be able to compete with the power centers of Japan, Singapore, and North America. One of the major ways to do this is to overcome the national fragmentation inside the EEC by creating an open internal market in order to boost the ability to accumulate capital on a larger scale. This process is currently in full swing through processes of "structural adjustment" or pan-European harmonizations and is expected to be accomplished in the near future.

The second trend, which is a consequence of the first one, is that each of the nations within the EEC has slowly undergone a transformation in its constitution. As a consequence of the opening up of Europe, the concept of nation and thus nationalism is slowly losing its usefulness as a focus for the processes of identity formation. As the nation-state dissolves as a result of increasing transnationalism, so too will the legitimating forces behind the perception of nationhood dissolve. The link between the institutional setup of the nation-state, which defines the territorial borders between the individual nation-states, and the ideological constructs of nationhood and nationalism that correspond to this institutional setup and create a sense of national cohesiveness, slowly loses its importance. As a consequence, the supremacy of national identity in relation to other kinds of identities—say, the many ethnic identities emerging in Europe—is thereby being undermined.

The asymmetry between two processes of identity formation is thus undergoing qualitative change. Not only is the asymmetry between national and ethnic ethos broken down and leveled, but also a process of additional cultural fragmentation is occurring. The relations of ideological domination are thus eroding. This development might be one of the reasons behind the pan-European rise of regional and ethnic groups and movements, which demand autonomy from the individual nation-state but nonetheless still depend for their reproduction on now transnational relations of production (see Björklund 1986).

What confuses one here, when analyzing these processes, is the rhetoric used by the different ethnic groups themselves. They proclaim they want their own "state," and several analysts define this rhetoric as being nationalist. I think this is an expression of conceptual conventionalism on behalf of both the ethnic groups and the analysts. Looked at objectively, are most of the "states" people are fighting and dying for at the moment really capable of reproducing themselves as independent nations in the generally accepted sense of the term? What does an "independent nation-state" mean today? How can any nation-state become independent in the face of an increasingly competitive international and diffusionist capitalism, one that demands cooperation and societal flexibility of the different national entities in order for them to exist as distinct societal units? I think we are witnessing, especially in Eastern Europe, the production of new societal constructs founded on ethnic identities as the common denominator, societal constructs we cannot but perceive as "nations" and "states" because we have to define them in known terms to understand and classify them. But this is unfortunate, because then we cannot perceive the novelty and distinctiveness of these societal developments.

If the present societal developments in Europe are resulting in the creation of more stable societal constructs, based on the principle of ethnic and/or regional identities, then these will be perfectly capable of coping with the new demands for identity formation in a postnational and postnationalist Europe. The European capitalist economy has thus cultivated the ground for the creation of ideal societal constructs for its own further development, once freed from national and nationalist constraints, thereby becoming perfectly equipped to meet new demands from a constantly transforming global economy.

Conclusion: A Melanesian Confederacy?

So far I have argued that the nation-states of Europe hinder the expansion of capitalism; this situation has provoked a reorganization of the different national entities. This reorganization, in turn, has resulted in the emergence of new forms of societal (dis)organizations—proliferating ethnic groups, cultural fragmentation, the development of regionalism—thus making the overall European social landscape more fluid. This development prompts one to question the appropriateness of nationhood and nationalism in a Melanesian context, especially in Papua New Guinea.

It is obvious to most observers of Papua New Guinean politics that regionalism is on the rise, causing serious problems for the nation-state as a coherent entity. Leaving aside their description by the authorities as minor domestic problems within the nation Papua New Guinea, are these developments in reality governed by the same forces that govern developments in Europe? Does the nation-state of Papua New Guinea constitute a straitjacket for the further sociopolitical development of Papua New Guinea?

Witness the Bougainville crisis, as well as the opening up of new mine and oil fields in the Highlands region which creates tension between national and local interests, not to mention problems with local landowner associations nationwide. The nation-state Papua New Guinea is trying to contain these potential dangers to national coherence, and at the same time legitimate its position as the ultimate power center, configured in the state (see LiPuma this volume).

If the Papua New Guinea state fails to maintain coherence in the nation Papua New Guinea, and if the individual regions begin to deal directly with the international economy,[12] is Papua New Guinea then moving toward a postnational and postnationalist epoch, as in the case of Europe? Is regionalism, which has its roots in the early days of colonialism, more suited to handle the fluidity of the world economy, thereby leaving the nation Papua New Guinea to act as an intermediary link between the individual regions and the world economy?

Other important features come to mind when comparing the development of nationhood in Papua New Guinea with the ongoing reorganization of Europe. For example, whereas the developments in Europe are partly caused by the fragmentation of the capitalist economy, the fragmentation of Papua New Guinea as a coherent nation-state is mostly caused by sociopolitical forces, because Papua New Guinea is not yet capitalized to the same degree as Europe. Furthermore, as Papua New Guinea has never been fully penetrated by capitalist relations of production, its discrete fragments constitute relatively autonomous societies in their own right. This status implies that their relation to international capital is different from that of Catalonia or Bretagne, which, to a great degree, still depend on capitalist relations of production for their reproduction as ethnic entities.[13] The outcome of the Papua New Guinea case will thus be different from that of its European counterparts.

What would happen if the nation-state Papua New Guinea were transformed into a confederation of the four regions that today make up the country: Papua, the Highlands, Mamose,[14] and the Islands? Present-day nationhood obviously has its limitations and drawbacks when embracing all four regions at one time. And what effect would that have on the other Melanesian nation-states? They are just as much creations of colonialism as Papua New Guinea is. Maybe one day in a not too distant future, we will see the rise of an integrated Melanesian confederacy, and the old conceptions of nation and nationalism will be regarded as blind alleys of history.

ACKNOWLEDGMENTS

I am grateful to Robert Foster, Jonathan Friedman, Ellen Facey, Nicholas Thomas, and James Carrier for the incisive comments they made on earlier versions of this chapter.

NOTES

1. According to the 1990 census, the total population of Papua New Guinea (PNG) is 3,576,066, with 565,018 people living in urban areas and the rest in rural areas (*1992 Statistical Yearbook for Asia and the Pacific*. Bangkok: United Nations Economic and Social Commission for Asia and the Pacific).

2. In defining a national culture in this context, I here follow Eric Hirsch (1990, 19): "[a] national culture (is) a system of ideas and practices which transcend individual linguistic/cultural units and have a roughly uniform significance within flexible, but generally well-defined political boundaries."

3. "The social relations of production encompass and relate the relations of production, appropriation, distribution and utilization of the social product as a whole" (Bernstein 1979, 422).

4. For a detailed discussion, see Conyers 1976, 38–50.

5. For a detailed discussion, see Conyers 1976, 41–42, and Standish 1979, 14–18.

6. See Preamble, especially National Goals and Directive Principles, No. 5: Papua New Guinean Ways (pp. 4–5), and Schedule 2, Part 1, Custom 2.1 (pp. 1–3).

7. See Part III—Basic Principles of Government, Division 3: Basic Rights, Subdivision A–D.

8. I owe this insight to Kapferer (1988, 1–26). However, it must be emphasized that there are great differences between the Sri Lankan nation-state, which Kapferer writes about, and the Papua New Guinean nation-state. Taking these differences into account, I still maintain that it is fully defensible to use Kapferer's analysis of the relationship between state and nation.

9. For a detailed discussion of this interesting relationship, see Jacobsen 1991a.

10. Wohlt and Goie (1986, 7) observed among the peoples of North Simbu that: "Most young men who are natal clan members inherit an adequate selection of land. If for some reason they do not, they have alternatives. Their brothers or other clansmen (probably a bigman who has or looks after much land) can usually provide a piece of ground. Alternatively they must look to their wife's or mother's clansmen."

11. For example, a general redeployment of production made possible by multinationalized capital in the manufacture of automobiles, electronic equipment (especially computers), textiles, and so forth.

12. An example is the application of Western Highlands Province to have its airport upgraded to international standards.

13. I owe this insight to Jonathan Friedman, personal communication, 1991.

14. This term covers the north coast of Papua New Guinea and includes the provinces of West Sepik, East Sepik, Madang, and Morobe.

REFERENCES

Anderson, Benedict. 1983. *Imagined Communities: Reflections on the Origin and Spread of Nationalism*. London: Verso.

Bernstein, Henry. 1979. African peasantries: A theoretical framework. *Journal of Peasant Studies* 6:421–43.

Björklund, Ulf. 1986. World-systems, the welfare state, and ethnicity. *Ethnos* 51:285–306.

Conyers, Diana. 1976. *The Provincial Government Debate*. Boroko, Papua New Guinea: Institute of Applied Social and Economic Research.

Fitzpatrick, Peter. 1985. The making and unmaking of the Eight Aims. In P. King, W. Lee, and V. Warakai, eds., *From Rhetoric to Reality? Papua New Guinea's Eight Point Plan and National Goals After a Decade*, 22–31. University P.O.: University of Papua New Guinea Press.

Friedman, Jonathan. 1989. Culture, identity, and world process. *Review* 12:51–69.

Geertz, Clifford. 1973. After the revolution: The fate of nationalism in the new states. In *The Interpretation of Cultures*, 234–54. New York: Basic Books.

Gellner, Ernest. 1983. *Nations and Nationalism*. Oxford: Basil Blackwell.

Ghai, Yash. 1983. Constitutional issues in the transition to independence. In R. Crocombe and A. Ali, eds., *Foreign Forces in Pacific Politics*, 24–65. Suva, Fiji: University of the South Pacific, Institute of Pacific Studies.

Hirsch, Eric. 1990. From bones to betelnuts: Processes of ritual transformation and the development of "national culture" in Papua New Guinea. *Man*, n.s., 25:18–34.

Jacobsen, Michael. 1991a. Papua New Guinea—Between or betwixt? Some experiences from Eastern Highlands Province. University of Copenhagen. Mimeograph.

———. 1991b. On migration and societal reproduction among the Dom people of Simbu Province, Papua New Guinea. Paper presented at the workshop "The Global Anthropology of Oceania," 18–19 October, at University of Lund, Sweden.

———. 1992. In the shadow of Mt. Digibe: Persistence and social change among the Goreku-Kopan people of Dom. Ph.D. diss., University of Copenhagen.

Kapferer, Bruce. 1988. *Legends of People, Myths of State: Violence, Intolerance, and Political Culture in Sri Lanka and Australia*. Washington: Smithsonian Institution Press.

Loveday, Peter, and Edward P. Wolfers. 1976. *Parties and Parliament in Papua New Guinea, 1964–75: Two Studies.* Boroko, Papua New Guinea: Institute of Applied Social and Economic Research.

Narokobi, Bernard. 1980. *The Melanesian Way.* Port Moresby: Institute of Papua New Guinea Studies.

———. 1983. *Life and Leadership in Melanesia.* Port Moresby: Institute of Papua New Guinea Studies.

Papua New Guinea. 1976. Constitution of the Independent State of Papua New Guinea. Port Moresby: Government Printer.

Standish, Bill. 1979. *Provincial Government in Papua New Guinea: Early Lessons from Chimbu.* Boroko, Papua New Guinea: Institute of Applied Social and Economic Research.

Tordoff, William. 1985. Provincial government in Papua New Guinea, 1974–82. In P. King, W. Lee, and V. Warakai, eds., *From Rhetoric to Reality? Papua New Guinea's Eight Point Plan and National Goals After a Decade,* 197–208. University P.O.: University of Papua New Guinea Press.

Wohlt, Paul B., and Anton Goie. 1986. *North Simbu Land Use* (*The Research Report of the Simbu Land Use Project, Volume V.*) Boroko, Papua New Guinea: Institute of Applied Social and Economic Research.

Epilogue

John D. Kelly

The Privileges of Citizenship:
Nations, States, Markets, and Narratives

Suppose we step back far enough to consider strange, rather than obvious, these ethnographers' desire to study nations and nation making. It is obvious that questions about present and future nations are important. But there is nothing obvious about the project of ethnographic research and writing about them. Here I will consider how these ethnographers have constituted the nation and nation-making processes as ethnographic objects, with special attention to the relations found among these nations, states, capitalist markets, and narratives, as observed.

I want to try to put these ethnographies of nation making in the context of recent trends in ethnography making. Ethnographers are still writing about people and things, but they are now centering ethnographic studies on things of a much larger scale and a different order of reality than was once normal for ethnography proper: things like nations, states, capitalist markets, and narratives. Let's compare what is changing in anthropological practice with what is dreamed of by our in-house philosophers.

There have been many recent efforts to capture changing ethnographic practice in images, generalizations, and recipes for future work, producing some important but particularly partial truths. One deliberately provocative school of thought, led by Clifford and Marcus (see Clifford 1986), presents the moment in images almost wholly focused on the ethnographers. The tale is told of a crisis in anthropology, an epistemological break, an end of modernism, and the emergence of a new sort of ethnography: an ethnography deliberate in its literary cunning, aware of its social grounding, flamboyant in acknowledging its dependence on subjective interests and experiences, the purveyor of partial truths indeed. This "reflexive" enlightenment is portrayed as if it came late to ethnography, but the "self-reflexive" ethnography is at least as often used as a vanguard instance of a new kind of social science, a social science more fully aware of the partial truth (at best) that its dependence on prose makes it, in this way, a subdiscipline of literary criticism (see, for example, White 1978).

The authors of the chapters in this volume are no doubt aware of this strand of current depiction of their discipline, but none seem to have found it useful to make their selves part of the ethnography. What they do find it useful to examine—things on the order of nations and processes on the order of nation making—makes more salient other recent efforts to capture the current situation in ethnographic work. These efforts focus less on the producers of ethnographies and more on the subjects of ethnographic depiction, and on changing research situations, relations and techniques. Asad (1973, 1986) and others have advocated increasing our attention to colonial and postcolonial context. Many scholars stress the need for more attention to migrating, displaced, uprooted people, and an end to the paradigm of a stable locatable community (for instance, a "village") as the proper unit for an ethnographic depiction (see, for example, Wolf 1982, Ferguson and Gupta 1992). Others declare a transformation of the world and seek ethnographic specification of a "postmodern" reality, often figured especially as a consumer-culture, global economy of "late capitalism." Here some of the most influential economic theorists are actually philosophers and literary critics (especially Baudrillard and Jameson), and the notion that we are past capitalism's half-life seems more a cunning effort to make a truth than a product of any kind of observation of anything. However, much of interest is being written under this rubric within anthropology, notably Appadurai's (1990) effort to figure an ethnography of disjuncture and Hannerz's (1989) effort to refigure Kroeber's (and indeed Wundt's) idea of a global, cosmopolitan cultural ecumene.

The result is not so much a crisis as a big mess, and an interesting one, within the discipline. It is perhaps better summarized as the collapse of a working research program than yet as the consolidation of a new one. If the end of the nineteenth century was marked by the collapse of the premise that ethnographic facts could find their place within stages of human evolution, the end of the twentieth century seems to be killing the premise that ethnography is the depiction of distant localities. The common product of the Boasian Americans and the British structural functionalists—detailed monographic depiction of coherent, whole, and small-scale social-cultural systems off somewhere separate from "us"— now seems quaint at best, and fatally flawed. Now the world seems irreducibly connected by complex and controlling lines of force, and ethnography requires techniques for depicting these connections and forces as well as differences and local systems.

Here we can leave aside interesting questions about whether the epistemic shifts within the discipline reflect changes in the world, and if so, how quickly and/or closely (see, for example, Smith 1991), and thus such problems as whether it is the world, or the ivory tower, that is now a postmodern global ecumene. Instead, working with the efforts to make sense of the contemporary Pacific that are collected here, we can reflect on the target and methods of study in this sort of ethnographic effort. Here the target is nations. But what is a nation, and how do you know one? To this question, what difference does an ethnographic approach make? These ethnographers resist simple answers, which I will now rush in to propose.

Questions

In this volume, Edward LiPuma provides us with a nuanced vision of a play of forces and connections in nation making. Nation-state mediations relate localities to larger wholes in complex social formations, without one determining vector or type of causality despite the real presence of a capitalist world. Here, and in Robert Foster's introduction, the capitalist market is measured for its epistemological impositions more than for its practical pressures, powers, and limits; it appears again, but with an aesthetic face, in Foster's chapter on print advertisements and nation making. What is the relation of these markets and nations? We have to consider both the practical and the aesthetic or epistemological aspects here.

The state is also an object for ethnographic assessment. In LiPuma's model and in many of the ethnographic chapters, especially Christine Jourdan's, the state is crucial as promoter of the nation via state ideological apparatuses, and it is difficult to imagine nation making outside of state institutions. Things are different, however, in Fiji, where an ethnic Fijian nation contests received definitions of citizenship and, through a coup, takes control of the state. Here, with the help of Henry Rutz and Martha Kaplan, we can ask questions about nations made against as well as within existing state apparatuses. Finally, these and all the chapters virtually require attention to the question at root of much current academic debate, the relation between nations and narratives.

States, Nations, and Narratives

Turning from questions to answers, I propose that the state, as it appears here, is generally the institution or set of institutions trying to define and defend property rights, to organize and control the division of labor, and thus to regulate the capitalist markets in a given territory. There are moments, here and there, of a more autonomously dynamic, Foucauldian, codifying state in action, a state whose center is ideological apparatuses.[1] But if we closely inspect these persuasive depictions (here see especially the chapters by Jourdan, Hirsch, Facey, and Jacobsen), "the state" in the Pacific has not been quite the same autonomous centralizing historical force that it has been, say, in France. Instead, here, we have states that came into being as the force and law organizing colonies, colonies mainly in the late-nineteenth-century imperialist flurry.[2] In these colonies, with their administrations acutely monitored for cost-effectiveness, the regulation and promotion of commerce was the center of the state mission, and the educational and other ideological apparatuses, such as they were, promoted an imperial social conception, not a national one.[3] Already, then, ethnography raises problems for theory: Is the state essentially capitalist? Is it essentially an officializing, truth-producing, and regulating disciplinary regime? If the chapters here in sum cast some doubt upon the latter, I also doubt the former. At least, states are not a necessary concomitant of capitalism in my view, as I will explain. But in the Pacific, they have clearly focused their regulating on topics of foreign and capitalist interest.

This makes the Pacific, in particular, a region where "the state" and "the nation" were least kindred, at the moment when the colonies gave way and "independent" regimes were fashioned. Perhaps, to keep things simple, it is the Foucauldian state that is so closely related to its people to deserve, after all, the title *nation-state*, the oneness of its people a product of its linguistic, social, and cultural regulating. Weber (1976) and Bourdieu (1991) are persuasive when they emphasize that the relative homogeneity of language and culture in nations in Europe was an outcome of state standardizing. But LiPuma (this volume) is also persuasive when he points out that the colonized regions made into states by the colonial powers in the Pacific (and many other places) were much more diverse, uneven, and culturally and linguistically complex than any region ever made into a nation-state in Europe. In any case, in the Pacific, we begin with states without nations. Then, in the Pacific as in other places, including Europe, we have candidate nations not originally connected to states: Kanaks, Bouganvilleans, the "ethnic" Fijians. What makes a nation if a state doesn't (and perhaps, even if a state does)? A narrative.

In fact, we might make the idea even simpler. "The nation" itself is a narrative. "The nation" is a narrative constituted dialogically and useful and important politically, for a state trying to regulate a capitalist market or for people to contest politically within and against the institutional framework of a state. "The nation" is the "we," the collective protagonist that the state should obey, foster, protect, and serve, a "we" only graspable through its own story, a "we" with a known past and present and thereby a will for its future. This idea, that "the nation" is a narrative, is present in most of the chapters, especially where they look at dialogues about the history of peoples as the process of nation making. It is also widely under discussion, especially in the wake of Homi Bhabha's *Nation and Narration* collection (see, for example, Borneman 1992; Malkki 1992).

Some theorists, notably Benedict Anderson (1991), argue for a general content to the idea of a nation. Though we also owe to Anderson the vivid image of variants of "the nation" produced as the idea is "pirated," he is best known for the idea of the nation as a specific form of "imagined community": a "horizontal" community composed of similar individuals in a bounded territory. Richard Handler (1988) has carried this farther, using also the ideas of Louis Dumont to constitute in "entitivity" a general or essential definition of what a nation has to be. But here, ethnography is again the graveyard of theory. I think many of the chapters show that there can be more complicated contestation about what a nation is, and lots of versions of nationness. For example consider Fiji: not only is the contestation complicated among "ethnic Fijians," but one point of agreement among them is that the true Fijians are *not* egalitarian, *not* horizontally related, but rather, on some other principle—divine mandate, royal mandate, land ownership—necessarily hierarchical, ruled by chiefs. "The nation," as a narrative fashioned dialogically, can take on more forms and features than can be imagined in one (no matter how paradigmatic or world-connected) epistemology.

Accepting that nations are narratives frees us from the need to determine an essential substance to the national form and allows us to recognize such ethnographic variety. It also opens up new questions to ask. Edward Said, in his writings not as an analyst of political discourse but as a literary critic, makes a relevant point here. He argues that for narratives, and for discourse and texts in general, beginnings are crucial things (Said 1985). If nations are narratives, the question of beginnings is crucial for them, too—beginnings as imagined in the narrative. Nations don't have to imagine themselves to be primordial, another idea floating in nation theory since Herder, but also doomed ethnographically. Primordiality, or antiquity, is only one sort of beginning a nation might claim. Understanding this makes it easier to accept readily observable facts—not only that nations are not primordial in real time, but also that for all that some nations find it vital to claim antiquity, many others are pleased to specify quite recent historical origins. Nations, as narratives, just have to have beginnings that are clear, uncontested, and meaningful. Rutz (this volume) makes a major point for Fiji scholarship when he notes that, unnoticed by the Fiji scholars for years, the Fiji chiefs have long been stressing a historical beginning of their license to rule, the Deed of Cession, rather than some more primordial basis for their authority. The nonprimordial, historical beginning of the United States is obvious, in the Declaration of Independence and so forth. But there is more to this than nonprimordial identities. Jourdan (this volume) suggests that in the Solomons, the sense of a possible nationhood lies not in a shared past, but a shared future: a narrative claiming the beginning to be the present. Jacobsen (this volume) neatly observes the same thing, in reverse lighting, for Papua New Guinea, that "there is no room for the real past in the real present" of PNG as a nation-state.

What is "nation making," then? Not only elaborating a narrative about a people and its history and future, its beginning and its plans and problems. The issue isn't just the existence of a narrative defining identity, but its reaching the standing of consensus acceptance: naturalness and necessity as the explanation of the order of its state and place. When the narrative is generally accepted, or better, when significant parts of it are generally accepted and seem incontestable, then and to that degree the nation is established. Rutz and Kaplan in their chapters give us the senses of dialogues in the process of making these narratives, efforts to make them incontestable, and vivid events in dialogic disruption of versions being propounded. Thus, in Fiji, we see the movements in ethnic Fijian political discourse from royalism to chiefly betrayal of the land, to the divine encompassment, the establishment of national symbols and rituals commemorating key elements and moments of the stories (a three-legged stool; chiefs sitting at the center of national ritual, receiving and giving gifts). And then we also see the elaborate construction by a visionary mystic of a pan-Fijian identity and history far more cohesively, but even less plausibly, encompassing the virtually unassimilable Indians and indigenes, including rituals, flags, uniforms, monuments, cosmology, history, and prophecy partly prescient. As Kaplan (this volume) argued, the main point to be learned from this story was the failure of an elaborate synthesis to resonate, and inversely the shallowness of official efforts, the intractability of real and present differences. Revealed are real limits on the imagination in the imagination of community.

If we accept the methodological move of regarding a nation as, by its nature, a narrative that establishes the identity of a people, then the claims about communities "invented" and "imagined," "constructed," and so on lose their air of mystery, their obscurity, and their whiff of ungrounded idealism. There is nothing odd about regarding narratives as invented, imagined, or such. To ground the study of nations in the real world, we need then to specify processes of formulation, promotion, and reception of these narratives, and to observe the techniques used to efface particular authorship and constitute consensus acceptance and possession of the national narrative. How does the dialogical process generating the narratives via contesting versions reach consensus about at least some points in the stories, especially when so much is always available to be gained by reformulating the story to the detriment or favor of particular constituents of it?

This question leads us to consider more about the people on both ends of the narrative building—as Jourdan (this volume) called them, "the builders and the buildees"—and the things connecting them. How do you experience a narrative not only as good or entertaining, but also as true and incontestable? How do you make others experience a narrative as true and incontestable? Kaplan and I agree that one place to look is ritual. Kaplan (this volume) discussed "the ritual requirements of nationhood" and described how the British and Fijian chiefs together regulated the rituals of chiefship in the colonial period, allowing them for the British governor but not for would-be business founder Apolosi Nawai, and how the rituals of nation in precoups independent Fiji were an uneasy synthesis of chiefly ritual and Indian garlanding, the latter usually by a young girl. Another place to look is police and legal procedure. In part, legal procedures could be regarded within the question of national ritual, or both could be subsumed, in most cases, within a conception of ideological state apparatuses (following Althusser) or within a conception of rituals and routines of rule (following Corrigan and Sayer). In any case, the methods for announcing, enforcing, and contesting law provide occasions inviting and sometimes virtually requiring reference to constituting moments, principles, and agencies. A third critical area of social routine, often but not always a state apparatus, is education. Institutionally organized education is simultaneously authorized by and productive of consensus conceptions of larger social identities and powers. But these consensus conceptions are not necessarily of states or nations, especially in a region where religious missions have been such a key player in the past and present of educational institutions. We come then to a key point. Not all rituals, schools, or even policing and arbitrating procedures are always state controlled; thus, the real history of state apparatuses in these areas can help us track, rather than presume, the role of states in nation making.

Similarly, if we are going to recognize as ethnographically variable these modes of connection between builders and buildees, these sometimes state apparatuses, then we should also scrutinize our conceptual vehicles for depicting the people, the narrative builders and buildees. In the conference sessions that led to this volume, terms such as *grass roots* and *folk*, *civil society* and *elites* came up. The scheme I am floating here relies, no doubt too heavily, on an unfocused concept of *elites,* in a way that is refined by more careful ethnographic histories of elite formation in the particular cases (here a host of questions about colonial relations can be raised). But consider the other terms. It is not really difficult to see *civil society*, a specific sort of community, come into existence as a phenomenon of capitalist epistemology: the public culture of market relations, spread through the proliferation of capitalist subjectivity, through such vehicles as advertising. This process is here discussed especially by Foster and LiPuma. An issue for comparison of the "civil societies" that go with new nations and states is their boundaries. What marks the limits, for various social circles in and out of the growing cities, of who is "civil," and thus suitable to be associated with? Here, as with the questions of colonially fostered elites, the Pacific cases generate contrasts as well as similarities. Pejorative stereotypes of noncapitalist peoples—*kanakas* or "bush people" in PNG, the Solomons, and elsewhere, *kai colo* or "hill people" in Fiji—vary markedly in their potency, as do the inverse denigrations (particularly powerful in Fiji) of people living in the way of money. At issue, in short, is the moral community, the civility of "civil society," which might or might not be construed as compatible with the custom (*kastom*) that "civil society" so busily commoditizes and sells. This boundary is not only regionally variable, but also contested in most Pacific cases; in any case, whatever its shifting and contested moral standing, "civil society" seems a useful construct, a locatable entity, in these Pacific societies.

Concepts of "folk" and "grass roots" types of people require more scrutiny, I think. I am especially skeptical of assertion of the reality of a folk or grass roots level of society as the natural polar opposite of the elite, especially if it is presumed, with Herder and the later German *geist* theorists, that the "folk" preserve a local culture that is more authentic and deeper rooted. Who the "buildees" of the nation are, where they are from, what they are doing, and the cultural and historical roots of their contemporary realities seem to me to be highly variant. For example, as the late Roger Keesing and others pointed out in the ASAO sessions, we tend to neglect and underestimate the history of labor migration and its cultural impact. Yet the other extreme view, that the "buildees" of the nation are passive, without cultural commitments or political agendas of their own, is also unpromising. I am merely cautioning, here, against a presumption that an authentic "folk" exists. The category itself, for all its connotation of innocence, was developed by an intellectual circle in Germany contesting the proper bases of law and order for a proposed nation there. It was, and still is, one of the key terms of contest in the building of national narratives in middle Europe. And isn't the best known use of the concept of "grass roots" in PNG, the *Post Courier* cartoon, an elite depiction of such "folk"? I think it is better to wonder whether we know the "buildees," than to know them as "the folk."

So, how does nation making work? Elite nation builders, justifying themselves with the narrative they embody and enact, repeat key fragments of their narrative (ad nauseam) in rituals and write its logic in the routines of education and law. The buildees experience their identity as depicted both in the national celebration imagery and, insofar as the elite control and use Foucauldian state instruments, in the quotidian operation of the state institutions they cannot avoid: census categories, tax distinctions, courtroom distinctions, medical, welfare, and educational programs, and so on. What those rituals and institutions are, and how much they really are avoided and contested, are then matters for comparative analysis, and in this volume we have the materials for such comparison, of nation making in the Pacific.

A first theme that is unmistakable, reading these chapters, is the weakness of these states. In the Pacific, and especially in PNG, as Jacobsen and Hirsch show clearly, the regularizing institutions can operate quite feebly and unevenly and can be experienced as something distant, sometimes fun, and sometimes troubling. The Fuyuge still await their first road. In the Solomons, as Jourdan points out, the colonial education curriculum concerned "Dick and Jane" in England, and only in the last five years has the central government tried seriously "to foster in the population the concept of a Solomon Islands nation." Elsewhere, the education system was similarly imperial and/or religious, as often sponsored by missions as the state.

Conversely, a second comparative theme is that Pacific efforts to make nations have deployed means not generally emphasized in the literature on state apparatuses, "modernization," or nation building. In Vanuatu, Fiji, and probably elsewhere, the emphasis on the Christianity of the "true nation" reduces to rubble the general theory of the nation-state as a secular break from feudal religious authority forms, but it makes perfect sense in light of the history of Christian education and community organizing. In the Pacific, with its cheapskate, budget-balancing, colonial states, it was perhaps the Christian ideological apparatuses, and not the state ideological apparatuses, that reached the farthest into the territorial peripheries. Christianity is not the only unusual nation-making vehicle noted in these chapters. Foster shows that, in PNG, the state is trying to harness advertising as an ideological apparatus. Advertising also may well be reaching farther than the roads, because it promotes nationally defined and marketed commodities. A third novel vehicle is that contested phenomenon on the boundary of "civil society" and "bush," reified custom (*kastom*). Facey describes how the Vanuaaku Pati licenses its rule by insistence on the priority of *kastom*, a vehicle of consensus by way of continuing, stabilized, and decentralized social domination by local "chiefs." But here comparison also finds difference. If appeal to reified custom is some Pacific nations' quietist solution to the problem of noncapitalist cultural diversity (the problem most forcefully outlined by Jacobsen for PNG), elsewhere (especially Fiji) reified custom is both a product of colonial paternalism and the banner of ethnic aggression.

So how does nation making work, in the Pacific? It is not clear, in any of the cases depicted, that nation making really does work. It is good, but also not good, they might say on Nguna. Or they might be harsher, with Jacobsen and his informants. There is a lot here, in all the chapters, revealing failures of nation making: clearly at least as much failure as success. We don't need to take states and nations for granted and, as LiPuma's chapter argued, we really should take the context of the expanding capitalist market seriously as a factor. Thus we turn to the relations of nation making to capitalist markets and to states as related to those markets.

Nation-States and World Markets

Beginning with the world capitalist context, with an eye on three levels—world, nation or state, and locality—I want to make one argument: that nothing in world capitalist markets per se requires the existence of states or nations. I would go so far as to say that nothing in capitalism *requires* their existence anywhere; for our purposes here, the more limited point is sufficient, that nothing requires their existence *everywhere*. In other words, though states and nations are hard to think out of in our current world, they are contingent, not necessary, for capitalism. In fact, crucial to my argument, they worked best when they were *not* existing everywhere. Thus, I disagree with the argument that there is an essential connection between capitalism and the nation-state, which seems to me to entail Fukuyama's (1989) argument as well as Handler's. I also disagree with the more practical, less essentializing argument that nation-states alone can provide the regulatory and coercive mechanisms necessary for capitalist markets to work. States do provide these mechanisms (minting money, for example), but they are only one means of doing so, and a means that has disadvantages as well as advantages for "multinational" capital.[4] Whatever the shape of its present and future, money has existed in non–state-licensed forms in the past, not only in the form of metals seen as intrinsically valuable (gold, silver, copper, brass, or, in Pennsylvania before suppression of the Whiskey Rebellion, nails), but also on paper. Seaborne Asian commercial capitalism, from China to the Red Sea, was conducted by means of promissory notes (*hundi*) guaranteed by famous trading houses until the Portuguese, British, and Dutch came to conquer, officiate, and tax.[5] States gained control over currency (U.S. dollar bill: "This note is legal tender for all debts, public and private") by force, as in post–Revolutionary western Pennsylvania, and continue to struggle for oversight and control over commercial transactions.

This argument puts in a different light the questions raised by

Eric Hirsch about "integrating trends" of the national state and the "countervailing forces" focused around local rituals. Both vantages, the local and the international, are valuable. Hirsch focuses on struggles for local and personal integrity. But how does the nation-state get integrity? The PNG case might be an instance in which it does not, recalling the urban anarchy and violence, the crimes not punished, the warfare in the hills, the rise of private security forces. (This point was also argued, on other grounds, by Michael Jacobsen in this volume.) Has this state failed to establish its hegemony even over coercive force?

In the absence of Foucauldian states, what makes integrity at the middle level, the nation-state posed between localities and world markets? Chapters here have posed at least two answers—ritual requirements of nationhood and a national order of commodities. As to the latter, Foster makes a case for the importance both of the rise of a national marketplace, with its own commodities and marketing, and of particular nation-invoking forms of advertising that objectify both the nation and the consumer at once. Taking Hirsch's and Foster's chapters together, how are the local rituals and the urban consumerism related? Can we view the urban commercial exchanges also as a kind of ritual? Can we carry out Hirsch's effort to trace their disruption and/or articulation with other exchange cycles, by figuring—with full attention to gender, class, cross-ethnic relations, and the like—how a cycle of urban life and transactional identity is being imagined and lived? If there is an epistemological entailment to the capitalist market, an "entitivity," it is taught and lived in these rituals of the market, which make money and the individualist logic of property seem natural and obvious mediators between people and things. As Hirsch shows, it is possible for these things to be accepted, but only at a distance; as Jacobsen insists, they need not entail respect for nation or state.

But what of the practical entailments of the capitalist market? Here let us first consider what might be called the enticement question. Broadly, borrowing from Foucault, it is the question, not of repression and coercion (which we will consider next), but of incitement. We are talking principally about the relations between the world and the local levels, leaving the nation-state and even the national consumer culture out of the picture for a moment. LiPuma's depiction of world capitalism as "relentless," encroaching upon and encompassing local culture, is in the mainstream of depictions of relations between capitalism and its "third world." But if the image of world capitalism as relentless and encompassing invites us to imagine the encompassed as coerced, passive victims, I want to pose, heuristically, another extreme image: that of peripheral would-be players anxious to get into a game. If we add in the world of advertising, and the national-level consumer culture (with its brand name dominated store signs, billboards, and such), we can also switch metaphors and imagine a periphery enticed to want to get into the show, trying to get their hands on tickets. Enticement makes much more sense to me than coercion as an explanation for the movements of commodities and local markets in Pacific places, most of which have very little of real interest to world capitalism: a local capitalism whose social relations are driven at least as much by petty local demand as by significant outside capital out to exploit anyone. (I am not talking about resort islands or mining here, but about soda pop, chewing gum, tobacco, beer, and, indeed, betel nut sales.) If I am right, the ability of advertising to inform, direct, and intensify demand (depicted especially in Foster's chapter) is all the more important, and it requires conjunction with the sort of inquiries launched by Hirsch.

Whatever answers come of it, I think that this sort of inquiry could replace vague depictions of forces of "urbanization," "modernization," or even "commodification," especially insofar as the focus is squarely on agency. Real coercion does exist (and more often outside the Pacific than within it, I think), and enticement can lead to bad deals, like land sales, that leave no further options but dependence on a money economy. Also, there is room here for wondering about a spillover effect, of advertising devices designed to please and control people elsewhere working to enchant peripheral peoples as well: the enchantment of the world as an unintended consequence of a developed consumer capitalism. But it should be possible, I think, to find local agency playing an important and irreducible role, if we seek the operations of forms of capitalism within Pacific localities as well as the impact of outside capitalism upon them. In most respects, I think this argument fits with LiPuma's; my question is simply whether the mediations won't sometimes seem clearer if we run the stages in reverse, beginning with the local search for commodities rather than capitalist impositions. And, where there was or is coercive pressure, how often is it an invisible hand of the market, and how often is it the very visible hand of a foreign nation-state?

Nation and Predation

It is time, for a final time, to return to the broader question of "the nation" in theory and practice. The context is capitalism. But anyone who looks at all seriously will see a vast difference between nation making in the late-twentieth-century, formerly colonized Pacific and nation making in Western Europe in the late eighteenth and early nineteenth centuries, the heyday of European capitalist nation making. There is no doubt, for the emerging "Western" nations (England, France, the Netherlands, Germany, Italy, and the United States) that the rising, self-promoted national consciousness was especially the vehicle of political consolidation for expanding urban bourgeoisies. Whether they took over and made over existing kingdoms or pulled together political patchworks, the European nation-states were engineered by the new engineers of time-wage labor capitalism. The structure of relations to capital is entirely different in the new Pacific nations.

Hobsbawm (1990, 34) tells us that the stories that the nineteenth-century western European bourgeoisies were telling themselves about their nations were primarily economic stories. He quotes John Stuart Mill:

> Experience . . . proves that it is possible for one nationality to merge and be absorbed into another. . . . Nobody can suppose that it is not more beneficial for a Breton or a Basque of French Navarre to be . . . a member of the French nationality, admitted on equal terms to all the privileges of French citizenship . . . than to sulk on his own rocks, the half-savage relic of past times, revolving in his own little mental orbit, without participation or interest in the general movement of the world. The same remark applies to the Welshman or the Scottish highlander as members of the British nation.

Thus the title of this commentary: the privileges of citizenship. Here the national narrative is, precisely, the story of coming together for equal participation in the privileges of citizenship, some sort of shared stake or interest in what Mill calls "the general movement of the world." What is this, and can they get it in PNG or Vanuatu?

The citizens of Mill's nations, and of the Western and other privileged nation-states, still get to control their own, ample benefits packages, benefits that accrued and still accrue especially through international "participation and interest." By pressing the question of "the nation," the bourgeoisies of eighteenth- and nineteenth-century Europe were able to divert sovereign intervention from the defense of the profits of the few blessed with mercantile monopolies to the widest possible national distribution of the fruits of fair trade (cf. *The Wealth of Nations*[6]). But these nations, like the mercantile kingdoms that preceded them, were and still are economic predators. Thus, it was hardly an accident that the mid-nineteenth-century consolidation of their homelands was followed by a new imperial explosion. In short, these engineered nation-states were not only Foucauldian machines turning peasants into Frenchmen, they were also predatory by design, spreading their capital, their military, and much of their citizenry far beyond the territorial confines within which they distributed their benefits.

All this is a far cry from the Solomon Islands or Fiji, where still the capital is mainly controlled from outside the islands. In Fiji, even the multinationals that have developed locally tend to exit the system—the largest, Bhanabhai and Company, having moved its base to Hong Kong long ago—in part because their influence on nation and state is insufficient to secure their interests. These nations and states are something else. They are not machines engineered by rising local bourgeoisies specifically to express and advance their collective interests, to support local capital and extend its benefits. Instead, they are the outcome of a different process. In the twentieth-century Pacific, the idea of the nation-state arrived prefabricated and was fit into place, not a new machine but a well-worn, imported tool; not engineering, but bricolage.

If Anderson (1991) demonstrates that there are many instances (though none east of Indonesia in the Pacific) where a colonized bourgeoisie is the agency "pirating" the national form, Hobsbawm (1990, 132–34ff) helps identify the point at which the nation-state model also begins to be arbitrarily imposed from without. It was at Versailles, where the empires that lost a world war, Ottoman and Hapsburg, were redesigned by treaty into nations such as Czechoslovakia and Yugoslavia. Not the same success stories as were the nation-states, later including Japan, able to use the form to consolidate and radically expand the industrial capital of their world region. Verdery (as discussed in Foster's introduction) is surely correct that nations as ethnic congeries and as co-owners of state enterprises have followed in the wake of the original bourgeois nation-states. Yet surely the later ethnic and socialist forms were efforts to retool the original conception of national citizenship, retooling efforts following from the limits of the privileges of citizenship, where the hidden predatory dimension was missing. England, the Netherlands, and France could devote state resources and strategies to the aid of their citizens in a world largely devoid of similarly oriented state agencies; the sun never set on their resulting empires and they made large profits outside the territories they conquered and ruled as well. What vast pool of labor was Czechoslovakia going to exploit? Where would it find a frontier for its outposts? As the world shrank to a patchwork of competitively managed, commercially monitored, and coercively regulated enclaves, is it any accident that the ethnic and socialist nations have fared less well than the originals?

When nationalist movements in European colonies pirated the national idea, used it against their colonizers, and began to make their own nations and states in the ex-colonial, post–World War II world, several of them also launched significant engineering projects, trying again to retool the nation-state. But their engineering efforts—Gandhian socialism, Mao's cultural revolution—have been no more successful. Several of the efforts described in this volume could also, arguably, deserve description as engineering efforts. In PNG, as Jacobsen outlines, there was the importation of the cult of appropriate technology by the Australian and UN-sponsored English academic consultants, smuggling elements of the then fashionable Tanzanian state plan into their proposals for the constitution. In Fiji, they try to refashion the nation-state via faith in a Christian god; in Vanuatu, via *kastom*. They may or may not deserve the label *engineering*, but none seems particularly promising. The history of nationalism shows us, in sum, that it is easier to fashion a narrative that organizes a people, to consolidate it through apparatuses such as rituals and media, and to mobilize it to legitimate a state, or to capture control of one, than it is to realize, thereby, the elusive privileges of citizenship, as they were and are for the predatory "civil societies" of the leading nations.

For how long will we live in what Liisa Malkki (1992) calls a "national order of things"? On the one hand, when I read theory about "nation-states," I am haunted by Marx's line about European public discourse before the rise of the truly new nations: "Thus in the eighteenth century a number of mediocre minds were busy finding the true formula which would bring the social estates, nobility, king, parliament, etc., into equilibrium, and they woke up one morning to find that there was in fact no longer any king, parliament or nobility" (1978 [1846], 141). Is this us, the scholars of the nation? On the other hand, Dipesh Chakrabarty is also cautionary, when he writes that there is no a priori reason to anticipate the demise of the nation-states under the pressures of transnational capital, especially as long as the former have armies, and: "For me, the dead of Baghdad (or those of Kuwait) will always be far more dead than the lethal grand narratives of Freedom and Progress which killed them" (1992, 65). Even here we must pause. After all, the legislature that empowered U.S. President George Bush to fight, the legislature he worked over so tirelessly and attended to so carefully, was not the U.S. Congress, which he buffaloed in a weekend. It was the UN Security Council. Where, then, lies sovereignty, even now?

Leaving aside questions I cannot answer, and the messes of the world, I want to finish by returning to the kinds of questions we as anthropologists are trying to answer, and the interesting, productive mess that is the current state of our discipline. An ethnographic inquiry, in Geertz's (1979) classic twentieth-century definition, delineates a "native's point of view" by tacking dialectically between "experience distant," theoretical concepts, and the concepts "experience near" to those of a distant locality. This definition distills very nicely the method of much of the most successful ethnography of the twentieth century. However, we need a more generalized sense of how ethnography operates to grasp the sort of ethnography done in studies such as those collected here (not because they are exceptional, but simply because they embody other tactics). The ethnography collected here is still study of difference, of things outside "our" everyday experience, but a different sort of study of difference. In general, the point I see arising from this volume is not that Melanesian nations are different from others, nor that they are the same, not simply that Melanesian nations are the synthesis of Melanesian culture with a pirated Western institution, nor stridently that they are proof that Melanesia is not really different in culture or institutions from the West. Rather, the point I see made is that what is happening in the Pacific in particular reveals much about the tenacity, elasticity, and limits of the nation-state form in general. Fred Myers has remarked[7] that anthropologists change the social theories they deal with fundamentally by taking an ethnographic approach to them. Ethnography, then, is not just a matter of comparing "our" things with other things (though this can be done), it is also a question of looking at how people use things, including conceptions near and distant to their experience, and change them as life goes on.

Ethnography, uniquely, is not frustrated when its comparisons are not controllable. More than deconstruction is accomplished when we dis-- cover that there is no one essence to "the nation" or the "nation-state." Instead, intending to seek out what actually exists, rather than the best set of social laws (as Boas 1887 perhaps best explained), ethnography brings "the nation" into a different focus: once a revolutionary breakthrough, now in many ways a fetter, but however worn out, still a useful thing in ongoing bricolage.

NOTES

1. For Michel Foucault's thinking on state centralization and the "art of government," see his book *Discipline and Punish* and especially his essay "Governmentality."

2. The colonies established by Europe in a late-nineteenth-century com- petitive rush were in interesting ways the inverse of the ones established at the outset of European colonizing. The early European colonies were mercantilist monopoly outposts, usually established, especially in Asia, by trading compa- nies. As Cohn and Dirks (1988) and others have argued, these companies in- vented or developed many of the Foucauldian state techniques for population surveillance and regulation. These companies, private and exclusive interests, in service to their stockholders, experimented widely in social record keeping, observation, and analysis, to further their business interests and to discharge efficiently the sovereign responsibilities they had tactically assumed. For exam- ple, fingerprinting for identification was first widely utilized in colonial India. By the late nineteenth century, however, European states themselves took up sover- eign control over the new colonies, but they rarely deployed more than a small fraction of their (by then highly developed) techniques for observing, governing, and serving a subject population. The best schools and most carefully scrutinized public works were those devoted to the citizens of the homeland who had found their way to the colony; for the "natives," state observation, regulation, and service were far slower, especially the services, notably because the colony was usually under great pressure to "pay for itself."

3. This is notwithstanding the fact that anticolonial nationalist movements arose also in these newer, late-nineteenth-century colonies, though more often in Africa and elsewhere than in the Pacific. Regardless of the messages of state ideological apparatuses, print capitalism created a national information field, as Anderson (1991) points out. Further, Anderson's less appreciated point, the con- tradictions in colonial practice unintentionally created a homogenized colony- wide cadre of governing bureaucrats among the locally recruited staff, trans- ferred widely and frequently within the colony, but rarely out to the metropole. This praxis, and not an official ideological apparatus intent on determining a

national reality, created the self-imagining communities in the late-nineteenth- and early-twentieth-century colonies. In the Pacific, the longest-standing, most broadly based, and most sustained anticolonial efforts were no doubt those of the Fiji Indians, who imported and applied South Asian anticolonial discourse: ironically, ethnic Fijians now sustain the colonial depiction of them as thereby "disloyal" to Fiji. In addition, it is interesting to note that Fiji's administrative praxis did not constitute a homogenized "native" civil service elite in Fiji. There were relatively few administrative posts that were given indifferently to indigenous Fijians or to Fiji Indians, and many that were deliberately "racially" specific. Thus, while "Indian clerks" and Fijian "Native stipendiary magistrates" might be transferred throughout the island group, they were not substitutable for each other. See Kaplan 1989 and Kelly 1989, 1991.

4. Some writers now suggest that our new world order is actually a developing conflict between two different managerial classes, a conflict between the official elites of the nation-states, and the newer, transnational capitalist elite. If the former either work in the "public sector" or run businesses entwined with it, the latter are in service to multinational corporate capital, consumerist rather than patriotic, long ago "displaced" from any ethnic commitments, and tired of tariffs, customs, taxes, and passport hassles. In this volume, Jacobsen sees the nation-state as a doomed institution. For a counterargument, skeptical that the nation-state is doomed in this conflict with world consumer culture, see Chakrabarty 1992.

5. In precolonial Asia, coins were inconvenient and sometimes less trustworthy (often adulterated by inland sovereigns with less to lose in reputation than the merchant houses); merchant houses were fully "multinational," spanning the Indian Ocean and beyond, and it was possible (at high rates of interest) to transfer credit from almost any point in maritime Asia to any other without use of any coin (see, for example, Braudel 1982, 124–25). We still lose money in currency exchanges, and exchange rate uncertainties disrupt international trade. Imagine the world, or even just Europe, with one currency.

6. As the literature on mercantilism (Heckscher 1955; Coleman 1969) makes clear, the very idea of a state mercantilist policy was less a self-conception of the eighteenth-century European states than an imputation of their critics. In other words, the discourse on "political economy" that began with the work of Adam Smith (but see Tribe 1978) created the idea of mercantilist policy, starting from Smith's critique of the system of royal monopoly charters to colonial trading and shipping interests. When he compared the benefits *for the nation* of "mercantilist" and laissez-faire policies, he brought into being not only the doctrine of the free market and the doctrine of mercantilism, but also the epistemic commitment to the nation's benefit as the measuring stick. By the early nineteenth century, the discourses of the nation-state were transforming the colonial as well as the European world: company misrule was blamed for colonial insurrections in India and elsewhere, and thus the new, state-governed colonies come into being.

7. At the annual meetings of the Society for Cultural Anthropology, in 1992.

REFERENCES

Anderson, Benedict. 1991. *Imagined Communities: Reflections on the Origin and Spread of Nationalism*, 2d ed. London: Verso.
Appadurai, Arjun. 1990. Disjuncture and difference in the global cultural economy. *Public Culture* 2:1–24.
Asad, Talal, ed. 1973. *Anthropology and the Colonial Encounter*. London: Ithaca Press.
———. 1986. The concept of cultural translation in British social anthropology. In James Clifford and George Marcus, eds., *Writing Culture: The Poetics and Politics of Ethnography*, 141–64. Berkeley: University of California Press.
Boas, Franz. 1940 [1887]. The study of geography. In *Race, Language, and Culture*, 639–47. New York: The Free Press.
Borneman, John. 1992. *Belonging in the Two Berlins: Kin, State, Nation*. Cambridge: Cambridge University Press.
Bourdieu, Pierre. 1991. The production and reproduction of legitimate language. In *Language and Symbolic Power*, 43–65. Cambridge: Harvard University Press.
Braudel, Fernand. 1982. *The Wheels of Commerce (Civilization and Capitalism*, Vol. II). New York: Harper and Row.
Chakrabarty, Dipesh. 1992. The death of history? Historical consciousness and the culture of late capitalism. *Public Culture* 4:47–65.
Clifford, James. 1986. Introduction: Partial truths. In James Clifford and George Marcus, eds., *Writing Culture: The Poetics and Politics of Ethnography*, 1–26. Berkeley: University of California Press.
Cohn, Bernard, and Nicholas Dirks. 1988. Beyond the fringe: The nation state, colonialism, and the technologies of power. *Journal of Historical Sociology* 1:224–29.
Coleman, D. C., ed. 1969. *Revisions in Mercantilism*. London: Methuen & Co.
Ferguson, James, and Akhil Gupta, eds. 1992. *Space, Identity, and the Politics of Difference*. Theme Issue, *Cultural Anthropology* 7:3–129.
Foucault, Michel. 1979. *Discipline and Punish: The Birth of the Prison*. Translated by Alan Sheridan. New York: Random House.
———. 1979. Governmentality. Translated by R. Braidotti. *Ideology and Consciousness* 6:5–21.
Fukuyama, Francis. 1989. The end of history? *The National Interest* (Summer): 3–18.
Geertz, Clifford. 1979. From the native's point of view: On the nature of anthropological understanding. In Paul Rabinow and William M. Sullivan, eds., *Interpretive Social Science: A Reader*, 225–41. Berkeley: University of California Press
Handler, Richard. 1988. *Nationalism and the Politics of Culture in Quebec*. Madison: University of Wisconsin Press.
Hannerz, Ulf. 1989. Notes on the global ecumene. *Public Culture* 1:66–75.

Heckscher, Eli. 1955. *Mercantilism*. Translated by Mendel Shapiro. New York: Macmillan.

Hobsbawm, Eric. 1990. *Nations and Nationalism Since 1780*. Cambridge: Cambridge University Press.

Kaplan, Martha. 1989. *Luve ni wai* as the British saw it: Constructions of custom and disorder in colonial Fiji. *Ethnohistory* 36:349–71.

Kelly, John D. 1989. Fear of culture: British regulation of Indian marriage in post-indenture Fiji. *Ethnohistory* 36: 372–91.

———. 1991. *A Politics of Virtue: Hinduism, Sexuality, and Countercolonial Discourse in Fiji*. Chicago: University of Chicago Press.

Malkki, Liisa. 1992. National geographic: The rooting of peoples and the territorialization of national identity among scholars and refugees. *Cultural Anthropology* 7:24–44.

Marx, Karl. 1978 [1846]. Society and economy in history. In Robert C. Tucker, ed., *The Marx-Engels Reader*, 136–42. New York: W. W. Norton.

Said, Edward. 1985. *Beginnings: Intention and Method*. New York: Columbia University Press.

Smith, Gavin. 1991. Writing for real: Capitalist constructions and constructions of capitalism. *Critique of Anthropology* 11:213–32.

Tribe, Keith. 1978. *Land, Labour, and Economic Discourse*. London: Routledge and Kegan Paul.

Weber, Eugen. 1976. *Peasants Into Frenchmen: The Modernization of Rural France, 1870–1914*. Stanford: Stanford University Press.

White, Hayden. 1978. Introduction: Tropology, discourse, and the modes of human consciousness. In *Tropics of Discourse*, 1–25. Baltimore: Johns Hopkins University Press.

Wolf, Eric. 1982. *Europe and the People Without History*. Berkeley: University of California Press.

Contributors

Robert J. Foster is assistant professor of anthropology, Department of Anthropology, University of Rochester.

Edward LiPuma is associate professor of anthropology, Department of Anthropology, University of Miami.

Henry Rutz is professor of anthropology, Department of Anthropology, Hamilton College.

Martha Kaplan is assistant professor of anthropology, Department of Anthropology, Vassar College.

Christine Jourdan is assistant professor of anthropology, Department of Anthropology, Concordia University, Montreal.

Eric Hirsch is lecturer in social anthropology, Department of Human Sciences, Brunel University, Uxbridge.

Ellen Facey is regional coordinator, University of Northern British Columbia.

Michael Jacobsen received his Ph.D. in anthropology from the University of Copenhagen.

John D. Kelly is associate professor of anthropology, Department of Anthropology, University of Chicago.

Index

Advertisements: form of, 153; and nation making, 24, 152
Advertising, 151
Analogy, 191, 197, 203, 204
Anderson, B., 7, 71, 77, 98, 134, 153, 154, 186, 188, 257, 267
Appadurai, A., 153, 254

Balibar, E., 2, 6, 15, 17
Bavadra, T., 108
Bhabha, H., 257
Bislama. *See* Pidgin
Bourdieu, P., 256
British Residency, 207, 210, 211
Browne, B., 173
Butadroka, S., 22, 82

Calhoun, C., 35
Capitalism: epistemology of, 18, 40, 177, 255; encompassment by, 35, 38, 44, 59, 62, 242–45; global, 7, 37, 62, 88, 117, 234, 243, 246, 264, 265; and nation making, 18–21; social relations of, 6, 25, 170, 229, 236, 246, 260; and states, 256
Chakrabarty, D., 269
Chatterjee, P., 37, 48
Chiefs: divine, 75; discursive category of, 75, 76, 77, 84, 85, 86; Fijian, 79, 80, 86, 99, 257; Fijian Great Council of, 80, 101, 102, 108, 109, 116; Fuyuge, 192, 193, 196, 199; and land people, 82–84; Ngunese, 213, 217, 218, 221
Christianity, 84, 85, 86, 100, 143, 209, 211, 217, 228; chiefly, 115; colonial-chiefly narrative of, 103; and cus-
tom, 218; and nation making, 262; on Nguna, 213
Church: discursive category of, 75, 76, 77, 84, 85, 86
Citizenship, 16, 18–19, 36, 61, 266, 267; consumer, 24, 155, 165, 176; and individuality, 236
Civil society, 21, 39, 47–50, 260–61
Class relations, 42, 59
Commercial Advertising Act, 151
Commodity form, 20, 41
Common roll, 105
Community: dynamic of, 49; of language, 127, 129; local, 229, 238, 239, 240; imagined, 61, 98, 185, 188; narrative of, 48
Constitution, 235; of Papua New Guinea, 1, 232
Constitutional Planning Committee, 232, 233
Consumerism, 24, 155, 190, 191, 204, 264
Consumption: commodity, 153, 170, 203, 228, 264–65; communities of, 133, 155, 170, 171; mass, 151; middle-class, 171
Coups, Fiji, 74, 85
Cultural creolization, 144
Cultural system, Fijian, 75–78, 83
Culture: concept of, 5, 118; consumer, 152, 264, 265; generic, 143; local, 44, 48; and nationalism, 117; objectification of, 20, 222–23; popular, 23, 56, 127, 128, 129, 141–43; traditional, 25; urban, 142, 144–45, 152. *See also* National culture
Currency, 160